FOLKTALES OF *France*

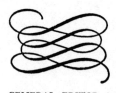 *Folktales*
OF THE WORLD

GENERAL EDITOR : RICHARD M. DORSON

FOLKTALES OF
France

EDITED BY
Geneviève Massignon

TRANSLATED BY JACQUELINE HYLAND

FOREWORD BY
Richard M. Dorson

THE UNIVERSITY OF CHICAGO PRESS
Chicago and London

International Standard Book Number: 0-226-50965-6
Library of Congress Catalog Card Number: 68-14008
The University of Chicago Press, Chicago 60637
The University of Chicago Press, Ltd., London
© 1968 by The University of Chicago
All rights reserved
Published 1968
Third Impression 1973
Printed in the United States of America

Foreword

In the age of the sun king, Louis XIV, the fairy tales of peasants incongruously found their way into the glittering court at Versailles. The courtiers and their ladies amused each other with telling and listening to country stories, and one court attendant, Charles Perrault, printed some in 1697 in the first European book of folktales, *Contes de ma Mère l'Oye*. This title appeared on the frontispiece depicting an old woman spinning and telling tales to a little group, but the title page carried the phrase, *Histoires ou contes de temps passé. Avec des moralités*. Perrault had mingled with the Versailles nobility while enjoying an appointment (1663–83) with Jean-Baptiste Colbert, controller general of finances, to assist in superintending the royal buildings. Hearing the tales at court, and having a bent for letters, Perrault set down in verses, in the manner of La Fontaine, "The Silly Wishes," "Griselda," and "Ass's Skin," published in a little magazine by Moetjens in 1694 at The Hague; he reprinted them that year as a book that received unkind notices. Then Perrault attempted prose versions, in Moetjens' miscellany, and they were collected in Paris in a little book destined for fame. The given author of these *Contes de ma Mère l'Oye* was Pierre Darmancour, the son of Perrault, who heard them from his nurse. Presumably the versions of the boy stimulated his father, recalling the recitations at Versailles, to write out the eight tales since become immortal: "Sleeping Beauty," "Red Riding Hood," "Bluebeard," "Puss in Boots," "The Fairies," "Cinderella," "Riquet of the Tuft," and "Hop o' my Thumb."

The *Contes de ma Mère l'Oye* proved to be a landmark in literary history and the history of folklore. Direct communication between the intellectuals and the folk would have to wait until the Grimms' collection of German Märchen in 1812, but still France could lay claim in 1697 to the first sampling of traditional tales. Perrault's styling is evident in occasional moral asides and personal witticisms, in some created characters, like his fairy god-mothers, in the removal of ugly incidents, and in the too perfect story line, but on the whole the manner is simple and plain and peasant-like. Only one of the Mother Goose tales, "Riquet of the Tuft," owed little to tradition, but the others have taken their place as household classics and are known to flourish in chimney-corner circles among many peoples. Perrault added little rhymed "Moralités" at the end of each conte. After Little Red Riding Hood is devoured by the wolf in the clothes of her grandmother, the point at which Perrault ends his version, he adduces the moral that genteel young ladies should beware of all sorts of strangers; a quiet-voiced Wolf may be the most dangerous.[1]

Perrault's *Contes* ushered in a long century of literary imita-tions, powdered and perfumed and prolix. An embroidered rendi-tion of *Beauty and the Beast* in 1742 ran to 362 pages. Usually they were written by ladies of the boudoir, and preserved in an endless series under the title *Le Cabinet des fées*. For the student of folklore these contrivances by Mme d'Aulnoy, Mme l'Héritier, and other estimable ladies hold little interest except to illustrate how the literary genre of the fairy-tale novelette grew and de-parted from Perrault's simple contes. The salon fashion of recit-ing tales aloud shifted to reading them in the cabinet. Well into the nineteenth century, the concern with folk tradition remained in France a sterile scholastic exercise, as in Baron Charles A. Walckenaer's *Lettres sur les contes de fées attribuées à Perrault et sur l'origine des contes de fées* (1825) and Alfred Maury's *Les Fées du moyen âge* (1843). In spite of the exemplary col-lections of the brothers Grimm and their emulators throughout Europe, fieldwork lagged among the French. When Lang wrote about "The Folk-Lore of France" in 1878, he observed that the folktales of France had not yet been collected with "method and system."[2] Then between the Franco-Prussian War of 1870

---

[1] Andrew Lang's introductory essays to *Perrault's Popular Tales* (Ox-ford, 1888), pp. vii–cxv, give valuable biographical and critical details.
[2] Lang in the *Folk-Lore Record*, I (1878), 113.

and the outbreak of the First World War, the French folklore
movement suddenly flowered, with the quickening of interest
in philology, archaeology, and ethnography. These were the
years of the founding of journals and societies, of the cultivation
of the cultural sciences, of the quest for Celtic, Romanic, medieval, and peasant contributions to the French soul. In particular
three giants emerged as French savants of folklore, all born in
the 1840's. The careers of Emmanuel Cosquin (1841–1921),
Henri Gaidoz (1842–1932), and Paul Sébillot (1846–1918) would
intertwine in curious ways.

The line of influence from the Grimms to Cosquin is direct
and clear. In 1862 Cosquin, then a youthful law student, is
writing the brothers Grimm in admiration of their stories and
notes in the *Kinder- und Hausmärchen*. He expresses joy at
discovering in his natal Barrois one of their Märchen told in
French country dialect. In the house of his great-uncle he had
found a true old housemaid, serving in the family for fifty years,
who corresponded to the Grimms' "Viehmannin," their tailor's
wife, as a fountain of peasant fictions.[3] Cosquin would do for
France what the Grimms had done for Germany. Enlisting his
sisters to aid him, he gathered the folktales of Lorraine from the
village of Montiers-sur-Saulx in the Barrois region, publishing
them piecemeal in the journal *Romania* from 1876 to 1881. Such
eminent folktale scholars as Gaston Paris in France, Reinhold
Köhler in Germany, and W. R. S. Ralston in England praised
Cosquin's articles and urged his assembling them in book form.
In 1886 he brought out *Contes populaires de Lorraine,* a book
that marked the coming of age of French folklore. If stimulated
by the Grimms' *Kinder- und Hausmärchen,* and comparable to
it as a pioneer scholarly collection of national folktales, the
Contes populaires de Lorraine still possessed its own strong in-
dividuality, and in a sense even rejected the Grimms. For Cosquin analyzed his eighty-four tales three-quarters of a century
after the Grimms issued their first volume, and he stirred to
new concepts, apparent in the subtitle: "Compared with the

[3] Nicole Odette Stein-Moreau, "Les frères Grimm, conteurs, et la France
au dix-neuvième siècle," in *Brüder Grimm Gedenken 1963* (Marburg,
1963), pp. 553–54.

Folktales of Other Provinces of France and of Foreign Countries
and Preceded by an Essay on the Origin and Diffusion of
European Popular Tales." The opening essay firmly stated his
position. Cosquin was an Indianist and a diffusionist. So his
work offered not only a scientific collection of French contes
and impressive comparative notes but a strongly argued theory
of origin and transmission as well.

Cosquin began by saying that Perrault had not dared publish
humble contes under his own name, as beneath the dignity of
an Academician. In 1887 he would not need to feel this false
shame, but he would face another danger, that of being seduced
by vapory speculations why tales in far distant places resembled
each other. With this preamble Cosquin attacked the theory,
on the one hand, of the Grimms, Max Müller, and J. G. von
Hahn, who saw Aryan myths and beliefs preserved in contes,
and, on the other hand, the anthropological school led by Andrew
Lang, who beheld survivals of savage ideas in popular fictions.
In their place Cosquin advanced the argument of Theodor
Benfey, the German Orientalist who in his 1859 edition of the
Panchatantra presented with powerful evidence the case for India
as the original homeland of European Märchen. Actually Cosquin
could point back to a French predecessor, Auguste Loiseleur-
Deslongchamps, who in 1838 had written *Essai sur les fables
indiennes et sur leur introduction en Europe,* but it was Benfey
who aroused folktale scholars.

With his essay Cosquin announced himself as a polemicist
and not a mere collector, and he plunged into the debate between
the evolutionists and the diffusionists. He pointed out that American Indian tales differed considerably from those of Europe
while European contes showed a strong family likeness to the
popular fictions of India. English civil servants and their families
in India were now putting into print orally collected tales, sup-
plementing the great literary collections of the *Panchatantra* and
the *Katha Sarit Sagara,* and in his notes Cosquin indicated the
Indic similarities to the contes of Lorraine. His treatment of "Le
Loup blanc" (No. 63), the Cupid and Psyche story, illustrates
his method. The three pages of the story text are followed by
sixteen pages of "Remarques." Here he considered the question

of whether the conte of Lorraine and its relatives from Norway,
Germany, and Italy derived from the Latin example of Apuleius
and Greco-Roman mythology? Cosquin rejects the idea that a
myth of Cupid ever existed and turns triumphantly to a folktale
published in 1833 from the lips of a Benares washerwoman, telling, as in the fable of Psyche, of a monster wedded to the King's
daughter who shed his skin to become a handsome young man.
Cosquin concludes that "Le Loup blanc," its European counter-
parts, and Psyche herself derive from a common Indian source.

Such was the tenor of his argument, running squarely into the
survivalist thesis of Lang, who read in Cupid and Psyche the
remains of savage belief in transformation. Cosquin dealt with
Lang's critical reviews of *Contes populaires de Lorraine* in a
paper, "L'Origine des contes populaires européens et les théories
de M. Lang", presented to the Congress of Popular Traditions
held in Paris in 1889, and followed it up with "Quelques observations sur les 'incidents commun aux contes européens et aux
contes orientaux'" at the International Folk-Lore Congress of
1891 in London.[4] He averred that where Lang's method was
anthropological, his own was historical. Lang had cited resemblances between Zulu and European tales as proofs of the similar
stages of culture and human invention through which widely
scattered peoples all passed, and hence as evidence against borrowing. But, countered Cosquin, did not these resemblances
prove borrowing? Surely the contes of India could have reached
Egypt, Abyssinia, and Morocco with the extension of Islam and
been carried by the Berbers from the Arabs to west and central
Africa. Lang asked if the ideas of folktales found in India do not
appear in other countries. This was not the point, responded
Cosquin, but rather, did the ideas in the tales, such as speaking
animals, transformation, and magic objects, contradict the ideas
of Indian culture? Since they did not, the assumption could be
made that many of the master tales originated in India and
found their way in popular storybooks and on the lips of traders
and travelers to Europe. Can the theme of a maiden saved from
a dragon by a hero, for instance, clothed in local details by

---

[4] Cosquin's papers at the 1889 and 1891 folklore congresses are reprinted in his *Études folkloriques* (Paris, 1922), pp. 50–64, 65–72.

modern Greeks, Nubians, and Armenians, have developed from
the savage idea of a person being periodically sacrificed to a
monster? No, such a specialized theme could only have entered
the heritage of many different peoples by being transmitted
from one to another.

The wave of the future indeed lay with Cosquin, for each new
field collection revealed fresh specimens of familiar plots and
strengthened the case for diffusion. As Lang had discredited
Müller the solar mythologist, so now Cosquin drove Lang the
evolutionist to the wall, compelling him to acknowledge the role
of borrowing to explain the world community of oral narratives.
Yet Cosquin did not long enjoy his triumph.

In 1893 Joseph Bédier crushed Cosquin's hypothesis in his
treatise *Les Fabliaux*. This study of popular literature of the
Middle Ages was dedicated to Gaston Paris, Bédier's own teacher
and celebrated scholar of medieval literature, who himself had
said that fabliaux derived from India. Bédier concentrated not
on the theory of transmission but on the theory of origin advanced by Cosquin as twin parts of his argument. For his test
cases Bédier turned to the humorous verse narratives of the
thirteenth century—the fabliaux—since they were traditional and
were preserved in writing in Europe at a relatively early date.
Did the fabliaux betray debts to India? Meticulously Bédier
marshaled the facts. Only thirteen of the four hundred tales
known in 1300 in French, German, and Latin appear in Oriental
collections (six fabliaux, five exempla, two French contes). In
these few similar cases, the Indian examples seem fragmentary
and the European ones the older. The reason India receives so
much attention from folklorists is that Buddhism by its nature
attracted parables which were written down, while Greek and
Roman authors felt no such religious compulsion to record oral
stories. When a conte does appear among the ancient Greeks,
Cosquin perversely calls it a myth. Yet some contes did indeed
get written down by the Egyptians, as Gaston Maspero's *Les
Contes populaires de l'Égypte ancienne* (1882) had demonstrated
and Cosquin himself had recognized. Bédier concludes by assert-
ing the French provenience of most fabliaux, crediting Picardy
with the lion's share; and he denies the possibility of tracing the

origins of any but purely ethnic folktales. How fruitless is the
piling up of variants that breed upon each other and never lead
to any source!

The Indianist theory suffered heavily from the hammer blow of
Bédier, and folktale scholarship on the whole suffered a setback
since the search for origins of any sort seemed discredited. Cosquin continued to write his essays and notes tracing the migration of tales from Orient to Occident and tinkering with the
ideas of Benfey, whom he felt gave too much credit to the
Mongols in transmitting contes. These essays were gathered
together in 1922, four years after his death, in *Études folkloriques*
and *Les Contes indiens et l'occident.*

Meanwhile another battle front was forming that would en-
gage the talents and energies of other illustrious French folklorists. In 1877 the first journal exclusively devoted to folklore
appeared, under the title *Mélusine,* named for the swan-maiden
of a cherished fairy tale, with the subtitle "Miscellany of Popular
Literature, Traditions and Usages." Henri Gaidoz and Eugène
Rolland were the founders and co-editors. *Mélusine* was printed
in a folio format, numbered according to the two columns on
each page, and at first the contents consisted of small collections,
notes, observations, "facetiae," "variétés," notices, and engravings.
Volume one offered an opening piece "On the Study of Popular
Poetry in France" by Gaston Paris, an appraisal by Gaidoz of
Mannhardt's work on Indo-European mythology of the fields and
woods, and an exchange between Loys Brueyre and Cosquin.
Loys Brueyre, while admiring Cosquin's texts and comments on
the tales of Lorraine, protested against his citing a Japanese tale
from a literary source to strengthen his thesis of the migration of
tales from Asia to Europe. Literary sources could well be influenced from outside the country, as with the *Arabian Nights,*
which actually came from India. Loys Brueyre had a point,
since the tale of the Good and Evil Hunchbacks which he cited
is today identified as a well-known European tale type (Type
503, *The Gifts of the Little People*). But Loys Brueyre's illustration of the *Arabian Nights* coming from India simply played
into Cosquin's hand.[5]

[5] *Mélusine,* I (1878), cols. 235–39, 276–79.

The second volume did not appear until 1884-85, and its Foreword specifically spoke of "folk-lore" as the object of study in the journal, to achieve for France what folklore societies in England and Spain and folklore periodicals in Italy and Portugal had accomplished. Gaidoz and Rolland announced plans to enlarge their domain. In the first volume they had shown France to Frenchmen; now they would show humanity to itself, and they invited their readers to join in making *Mélusine* the central organization of universal folklore. Yet Gaidoz and Rolland soon faced Parisian rivals in the *Revue des traditions populaires*, founded in 1886 by Paul Sébillot for the publishing of current field reports, and *La Tradition,* initiated in 1887 by Emile Blémont to maintain old traditions and regional values. Sébillot's journal served as the organ for the newly founded Société des Traditions Populaires, printing its program on the opening pages, and stating how France after a long sleep was now vying with its neighbors in the investigation of oral literature and popular arts. Supernatural legends, sayings, folksongs, proverbs, charms, riddles, games, customs, linguistics, imagery, chapbooks—all would come under the umbrella of the new science. Besides these journals, two extensive series of folklore collections were launched in the 1880's, *Contes et chansons populaires* (1881-1930, Éditions Leroux, 44 volumes) and *Les Littératures de toutes les nations* (1883-1903, Éditions Maisonneuve, 47 volumes). And the first international folklore congress was held in Paris July 29 to August 2, 1889.

So well established had the study of popular traditions become in France that it could even nurture a bitter factionalism, based not on conflicting theories but on claims to priority and preeminence and scholarly integrity in the development of the subject. The two dominant figures of Gaidoz and Sébillot, with their respective journals and coteries, presided over the opposing camps.

Henri Gaidoz was the academic scholar, trained in Romance philology and Celtic studies, and a founder of the *Revue celtique* (1870). Neither the field collector nor the producer of general books, he specialized in the erudite monographic essay, frequently reprinted as a separate brochure, on such varied Romanic subjects as Gargantua in Celtic mythology, Latin inscriptions in Ireland, the religion of the Gauls, Rumanians in Hungary, and rabies and St. Hubert. Some of his papers dealt purely with folklore matters: a comparison of Cuchulainn, Beowulf, and Hercules; the study of popular traditions in France and abroad; and the change of sex in Celtic folktales. He published these pieces of varying length in numerous journals, proceedings, and encyclopedias, while filling his own *Mélusine* with caustic reviews and commentaries deflating meretricious folklorists.

Paul Sébillot, by contrast, was the independent artist of the seaside and the country who became a prodigious collector and assembler of French folklore. His beloved province of Haute-Bretagne, the French-speaking section, as opposed to the Breton speakers of western Brittany, provided his first hunting ground, and he published in separate volumes its folktales, oral literature, traditions and superstitions, popular customs, and local legends. His talent as a marine painter led him to collect the lore of fishermen and the legends, beliefs, and superstitions of the sea. From fishing to other occupations was a logical step, and Sébillot pioneered in exploring legends and curiosities of trades. His success as a collector of regional and occupational traditions gave him national authority, and he broadened his scope from regional folktales of the moor and the strand, the earth and the sea, to folktales of all the French provinces and ultimately to his major four-volume encyclopedic inventory *Le Folk-Lore de France* (1904–7). Here he systematically grouped peasant beliefs and legends about the heavens and the earth, the ocean and the rivers, animals and plants, prehistoric remains, historical monuments, and traditional history. His short survey *Le Folk-Lore* (1913) condensed these materials of oral literature and traditional ethnography. In addition he wrote poems, stories, and plays based on Breton folk themes.

Such were the two dissimilar figures who moved into the center of French folklore activities. Where Gaidoz tracked Gargantua into ancient Gaulish religion, Sébillot pursued him in the spoken traditions of the people. Yet the two joined forces for a brief period. They planned a series on the marvelous and legendary history of France, published parts of a bibliography

on the traditions and popular literature of France, and collaborated on one book, *Blason populaire de la France* (1884).
This ingenious work has given its title to a folklore genre in English, the *blason populaire* that wittily gibes, in rhyme or saying or cryptic phrase, at a nationality, a region, a city, or a village. The honeymoon ended with a devastating review by Gaidoz in the third volume of *Mélusine* of Sébillot's *Coutumes populaires de la Haute-Bretagne* (1886).[6] Here the precise library scholar goes to work with his scalpel on the mass traditions, assembled in seemingly orderly fashion by the prolific collector, dealing with the life cycle, household affairs, occupations, and recreations of north Breton peasants. First there are the omissions. Why not discuss costumes and popular jewelry as well as furniture, inns as well as houses, aphorisms inscribed on the façade of houses or at the bottom of chimneys? If Sébillot is reserving the customs of fishermen for another book, why does he leave out the customs of hunters? If he gives formulas for greeting, why does he neglect oaths? On these and other matters Sébillot would have profited from reading recent articles in *Mélusine*.

Further, Gaidoz chides Sébillot because he, along with other provincial writers, neglects to do the necessary historical research on the background of the customs he observes. Folklore to be more than an amusement or curiosity, and to become a proper scientific study, depends on history to explain genesis and on comparison to explain psychology. Sébillot's carelessness is evident in his loose manner of citation, his stringing together notes without proper synthesis, and his repetitions from his own previous publications, particularly *Traditions et superstitions de la Haute-Bretagne,* sometimes without acknowledgment! Thus he repeats himself on well worship and saints' offerings to fatten pigs. He even repeats passages in the present work, for instance on January 25 as a lucky natal day. Will he use the same items in subsequent inflated volumes of his inflated list of publications? Like theater revues in which dancers enter by one wing and leave by another, then reenter again, the books of Monsieur

[6] *Mélusine,* III (1886–87), cols. 220–22.

Sébillot give a pleasing illusion of an army of facts—but they are always the same.

After this review, Gaidoz and Sébillot ceased to collaborate. Sébillot continued rapidly to turn out his repetitive books, and Gaidoz his learned articles, and each edited his own journal. Then in the years preceding the First World War, the latent hostility between them flared forth in a *cause celèbre* illuminating in comic relief the whole French folklore movement. This was the affair of the Dinner of Mother Goose.

It began innocently enough with an obituary in 1909 of Loys Brueyre by Paul Sébillot in the latter's journal, *Revue des traditions populaires.*[7] Sébillot praised civil servant Brueyre's accomplishments in comparative folklore,[8] and incidentally mentioned that when "le Dîner de ma Mère l'Oye" was instituted in 1882 as a means of bringing together French folklorists, Brueyre and he had signed the invitations; at the one hundredth dinner Brueyre had given a highly applauded speech.[9] This innocent aside triggered off a violent if delayed reaction by Henri Gaidoz, "Eugène Rolland et son oeuvre littéraire," appearing in 1912 in *Mélusine.*[10] In this lengthy essay on the career of his lifelong colleague, Gaidoz dwelt on the Dinner of Mother Goose and credited Rolland with its conception. In the 1883 volume of the *Almanach des traditions populaires,* which Rolland had edited from 1882 to 1884, Sébillot himself told how Rolland had planned a monthly dinner to assemble the steadily growing group of French savants interested in oral literature. In order to give the dinner a French title, rather than the English "folklore," the name *Dîner de ma Mère L'Oye* was chosen, with the subtitle, "Réunion des folkloristes." The first meeting was held February 14, 1882, under the presidency of Gaston Paris, the famed

[7] *Revue des traditions populaires,* XXIII (1908), 459–60.

[8] Loys Brueyre's article, "Littérature orale et traditionnelle, éléments de folklore," in the *Revue de la société des études historiques,"* LXII (1896), 10–35, presented the first general theory of comparative French folklore, including the Creole.

[9] Loys Brueyre's speech is printed in *Revue des traditions populaires,* X (1895), 132.

[10] *Mélusine,* XI (1912), cols. 417–40.

author of, among many notable works, *Le Trésor du roi Rhamp-sinitus* (1874), suggesting that folktales originated in ancient civilizations.

Gaidoz could not recall the author of the poetic title for the banquet, but the important point was, he proclaimed, that the namer was only the godfather and Rolland the true father. Yet Sébillot had taken unto himself the mantle of the originator of the dinner, much as Amerigo Vespucci had sought to eclipse Columbus, the true discoverer of America. Gaidoz liked this analogy and repeated it in later ripostes.

From his country residence in la Beauce, at Aunay-sous-Auneau (Eure-et-Loir), Rolland designated Brueyre and Sébillot as his commissioners to make arrangements with the Parisian restaurateur and to send out the invitations. This fact, alleged Gaidoz, had been carefully concealed by Sébillot until the death of Rolland in 1909, when in writing his obituary Sébillot did acknowledge Rolland as one of three discoverers of America.[11] But still this was inexact, a grudging concession to the true and sole founder of the Dîner de ma Mère l'Oye. And Gaidoz again printed, this time in capital letters, the tell-tale phrase from the 1883 publication:

M. EUGENE ROLLAND SONGEA QU'UN DÎNER MENSUEL . . .

Signé: Paul Sébillot

Furthermore, continued Gaidoz, on the occasion of the one hundredth Dinner of Mother Goose, February 28, 1895, Sébillot had the irony to invite Rolland on a printed card in an open envelope with a five-centime stamp. Rolland and Gaidoz had laughed philosophically about this "love letter." Needless to say, neither attended the dinner, which was described at length in the *Revue des traditions populaires.*[12]

Reading about the dinner must have severely agitated the editors of *Mélusine.* It was apparently a joyous and self-gratula-tory occasion for the participants, who complimented each other on the durability of their gatherings now fourteen years old and

[11] Sébillot's obituary of Rolland appeared in *Revue des traditions popu-laires,* XXIV (1909), 250–52.

[12] *Revue des traditions populaires,* X (1895), 129–35.

on the consequent gains for the cause of scientific folklore. According to the printed account, the president, E.-T. Hamy, toasted Sébillot and Brueyre as the founders and preservers of the dinner, in spite of the indifference and hostility of certain other persons. Brueyre toasted his fellow-founder Sébillot as one to whom the science of folklore owed much. Sébillot toasted the foreign visitors present and the foreign folklore societies which had sent their emblems in honor of the occasion (the Chicago Folk-Lore Society sent their ornament, but the American Folklore Society had none). The table was decorated with bouquets of hollyhocks, whose leaves were customarily plucked by country folk to divine their future, and before each banqueteer was placed an earthenware dish with minced pork bearing a likeness of Mother Goose as an old lady and a small loaf of bread shaped like a goose. After the report there were melancholy and happy French folksongs and a sidesplitting folktale of the wolf and the gendarme and poems based on popular themes. It was an evening to remember—by those present and by those absent.

Accompanying Sébillot's account of the dinner was a spirited full-page illustration by Félix Régamey with a flapping goose in the foreground spreading its wings over an open volume of the *Revue des traditions populaires,* surrounded by goslings in the foreground and folktale characters in the background. A caption read, "Centième Dîner de Ma Mère L'Oye."

Eugène Rolland (1846–1909), the hapless pawn in this vehement controversy, was born at Metz and died in Paris after spending forty years doing research in the Bibliothèque Nationale to the neglect of his bookshop. He devoted all his available energies to diverse folklore collections, although the folktale escaped his net. In 1877 he compiled a volume of French riddles, *Devinettes ou énigmes populaires de la France,* to which Gaston Paris contributed a preface and examples; and in 1883 he prepared a book of children's games, *Rimes et jeux de l'enfance,* which Sébillot called one of the best volumes in the *Collection des littératures populaires de toutes les nations* and van Gennep called one of the weakest. But his major efforts were reserved for heroic series: the compilation of French folksongs, *Recueil des chansons populaires de la France* (6 volumes, 1884–90), and the folk dictionaries of French flora and fauna, *Faune populaire de la France* (13 volumes, 1877–1911) and *Flore populaire de la France* (11 volumes, 1896–1913), which brought together patois names, proverbs, charms, and superstitions linked by the peasantry with local animals and plants. In 1877 and again from 1884 to 1887 he collaborated on *Mélusine* with Gaidoz, who now sought to honor his late comrade at Sébillot's expense. In his biographical sketch of Rolland, Gaidoz intensified his complaints against other folklorists. He stated that Rolland, on returning to Paris in 1884, disinterested himself in the Dinner of Mother Goose since he could now regularly see his confrères in folklore. Sébillot continued the dinner and used it as a springboard for his *Revue des traditions populaires,* founded in 1886. Accordingly Rolland organized a simpler weekly dinner at the Café Voltaire, where Gaidoz frequently joined him to talk of folklore. In April, 1884, Rolland and Gaidoz resumed *Mélusine,* which they had let lapse in 1878. (Sébillot wrote in his obituary of Rolland that he had never heard of it in 1877 and that it reached only twenty subscribers.) The weekly dinners gradually limited themselves to the circle of *Mélusine* contributors and friends, to whom Rolland offered an informal course in folklore. Because of its high standards, continued Gaidoz, *Mélusine* antagonized rival·journals which sought to emulate it but printed inferior materials. Gaidoz himself had on an earlier occasion pointed out, as he reminded his readers, that dilettantes in folklore were forming a mutual admiration society. In that earlier article of 1890 Gaidoz had expressed his surprise that Sébillot had lifted a quotation from an old song first quoted by Rolland without acknowledgment in a miscellany edited by Henry Carnoy, and he now repeated his charge.

This outspoken piece of 1890, titled "La Collection internationale de la *tradition,"* and reviewing a new series bearing that title, was indeed not calculated, as Gaidoz recognized, to win friends, but its severe chastisement of popularized and pretentious scholarship still hits the mark.[13] Gaidoz began with an appraisal of a new series of small works on folklore initiated by Émile

[13] *Mélusine,* V (1890), cols. 25–36.

Blémont and Henry Carnoy, the editors of the journal *La Tradi-tion*. This series dealt with books of divination translated from a Turkish manuscript; with music and dance in the traditions of Lithuanians, Germans, and Greeks; and with Japanese musical folk arts. Gaidoz scorned the editors (even though he considered Carnoy one of his disciples) who would reprint an ancient manuscript on books of divination with no indication of its age or provenience. He derided Carnoy for declaring that Edmond Veckenstedt, editor of one of the booklets, was introducing in France his novel theory of interpreting popular traditions that had obtained a wide success in Germany. Bold words, worthy for presenting a Max Müller or an Andrew Lang! But this theory turns out to be a commonplace statement that the science of tradition should investigate the changes in tales and myths effected by the language, customs, and ideas of a culture. And nowhere does Veckenstedt apply the method. As for Veckenstedt's fluvial, verdant, and astral explanations of the origins of the Greek dance, who can fathom them! For all his pretensions, Veckenstedt now reveals himself as belonging to the rejected school of nature mythologists. Why should this old-hat theory be translated from German into French?

The only reason, conjectures Gaidoz, seems to be that Veckenstedt has initiated an international group of mutually admiring folklorists. He had founded in Leipzig a folklore journal, *Zeitschrift für Volkskunde,* serving as the German counterpart to Sébillot's *Revue des traditions populaires* and Blémont and Carnoy's *La Tradition.* The able Breton collector François-Marie Luzel had recently derided eulogistic articles written by folklorists in praise of one another. But now Veckenstedt had come up with a still more ingenious idea—that of international exchanges of folklore. He would print in his journal, in German, articles by editors of folklore journals in different countries, who would then return the favor. Thus pieces by the Frenchman Henry Carnoy, the Belgian Auguste Gittée, and the Italian Giuseppe Pitrè have appeared in the *Zeitschrift für Volkskunde,* and writings by Veckenstedt turned up in the respective journals of those folklorists. New journals with similar aims keep emerging. Here from Italy was the first number (January, 1890) of

Rassegna di letteratura popolare et dialettale, avowedly devoted
to serious criticism of new publications in place of sterile praises,
and yet indulging in just such sterile praise of the *Collection
internationale de la tradition!* Furthermore, a third of the *Rassegna* was occupied with summaries of such journals as *La
Tradition* and *Zeitschrift für Volkskunde.* So did the folklore
journals batten upon each other, filling up their pages with
rubbish which would have been better placed in cheap news-
papers (as *Romania* said of *Revue des traditions populaires* and
Tradition). These long summaries are but the shadow of a
shadow.

Thus the biting Henri Gaidoz, striking home, for the Veckenstedt of his gibes would be publicly exposed in *Mélusine* as a
plagiarist.[14] But there was more to come. Gaidoz now turned
to an impartial commentator, the German philologist Karl Weinhold, professor at the University of Berlin, who had written in
the *Zeitschrift für Völkerpsychologie* (XX, no. 1) on "Was soll
die Volkskunde leisten?" ("What services can the study of folklore perform?"). Weinhold acknowledged the scholarly international status of the subject, made manifest in the 1889 congress
of folklorists held at Paris. Yet the professed science was no more
than a sport, a vogue. The journals rarely contained serious
articles based on methodical research but mostly a frightful ac-
cumulation of small broken pebbles or a heap of straw thrown
to the wind. Properly the science of folklore demands familiarity
with history and linguistics, anthropology and psychology, as well
as legal history, political economy, the arts, literature, and natural
sciences.

Gaidoz thoroughly approved this large view of the subject,
except that he would go even farther than Weinhold, who restricted folklore to the study of one people. While it was true
that certain parts of folklore, falling under ethnography, such
as dwellings, costume, and material culture in general, were
fixed in a regional place at an historic time, when it came to
beliefs and oral literature Gaidoz considered folklore a science

---

[14] For the exposé of Veckenstedt, see E. Sidney Hartland in *Folk-Lore,*
II (1891), 100–107, summarizing the charges made against Veckenstedt
in *Mélusine* in 1890.

as much international as national, as much comparative as historical. Actually the history of popular literature presented a second, later division of folklore, dependent on the first—the history of beliefs and customs.

Is folklore then a science? Gaidoz preferred to call it a new method of research. The method consisted in the study of a religion, a mythology, an institution, a belief, a custom, not in its final and complete crystallization, but from the germ of its origin, following it through all the degrees of its development, taking account of all the influences shaping it, and at the same time determining (but in an experimental manner) the psychological point of departure of this or that cultural item. These researches, which are a branch of "demopsychology," depend especially on direct observation of the people and on documents dealing with popular origins. One must pay the closest scrutiny to the manifestations of the popular soul, whether as survivals in civilized societies or as parallels among less advanced peoples. One must search for the links of the chain scattered among many countries and peoples, just as the naturalist must search for and juxtapose fragments of an extinct species scattered over a vast continent. Such, thought Gaidoz, was the method of folklore study.

But who, he asked, has the erudition and the patience to cover this vast realm? The few savants in France occupied with these studies are swallowed up like trappers in the American Far West. Too many folklorists on the continent discredit their subject in the eyes of the knowing public with vain and arid agitations. The numerous works on folklore, falling thick as autumn leaves, suggested to Gaidoz Voltaire's witticism in *Candide.* "Sir, how many theatrical pieces are there in France?" asked Candide of the abbot, who replied, "Five or six thousand." "That is a good many," said Candide. "How many of them are good?" "Fifteen or sixteen," replied the other. "That is a good many," said Candide.

The severe judgment of Weinhold, perhaps even involving *Mélusine,* should warn all folklorists seeking popularity at the expense of scientific merit. So concluded Gaidoz in his editorial pronouncements of 1890, appraising the state of the field, and sideswiping several of his close competitors in a manner strangely prophetic of the "fakelore" controversy of mid-twentieth century.

Resuming the thread of his biographical essay of 1912 on Rolland, Gaidoz continued his innuendos against Sébillot, whose abilities he did not deny. Rather he made of Sébillot a diligent pupil learning from Rolland, who introduced the Germanic mode of scholarship into France. Before Rolland, amateurs presented folklore materials in florid style, with moral reflections and comparative commentary on superstitions and customs mixed together. Rolland confined himself to facts, and, from 1880 on, others observed and followed his method. Unfortunately, gibed Gaidoz, those who followed were men of letters rather than philologists; hence the great inferiority of French as compared with German folklore studies. In France the amateurs endlessly report local examples of "If the slow worm sees . . ." and "Bees, your master is dead." To correct this amateurism, Rolland undertook in 1884 to revive *Mélusine* with Gaidoz, changing the format of 1877 from an anthology of French traditions and popular literature to a medium for comparative studies. Rolland contributed the idea, copied by rival journals, of cooperative investigations, in which readers could add their notes, documents, and ideas to topics presented in *Mélusine*. And it was Rolland who first investigated meteorology and the folklore of the sea, subjects since vulgarized in France and English-speaking countries. (Again this was an obvious dig at Sébillot, who wrote on traditions of fishermen and beliefs connected with the heavens.) Further, Rolland refused to print in *Mélusine* articles or documents their authors had published elsewhere, a common practice of folklorists seeking to expand their bibliographies, nor did he invite such "repreneurs" to collaborate with him on the new journal.

Gaidoz praised the field method employed by Rolland in gathering data for his *Faune* and *Flore*. Like the Russian nihilists from another point of view, Rolland practiced "going among the people." When he spotted a man of the people adept in his patois, whether a peddler, street merchant, or other vendor, he engaged him for about forty sous an hour to discourse on folklore. Rolland revealed neither his name nor his address, which would have been dangerous, but led his man to a café or a cabaret, where they could order and reorder refreshments, and there, notebook in hand, he interrogated the "son of the earth" on the local names of animals and plants. Rolland would draw from his pocket a botanical album with colored plates that never left his side. "Do you know this plant? What do you call it in your town? What do you do with it?" he would ask. Sometimes his subjects were suspicious, wondering why this bourgeois so interested himself in the village affairs and whether he was from the police. Rolland had a ready response: "I am doing a book for pharmacists; they need to know the names of the plants to gather them in the countryside." If one meeting did not suffice, Roland made a rendezvous for a second. Rolland once told Gaidoz that with money he could collect all the folklore of France right in Paris. Upon the death of Rolland in 1909, Gaidoz acquired his books, manuscripts, and working notes in order to continue and complete the *Faune* and *Flore* as far as possible during his remaining years.

Besides his well-known works, Rolland conceived the idea for publishing a "secret museum" of the folklore too free and raw in character to be issued through ordinary channels. He discussed the idea with Gaston Paris, who approved and suggested the discreet title *Kryptadia* (*Secret Things*), and recommended the translation of a certain collection of Russian tales for the first volume. Brueyre collaborated on volume one and Gaidoz on subsequent volumes, which could be considered as the "subterranean overflow" of *Mélusine*.[15] (The *Kryptadia* does indeed represent one of Rolland's most permanent and courageous contributions to folklore researches, making available in print, although necessarily in a highly restricted edition, the obscene texts that flourish orally but are screened from pretty collections of tales and ballads.)

So ended the lengthy obituary essay on Rolland. The gauntlet was now thrown to Sébillot, who responded with equal ampli-

---

[15] Details about *Kryptadia,* initiated in Heilbronn, Germany, in 1883, are given in Gershon Legman, *The Horn Book* (Hyde Park, N.Y., 1964), pp. 477–78, but he does not mention Rolland as an editor.

tude and also in a personal and revealing manner, in the *Revue des traditions populaires* for 1913.[16] Sébillot titled his two-part article, "Notes pour servir à l'histoire du folk-lore en France." He cast it in autobiographical vein to refute immediately Gaidoz's assertion that Sébillot changed from a painter of the scenes of Haute-Bretagne into a folklore collector after reading the first issue of *Mélusine* in 1877. Sébillot had, as he reminded Gaidoz, related in his preface to the *Contes populaires de la Haute-Bretagne* having collected in 1860 about twenty tales, of which half a dozen were printed in that book. Rolland himself had suggested in a letter of 1884 that Sébillot describe in his prefaces how he came to discover folklore, as a contribution to the history of folklore studies in France. In these "Notes" Sébillot retraces the circumstances of his early life that brought him into contact with oral traditions before he became professionally committed to folklore. He had indeed already begun a manuscript autobiography of *Mémoires,* at the request of his children.

From his earliest recollections, Sébillot had the taste for folklore. As a schoolboy he set down in his notebooks songs, riddles, rhymes, and such scraps of tradition sung or recited by peasants and domestics. At the college of Dinan in 1860 he maintained the practice but added other materials—things seen or legends heard. While at college Sébillot chanced on the book *Foyer breton* (*Breton Hearthside*), and was entranced by the drawings of Breton scenes and the accompanying contes, of Sleeping Beauty, the Golden Bough, and Beauty and the Beast, taken from Perrault, Madame d'Aulnoy, and Madame Leprince de Beaumont. The illustrations of the peasant costumes of Vannes in Souvestre recalled to his mind those he had seen while visiting his father's farms at Merdrignac (Côtes-du-Nord) at the border of Morbihan. And the contes related by the laborers, artisans, and sailors of Souvestre seemed more real and familiar than ones Sébillot had encountered in other collections. Narrative incidents about the world of the dead recalled to Sébillot incidents he had heard in his childhood, and he decided to search in his native country during his vacations for marvelous or fantastic stories worthy

[16] Paul Sébillot, "Notes pour servir à l'histoire du folk-lore en France," *Revue des traditions populaires,* XXVIII (1913), 49–62, 171–82.

of a Gaelic "Hearthside." At the time he did not contemplate publishing them but rather of bolstering his local pride, deflated at all the talk about the picturesqueness and the legends of Basse-Bretagne. Surely the Gaelic country, in particular that of Penthièvre, could not be so barren as one supposed.

Now Sébillot charmingly tells of his first tentative probings into local tradition. Back in Matignon he hunted up his old nurse, Vincente, who at first claimed that she had forgotten all the old contes but, prompted by the mention of Jean de Diot and the thief Finn, began to recall them from her service in Saint-Pôtan, one of the most rural regions of the canton of Matignon. There shepherds gathered in the open air to cook apples in hollowed-out bake ovens in the earth, while posing riddles, singing songs, and relating contes about ghosts and drolls but not about fairies. Twenty years later Sébillot published Vincente's tales with small changes and other contes from different storytellers whom he also described.

But, beginning in 1867, he turned to marine painting and for a decade neglected contes. In 1870 the pioneer Breton collector, François-Marie Luzel, sent him a copy of his article "Contes bretons," one of a series of field reports finally published in 1879 in the book *Veillées bretonnes*. Luzel employed the literal rather than the embellished style of presenting tales, which thenceforth Sébillot followed. It was Luzel who gave Sébillot the Paris address of Gaidoz early in 1879 and wrote Gaidoz in advance about Sébillot's work with the Gaelic patois and his collecting the traditions of Haute-Bretagne. The same year Sébillot met Rolland at the home of Gaidoz. Common interests stimulated friendship and exchange of ideas among the three. Gaidoz wrote Sébillot in 1881 about their collaborating: "I have in my head several books that we could easily do together. Rolland is strong, like the champion whose name he bears; but I have the idea that we could be supporting pillars for each other, that we could accomplish great things." In January, 1883, Gaidoz proposed the title "France Marvelous and Legendary" for a series of some sixteen volumes they would jointly edit on various aspects of folk tradition—a series that never materialized. In his *Traditions et superstitions de la Haute-Bretagne,* Sébillot adopted in large part

Rolland's classification in his *Faune* of animal names, adding
contes to the proverbs and beliefs. But Sébillot had investigated
folklore of sailors and the sea before he ever met Rolland.
Thus Sébillot assembled memories and documents, in elaborate
detail, about his early career in folklore. He even printed a table
of the forty folktales he had collected before meeting Gaidoz and
Rolland. Now he turned to the Dinner of Mother Goose.

Sébillot quoted from a letter Loys Brueyre had sent him in
1880 saying, "I went Wednesday to the dinner of the Celticists
and we spoke of the Dinner of Mythographers." Rolland attended
the meeting of the Celticists and so must have gleaned the idea
at that time, and after leaving Paris he pursued it for the self-
interested motive of keeping up his contacts. Rolland in his letters to Sébillot asked him to serve as "commissary" for a mytho-
graphic dinner, but Sébillot coined "Dîner de ma Mère l'Oye."
Digging into his files, he produced letters from folklorists invited to the dinner, like Jean François Bladé, who preferred "Ma
Mère l'Oye" to "Réunion des folkloristes."

Sébillot sent the two copies of his journal to Gaidoz, who
addressed a letter to his donor, printed in the same volume of
Revue des traditions populaires. If it required a subtitle, Gaidoz
noted, he would call his epistle "Eugène Rolland, founder of the
Dîner de ma Mère l'Oye." He reprinted his documents in behalf
of Rolland, calculated the expenses of the dinner borne by Sébillot
and Loys Brueyre as two francs maximum for stamps, and
corrected Sébillot's use of the verb "neglect." "Rolland did not
neglect, he *disdained* to concern himself with material details
which were discharged by an agent, the commissioner of the
Dinner, and this commissioner was you—you chosen and instructed by Rolland." [17]

Following Gaidoz's letter, Sébillot printed his own remarks
in small type, headed *Simples Notes.* He deplored Gaidoz's ex-
travagant use of italics, capitals, and quotation marks; raised the
ante on the cost of stamps for the letters of invitation from five
to fifteen and twenty-five centimes and added the cost of printing; and claimed that he was preserving the credit due Loys
Brueyre as co-founder of the dinner. "All this luxurious typog-

[17] Gaidoz in *Revue des traditions populaires,* XXVIII (1913), 271–74.

raphy, all these argumentations could do nothing against the
fact that it is to me that the Dîner de 'ma Mère l'Oye' owes its
name, that Brueyre and I organized the dinner and made of it
a reality." [18]

Within a year Europe was devoured by war, and the Dinner of
Mother Goose faded into the antiquarian past. Yet the writings
it provoked testify today to the passion and dedication of strong
personalities at the height of the French folklore movement.
This was no tempest in a teapot but a scholarly debate over the
origins of folklore organization in France.

French folklore found a new titan in the person of Arnold van
Gennep (1873-1957) to carry its banner in the first half of the
twentieth century, a lean period for scholarship scarred by the
two world wars. As Sébillot had entered folklore from painting
and literature, and Gaidoz from Celtic studies, so van Gennep
approached folklore as an ethnologist and sociologist. He com-
menced his field researches with accounts of taboos and totemism
in Madagascar in 1904 and myths and legends of Australia in
1906, and his first-hand observations on the operation of traditions
in society led to two books of high theoretical importance,
Les Rites de passage (1909) and *La Formation des légendes*
(1910). In the first he considered the groupings of powerful ritual
ceremonies around the crucial events of human life—birth, initiation, marriage, death. In the second he dwelt upon the forms of
folk narrative, distinguishing legend from conte and myth as a
localized, individualized, and believed recitation, not connected,
like the myth, with the supernatural world and with magic rite.
Rejecting arid discussion on symbolic meanings or places of
origin for legends, van Gennep concentrated on their social and
psychical function among primitive and semi-civilized peoples.
His control of the sources for both savages and peasants gave his
comments special authority.

In later years he turned to the folklore of his own country, con-
tributing volumes on Côte d'Or in Bourgogne, on Auvergne and
Velay, Flanders and Hainaut, the high Alps and Dauphiné to
the series on folklore of the French provinces and the popular

[18] Sébillot in *Revue des traditions populaires,* XXVIII (1913), 275-76.

literature of all nations, maintaining his ethnological, linguistic, and psychological emphasis. He provided a brief but meaty overview of *Le Folklore* in 1924, avowedly to propagandize the field. But his magnum opus occupying his final two decades was the multivolume *Manuel de folklore français contemporain* (1937–58), a sweeping panorama of French life-cycle and seasonal ceremonies with a superb analytic bibliography of general, provincial, calendrical, and topical researches on French folklore. That van Gennep's sympathies lay with Sébillot and against Gaidoz is seen in his caustic critique of Gaidoz as exclusively the literary and Celtic folklorist failing to employ the direct method of observation. *Mélusine* died, he noted drily, after an enormous monograph by Tuchmann on fascination. Van Gennep contrasted the acerbity of Gaidoz with the diplomacy of Sébillot.[19]

Another intimate and involuted relationship bound van Gennep to an equally prolific contemporary, Émile Dominique Nourry (1870–1935), a publisher who doubled as an author of French folklore works under the pseudonym Paul Saintyves. In terms of personalities, van Gennep continued the caustic vein of Gaidoz and Saintyves the moderate tone of Sébillot. Saintyves (as Nourry) published van Gennep's *Les Rites de passage,* and the two collaborated on various scholarly undertakings, such as the *Corpus du folklore préhistorique en France et dans les colonies françaises* (1934), an assessment of legendary traditions attached to artifacts from the Stone Age. They united and disunited on journals. Van Gennep founded the *Revue des études ethnographiques et sociologiques* in 1908, to which Saintyves contributed. In turn Saintyves initiated the *Revue de folklore français* in 1930, with the support of van Gennep, who dropped out two years later when the journal added *et coloniale* to its title. As with Gaidoz and Sébillot, these were two brilliant devotees of folklore with fundamentally different visions. Van Gennep was the ethnologist, sociologist, positivist, and agnostic; Saintyves, the rationalist, philosopher, and Christian moralist.

The emphasis of Saintyves' heavy output was on religious

[19] Arnold van Gennep, *Manuel de folklore français contemporain* (Paris, 1937), III, p. 119, no. 107; p. 122, no. 123.

folklore.[20] He scrutinized the documents of tradition in the manner of a biblical rationalist seeking to explain magic and miracles by natural phenomena and human conceits. Intellectually he was moved by Emile Loisy, the modernist philosopher who had written on initiation rites among the Australian aborigines. Loisy belonged to the school of Ernest Renan, author of a naturalistic life of Christ. So Saintyves ranged over biblical myths and marvels, popular astrology and lunar folklore, the Christian mythology of saints expressed in folk cults and legends, stories of virgin mothers and miraculous births. The saints of medieval and modern times had, he contended, succeeded the gods of the ancient world in popular belief. In his most influential work, *Les Contes de Perrault* (1923), he traced the origins of Perrault's eight prose and three verse contes to seasonal and initiation rituals by piecing together scattered evidence. Thus "La Belle au bois dormant" illustrates a primitive rite celebrating the sleep of the new year. The affinity of Frazer for Saintyves can readily be surmised, and the author of *The Golden Bough,* at one time a resident in Paris, financed the circular promoting Saintyves' *Revue de folklore français.* Posterity has judged both ritualists similarly.

Not Saintyves but van Gennep guided their younger contemporary, Paul Delarue (1889–1956), who carried French folktale scholarship to a new pinnacle. Delarue, like Cosquin and Sébillot, grew up in the countryside imbibing folklore as part of his milieu. He was born at Saint-Didier in Nevers to a family of small peasants, received the Legion of Honor in the First World War, served as teacher and schoolmaster of a school in the Morvan near Nevers from 1932 to 1936 and then for three years at a school in Paris until the Second World War, in which he took part as a battalion commander. After the war he briefly directed a school at Ivry, but retired in 1946 and devoted his full energies until his death to the cause of folktale studies. From 1946 to 1953 he presided over the Commission of Folklore in the League of Teachers. In 1947 he became vice-president of the

[20] A full bibliography is in P. Saintyves, *Manuel de folklore* (Paris, 1936), pp. 209–15.

Society of French Ethnography, of which van Gennep was president. Through the Centre National de la Recherche Scientifique he guided a young group of French folktale enthusiasts to the degree Master of Research. Meanwhile he was publishing regularly in the new French folklore periodicals, *Nouvelle Revue des arts et traditions populaires, Bulletin folklorique d'Ile-de-France,* and the *Mois d'ethnographique français.*

These activities accompanied Delarue's central enterprise—the systematic cataloguing and tasteful sampling of the whole body of French folktales according to modern methods. In a 1953 article in *Arts et traditions populaires,* he surveyed the state of folktale collecting and classification in France as a prelude to two major undertakings of his own. These were a series of volumes presenting the living folktales of the provinces of France, and an exhaustive tale-type index of the French *contes populaires.*

The systematic ordering of folktales in the twentieth century succeeded the bold theories of origin and meaning in the nineteenth, and to this vast international enterprise Delarue contributed a magnificent national index of French tale types, *Le Conte populaire français.* Volume I, covering Types 300–366 in the Aarne-Thompson index, appeared the year after his death, 1957; volume II, almost double in size, with 732 pages, covering Types 400 to 736, in 1963. Marie-Louise Tenèze, a faithful disciple of Delarue, served as co-author of the second volume and continues the monumental task from her position in the Museum of Popular Arts and Traditions in Paris, where Delarue's files are deposited, with the support of the National Center for Scientific Research. In brief, *Le Conte populaire français* presents a descriptive inventory of the printed and manuscript versions of folktales collected in France and in the French-speaking areas of North America and the West Indies. The tales are identified and numbered according to the system devised by Antti Aarne and Stith Thompson in 1928, and revised in 1961, *The Types of the Folktale,* primarily for the folk narratives of Europe. The French catalogue begins with Tale 300, "The Beast with Seven Heads," rather than with Tale 1, as the Aarne-Thompson index begins with animal tales, much less abundant in France than the popular fictions of magic and wonder (*contes merveilleux*), whose numbers start at 300.

Since the Aarne-Thompson index can give but a bare figure for the number of versions of a given tale type reported in each country, national indexes are needed as supplements in an ingenious interlocking apparatus. For the French catalogue, Delarue planned a sensible and informative scheme. Each tale type is given first its Aarne-Thompson number and title, then the text of a representative French variant, then a breakdown of the main divisions and episodes of the conte, and finally a tabulated list of versions with bibliographical sources and notes on deviations from the main form and a summary statement on studies of the tale and its world-wide distribution. Thus to one of the most popular of all French contes, Type 425, "The Search for the Lost Husband," a development of the Cupid and Psyche story intermixed with "Beauty and the Beast," the catalogue devotes thirty-seven pages (72–109), giving three sample texts, and listing 122 versions, with further references (a–m) to New World appearances. The long analytic bibliography begins with three references of 1697–98 to Madame d'Aulnoy's *Les Contes des fées,* and eventually includes texts from Cosquin, Millien (nos. 20–41), Luzel, Sébillot, van Gennep, and Massignon—almost all the great French collectors.

Besides the catalogue proper, the first volume offers an historical review by Paul Delarue of the collection and study of *contes populaires* in France, an analysis of its characters, supernatural and human, and an extensive, well-classified bibliography. In her informative Introduction to Volume II, Madame Tenèze speaks of the necessity to restrict the analysis of overseas tale variants, in order to make her efforts more realistic. The two volumes, running to more than a thousand pages, have still dealt with only 114 tale types (27 in volume I, 87 in volume II) representing a total of some 1,700 variant texts.

The books of folktales from French provinces were intended to sample the regional narrative traditions. Delarue described his plan for the series as follows:

> For folklorists, the annotated edition will furnish a new
> and abundant documentation on all the questions which

can interest them: comparative, stylistic, systematic study of themes; the portion of the individual contribution, of the collective contribution, and sometimes of the bookish contribution by the intermediary of peddlers, etc. . . . From certain comparisons will spring forth new insights. And this is the place to indicate how very different are the materials gathered together in our various collections, in their presentation externally identical. That of Nivernais and Morvan contains contes more developed and, in some part, worded with a concern for precision which applies more to content than to form, as was customary with the contemporaries of Achille Millien, Luzel, Cosquin, and Sébillot; that of the West (G. Massignon) restores to us faithfully the recorded language of the tellers; that of the Alps (Joisten) is composed from the most characteristic of six hundred stenographic versions, of which the whole furnishes, for a region limited enough, a practically exhaustive inventory of a tradition in the course of decomposing and dying; that of Bas-Languedoc and Gascogne (A. Perbosc and S. Cézerac) gives us the most typical forms of the Occitan country, while the original versions of the collection of the Audoises Pyrénées (Maugard) presents us with the oral literature of the neighboring Catalogne; that of Haute-Bretagne (A. de Félice) offers the repertoire of tellers who are carriers of a tradition still living in a milieu of basket-makers; that of Haut-Languedoc and Lyonnais (V. Smith) informs us of some of the most ancient forms of the contes of Perrault that have been gathered in the course of the great research undertaken in the last century; and the collections of French Canada, where the oral traditions of our western provinces are perpetuated, elaborated, adapted to the physical and human milieu and sometimes penetrated with Irish influence, will bring to us great recorded tales, certain of which are the veritable chefs-d'oeuvre of spoken style, thanks to particularly gifted tellers." [21]

For his series Delarue proposed a number of distinctive features. It would, in the first place, make available to the educated

[21] Translated from Paul Delarue, "Présentation de la collection," in A. Millien and P. Delarue, *Contes du Nivernais et du Morvan* (Paris, 1953), pp. viii–ix.

public the choicest specimens of French popular tales whose discovery, in the words of Gédéon Huet, himself an esteemed authority on the *conte populaire,* constituted one of the most remarkable scientific activities of the nineteenth century.[22] Second, he would restrict the contents of the volumes to authentic versions of tales preserving the simple syntax and direct story line of the *conteur,* without literary embroidery describing the features of the hero or depicting the landscape or moralizing on the events. (Delarue was not, however, modern enough to include scatological incidents, which he suppressed in the text and provided in the notes.) Third, he provided two editions of each volume: a popular edition that would supply with the tales full information on the methods of field collecting or procuring manuscripts and the regional areas explored, and an annotated edition for scholars with commentaries on each tale giving data on its variant forms and points of historical, comparative, and literary interest as well as its place in the international classifications of tale types. Fourth, the volume editors would divide their tales in sections according to specific genres, such as wonder tales, animal tales, jocular tales, and so on, rather than heaping them together indiscriminately. This series has indeed richly fulfilled Delarue's promises.

He himself prepared the first volume, for Nivernais and Morvan, based on the manuscript archives of Achille Millien (1838–1927), one of the greatest French collectors and also a reputed poet and a translator of Russian folktales and folksongs. Millien is known for the folksongs he published, but his precious trove of contes had, for the greatest part, never reached print. The discovery by Delarue of Millien's manuscripts in 1933 in the departmental archives at Nivernais, and Delarue's intimate account of his predecessor's life and work, in itself illustrates the continuities in the history of French folklore scholarship. Born in Beaumont-la-Ferriere and inheriting from his father large estates, Millien devoted himself to the collecting of songs and tales—"the flowers of the earth"—that he had learned about from his own peasant servant who became his wife. Nivernais, snuggled be-

---

[22] Gédéon Huet was the author of *Les Contes populaires* (Paris, 1923), a considered review of problems in folktale studies.

tween the valleys of the Loire and Nievre de Premery, bristled
with the activity of woodcutters, charcoal burners, lumbermen,
wagoners, and dairy farmers, while in the town of Beaumont
lived a mixed population of small gentry, peasants, day laborers,
and artisans working for the manorial lord or the forge master.
In this milieu traditions were faithfully conserved, and Millien
set out systematically to gather them on annual forays, contacting
the mayor, the school principal, and the curé, and asking them
to assemble informants for him at an inn, a farm, a school, or a
parish house. To these places he traveled by ferry, carriage, and
cart. Between 1877 and 1895, he collected more than twenty-seven
hundred melodies and texts of folksongs, more than nine hundred folktales, hundreds of legends, plus proverbs, *blason populaire,* beliefs, customs, folk zoölogy and folk botany in notebooks. He published parts of his materials in the journals spring-
ing up in the 1880's, including both *Mélusine* and *Revue des
traditions populaires,* and in a journal he founded in 1896, *Revue
du Nivernais,* with supplementary numbers presenting parts of
his collection, beginning with the songs. But partial paralysis
in 1909 coupled with financial reverses and the subsequent dis-
appearance of his parasitic friends prevented Millien from the
completion of his task. This remained for Delarue.

In this unusual liaison óf a nineteenth- and a twentieth-cen-
tury master folklorist born in the same region, Delarue visited
localities where Millien had collected and sought to clothe in
flesh and blood some of his six hundred singers and tellers of
half a century before. Millien had merely given their names and
place and date of birth. Now Delarue actually met some of the
old men and women who had heard of or known "Mossieu
Achille," and Delarue thus supplemented the information on
Millien's narrators. "In Morvan, at Glux, to which I bicycled in
1942, I found an old man youthful in spirit, François Berthier,
born in 1864, who had been present at the reunion organized
by Millien in 1887, in an inn of the countryside, and he had kept
a precious memory." The old man recalled that the person who
had furnished Millien the best of his contes was Jeanne Martin,
called Jeannie, born at Glux in 1862. Daughter of a roofer using
oak planks, she was unlettered and was considered simple-
minded. Jeannie had married a man come from the "country of

vines"—that is to say, neighboring Bourgogne; she spent all day tending two nanny goats while spinning at her spindle, and it was from the old shepherds that she acquired the contes which she repeated voluntarily at the evening socials.[23]

At the Colonial Exposition in Paris in 1937, an international congress of folklore was held during which Delarue reported on the manuscripts of Millien. In his first printing of Millien's texts, Delarue, hitherto a botanist classifying water plants, took liberties with the wording, but after coming into contact with van Gennep he learned and adopted scholarly procedures. Subsequently, the first volume in the *Contes merveilleux des provinces de France* brought together the work of two renowned folklorists who never met—Millien and Delarue.

Other volumes in the series lived up to the standard of the first. Ariane de Félice's *Contes de Haute-Bretagne* (1954) revealed a whole unsuspected tradition of storytelling among basket makers in the hamlet of Mayun. These artisans regaled each other with long contes while engaged in their tedious occupation, in order to keep themselves from falling asleep. Their *veillées,* or evening socials, vividly described by Mlle de Félice, were conducted according to ritual procedures; the *conteur,* urged to deliver, would suddenly ejaculate, "Cric," whereupon the audience would be expected to respond, "Crac." One narrator while being recorded uttered, "Cric" to the unprepared circle of museum personnel, and when they did not reply appropriately he desisted and the disk had to be recommenced, with the now alerted audience ready to sound out, "Crac." Mlle de Félice expertly analyzes the repertoires and styles of her basket makers, around whom the collection is grouped. She finds that certain passages in contes are fixed and stereotyped and others, usually involving descriptions of the milieu, are flexible and subject to enlargement.

Geneviève Massignon, inspired by Delarue to become the most active modern field worker in France, contributed in 1954 *Contes de l'Ouest,* dealing with the regions of Grande Brière, Vendée, and Angoumois. Among these conteurs of the West, Mlle Massignon discovered a reliance on numerous little formulas and rhymes, fixed passages in the tale aiding the memory of the teller. In 1963 Mlle Massignon published the results of field trips to

[23] Paul Delarue, in *Contes du Nivernais et du Morvan,* p. 247.

Corsica in *Contes Corses,* presenting 106 texts with full scholarly apparatus. Her first forays into the field had been directed to dialect, as charged by the National Center for Scientific Research, which was engaged in preparing a *New Linguistic and Ethnographic Atlas of the West of France;* but Delarue encouraged her in this work to seek contes, and classified her harvest in his great catalogue. Similarly he suggested that on her vacations in Basse-Bretagne she hunt for *conteurs,* and in consequence Mlle Massignon brought out in 1965 an unusual collection of tales told by flax strippers of the Breton-speaking region of Trégor, *Contes traditionnels des teilleurs de lin du Trégor.* Like the basket makers, the flax strippers told tales at work and recreation, localizing and coloring the contes according to their Celtic temperament and personal horizons. The odious priest and wealthy patron appear as hostile figures, matched in the supernatural world by giants and monstrous animals, but fairies do not appear in Trégor. Besides publishing these collections of contes, Mlle Massignon also distinguished herself for her recording of French folksongs and her study of French dialects in Acadia. During her trip to North America on an *enquête* of 1946–47 she also collected contes from French-speaking farmers in Maine.[24] For her research in Acadia, she was given the gold medal of the French Canadian Academy, the first foreign author to receive this honor.

A gifted and industrious field worker, alert to the new techniques of tale collecting that embrace the teller, the style, the dialect, and the milieu as well as the text, Mlle Massignon was superbly fitted to undertake the present volume, completed shortly before her premature death in 1966 at the age of forty-five. The *Folktales of France* is both her memorial and a testament to the illustrious tradition of French folktale savants.[25]

RICHARD M. DORSON

[24] Geneviève Massignon, *Les Parlers français d'Acadie. Enquête linguistique,* 2 vols. (Paris, 1962); *La chanson populaire française en Acadie* (Paris, 1962).

[25] Daniel Massignon, brother of Geneviève, has furnished valuable assistance in seeing the manuscript through the press. I am deeply indebted to Roger Pinon, visiting professor at the Folklore Institute in the spring of 1967, for suggestions on the sources for this Foreword.

Introduction

The traditional field in mid-twentieth-century France may seem an exhausted territory to many scholars. Nevertheless, it yields happy surprises to collectors if they are capable of infiltrating into rural areas far from modern life. There they can listen to the peasant voice of the craftsman or the mountain dweller still linked by their occupations to the traditional life.

The role of tales and legends, of sayings and folksongs still seems to be of some importance in the traditional thinking of many natives of the French countryside. At least this is certainly true when they think back to the early years of their youth.

A map of the French provinces drawn up in 1893 by Paul Sébillot shows an odd distribution of the twenty-five hundred tales collected at that time.[1] This distribution shows us not only the efforts of certain local folklore experts but also the richness of certain fields. If that map were redrawn now, the same would be true. (In 1956 Paul Delarue estimated that there was a stock of ten thousand French tales.)

It has definitely been established, for instance, that North and South Brittany are privileged to have been chosen areas for tales and legends, and have brought to light collectors such as F. M. Luzel, François Cadic, Paul Sébillot, and Adolphe Orain. But not all the provinces of France or its districts have the good fortune like Montiers-sur-Saulx to have had a master of folklore such as Emmanuel Cosquin. He dug out of this village the material for his famous *Contes populaires de Lorraine* (Paris, 1886) and used it as a background for his remarkable outline of the modern comparative method.

In 1953, when, Paul Delarue was bringing out the series *Contes*

[1] *Revue des traditions populaires,* VIII (December, 1893), 584–85.

merveilleux des provinces de France, he noted with bitterness the regrettable gaps in the documentation of folklore collected from provinces where regional flavor was particularly strong, such as Provence, among others. By the end of the nineteenth century, rural life in other regions had already been submerged by industrialization and with it the framework of the traditional life of yesteryear. Delarue patiently made a census of the manuscripts collected at the end of the last century and the beginning of this one. His predecessor, A. Millien, found twelve hundred variants for the regions of Nivernais and Morvan. Delarue rediscovered the volume of tales entrusted to Emmanuel Cosquin by Victor Smith, the famous folklorist of Forez and Velay, and managed to collect together, with the help of both families, tales in manuscript (or published in places almost impossible to find) in exactly the same way as many folktales were culled by Antonin Perbosc in Gascogne and François Cadic in the Morbihan.

A small group of young collectors, of whom I am one, that Paul Delarue had managed to interest in French folktales, extended their investigations into areas offered to them either because the *Musée des arts et traditions populaires* had diverted them in that direction or because the dialectic investigations of the *Atlas linguistiques et ethnographiques de la France* gave them the opportunity. Perhaps they were simply moved by a personal interest in tradition. Ariane de Félice has already given the public her research on the basket weavers of Grande Brière (*Contes de Haute Bretagne* [Paris, 1954]). Her complementary thesis at the Sorbonne deals with the tales from the Bocage Vendéen, and the material resulting from her search in Berry, Marche, and Combraille has been published in part by G. Hüllen and M. L. Tenèze in the bilingual collection entitled *Begegnung der Völker im Märchen* (1961 and 1964).

Charles Joisten stuck with unusual tenacity to the tales from the French Alps, combing through many a valley, where he picked up hundreds of variants in the past fifteen years. These variants belong to a tradition now coming to its close. He published a first installment in *Contes des Hautes Alpes* (Paris, 1956), devoted to Queyras, known as the last stronghold of the folktale. But this did not prevent him from extending his research to the Pyrenees. As for the abbot Jean Garneret, author of a remarkable monograph on the speech of Lantenne-Vertière (Doubs), which was his parish, he also gathered in this small area the last traces of tradition and handed them over bit by bit to Paul Delarue as he found them.

With the study of dialects as a principal aim, research was undertaken under the aegis of the Centre National de la Recherche Scientifique which led to the establishing of the *Atlas linguistiques et ethnographiques de la France*. However, when rural areas are penetrated by the researcher knowing the regional dialect, this knowledge allows him to gain contact with the country people who retain local tradition. These are the narrators of tales or legends or the singers of songs. Pierre Nauton is director of the *Atlas linguistique et ethnographique du Massif Central* (three volumes have already been published, followed by an extensive *Exposé général*), and has done all the research by himself. He has had the opportunity of picking up many folktales in the past twenty years, nearly all recorded on tape. This is for him the most valuable kind of material in the study of the style and grammar of a dialect. It also provides other folklorists with interesting versions of folktales. Marguerite Gonon, who helped in the making of the *Atlas linguistique et ethnographique du Lyonnais,* has collected tales from an old miller's wife in Forez.

Because I was responsible for the research work for the *Atlas linguistique et ethnographique de l'ouest,* I explored the departments forming the "Pays Nantais," the "Pays de Retz" (Loire-Atlantique), the Haut Poitou and Bas Poitou (Vienne, Deux-Sèvres, and Vendée), the Aunis and the Saintonge (Charente-Maritime), the Angoumois and the Ruffecois (Charente), the Basse-Marche (Vienne and Charente), and the borders of the Limousin (Charente). Wherever I found it possible, I gathered folklore material while doing research on dialects in the various districts. My collection numbers about two thousand songs and three hundred tales and legends, some of which have been published in the magazine *Arts et traditions populaires* (1953) and in my *Contes de l'ouest* (Paris, 1953 and 1954).

For more than ten years I was advised by my teacher, Paul

Delarue, whom I miss very much, to extend my research to a district where I had spent many a holiday, the Côtes du Nord in the Pays de Trégor, which Luzel had admired for its oral literature, calling it "the attic of Basse Bretagne."

A search made in the rural craftsman's world, particularly in the valleys of the Leff and the Trieux where the flax *teilleurs* are to be found, allowed me to pick up thirty-one tales. Another search launched into the peasant circles of Trégor enabled me to collect fifty-nine tales there between 1953 and 1954. More than thirty of these were narrated to me by the same informant.

A little later in Corsica, where I already knew the dialect, I undertook another search among the mountain dwellers of Castagniccia and Niolo. This was more detailed and led me to collect ninety tales. Paul Delarue studied and catalogued them for his *Catalogue des contes français*. His faithful collaborator, Marie Louise Tenèze, carried on the master's work, and it is with her that I checked my second collection of Corsican tales made in 1959 (sixty tales), as I mention in the preface to my *Contes corses*.

The liveliness of the French tale in the twentieth century depends very much on the preservation of traditional rural life. It is true that in certain areas this way of life is fast disappearing as traditional customs must give way to modern progress, but we still find that the mountain people of the Massif Central, the Alps, the Pyrenees, and Corsica have a rich repertory of tales today. It is equally certain that the existence of a language or a dialect very different from regular French has helped to preserve local tradition. This is the case in South Brittany, Corsica, and the Bocage Vendéen; a certain conservatism is evident in their customs and their way of life. In the case of the Bocains of Vendée on their widely scattered farms, or in the case of the basket weavers and eel catchers of Grande Brière (North Brittany), their isolation has helped to keep up the traditional evenings spent with neighbors. Then, too, some crafts produce favorable circumstances for the spreading of tales and songs. They tell stories as they weave their baskets or spin the flax, as they carve their spoons of wood or their clogs, because these are jobs done collectively.

How do our narrators of the twentieth century appear to us? They may be craftsmen spending an evening with the neighbors, shepherds gathered around the fire, or peasant grandmothers looking after the young children. All are holders of a tradition communicated orally by their parents and grandparents and neighbors. In rare instances, traditions may come from people passing through the district and staying only temporarily in the countryside through which they traveled. Such persons might have been basket peddlers or livestock dealers taking their flock to the nearest market. Our folktale narrators are filled with their traditions, which they try to pass on as truthfully as they can to an audience which wants to hear a good story of the old days. It is unusual for one of these narrators to hesitate or go back in the telling to some forgotten episode. Only for some tales would he use rhymed passages to help him remember or to embellish the story for his audience.

The way in which these folk narrators tell their tales differs markedly from one province to another. The dialect, which is the usual medium used, imposes its own forms on the narrator's recital, and even if he tries to tell a tale in French, there still remains something of the dialect. Thus the Corsican tale starts with *Una volta era* (*Une fois, il était*) an inversion of our *il était une fois*. Marguerite Gonon, who collected old tales from Forez, mentions one of the sayings prefacing one of the tales best loved by the French narrators, *"Cric Crac; Cuiller à pot; Marche aujourd'hui, marche demain; A force de marcher; On fait beaucoup de chemin"* (cf. our tale No. 52, The Four Friends).

The rhymes ending a tale also vary according with the region. If Corsica ends with *"Fola foletta, dite a vostra; a mea è detta* (Fable, little fable, tell yours; mine is told) (cf. our No. 69, The Shepherd and the Snake), then in the regions of Languedoc you find them often using this: *"Passa per un pitit crô dé rat; moun counte est acabat"* (I've been through a little mousehole; my tale is finished.) Our tale in Limousin speech, The Gold Ball, offers us a variant. Or else a still shorter rhyme shows how the spell is broken, *"Le coq chanta et le conte fut fini."* So goes a tale from the Massif Central (cf. our No. 50, "Jean and Jeannette").

The tale from Poitou and Angoumois and Ruffecois is adorned with rhymed spells whose tone often varies as the tale progresses. An example of this is the tale of The Goat, the Kids, and the Wolf (No. 36). Now and then the magic words are repeated without alteration but addressed to different speakers:

> N'avez-vous pas vu passer
> Mon Jean et ma Jeannette?
> Mon char et ma charrette
> Avec mes chevaux blancs
> Ferrés d'or et d'argent.

In certain tales the jingle is sung. The tale of The Little Devil of the Forest (here it is No. 63), picked up by Charles Joisten in Savoie, is an example of this quite frequent case in the variants of Type 500. On the other hand, a Pyrenean version of *L'os qui chante* (Type 780) entitled The Laurel Flower (No. 66) brings us jingles with a simple rhyme and not *psalmodiées,* as is commonly found.

The narrator's diction varies, not only with the people or with their gifts, but primarily with the area. The Breton narrator loves abundance of detail, especially in long descriptive tales sometimes inbred with mystery; and this is true of North and South Brittany as well.

On the other hand, the Corsican narrator makes the characters talk to each other, revealing little scenes of local life, and going gaily from one episode to another. Limousin tales are short and concise. The thoughts as well as the elements making up the tale are sometimes concentrated dramatically in very short sentences. The tales of Franche-Comté and Poitou, especially those dealing with animals, are spicy and full of imagery.

The gestures and the accents of the narrators also contribute to the appearance of the tale. A Corsican woman narrator used to take my hand and place it over my heart in order to link me with the parts of her tale which she thought most moving. Another one, who was blind, concentrated on vocal inflections to put over the most violent passions occurring in parts of her tales.

The fantastic creatures that you find in traditional French tales are widely varied. If Brittany calls ogres and ogresses *Sarrazins et Sarrazines,* the central area of France containing Poitou, Marche, Limousin, and Nivernais labels them mysteriously *brou, lebrou, loup-brou, malbrou.* (These beings are presumably variants of the French *loup-garou.*) The southern areas sometimes substitute *le drac* (dragon) or the Devil. Corsica has *maghi,* the wizards whose powers are more varied than those of the ogres. More often than the *fada* (fairy), there appears in this island the little old woman who gives good counsel.

The fairy, usually a friendly character (except when she thinks herself slighted), sometimes gives way to the Holy Virgin as godmother to orphans or protector of the persecuted, and this takes place not in the regions thought of as devout areas, such as Vendée or Brittany, but in the provinces of Centre-Ouest, actually thought of as turning away from the Christian faith.

The liking for tales of wonder is common to North and South Brittany and Corsica, but Brittany, which is reputed to be mystical, does not discard facetious tales either. As for animal tales, they seem to be more appreciated in the middle west and in Franche-Comté and the Massif Central.

Together with authentic folktales, three legends are included in this collection. One is linked with a definite place, The Little Elves of La Chausse-en-l'Air (No. 22), and the other is linked to an event thought to be true (discovery of hidden treasure guarded by a diabolical being): The Black Hen (No. 27). As for The Legend of the Oxen's Pass (No. 67), set in Niolo (Corsica), this is one of those oral tales made to explain the strange shape of a mountain, in this case that of the *Cabu Tafonatu,* or "mountain placed by the Devil."

Those who have the traditional tales handed down to them know just as much about the kingdom of legends as that of fictions; but unlike the tales, whose form is rigid and which are passed on word for word to folk who have excellent memories, legends, being more open to variation, travel farther, and many villagers who do not know how to spin a yarn, have heard and spread scraps of these stories. Few informants told me legends as well developed and perfected as the tales.

In this collection I have grouped the chosen stories into fifteen areas, arranging the tales within each region according to the international classification of the Aarne-Thompson *Type Index*. The notes for each version are aimed at placing it within the framework of French tradition and also explaining any local particularities.

GENEVIÈVE MASSIGNON

Contents

Part I
Lower Brittany

Yann the Fearless

• HE WAS A LITTLE BOY who had lost his mother and father and was being brought up by his uncle, the priest. The little boy had no evil in him, but he was a little tricky to manage, if you like, and his uncle was not succeeding in teaching him any discipline.

Once when the priest had put Yann in the church as a punishment, he forgot that he was there, and the child had to stay there all night long. When he saw dusk approaching, he went into a confessional to get out of the cold.

At about midnight he heard a noise in the church. "Get that out of here!" said a voice.

"What is the matter with you?" replied Yann, who was not afraid.

Said the voice, "When I was a priest, I decided to steal something. I pinched the priest's stole, and I also took a golden goblet, and in order to hide them I put them in the priest's garden."

This was the previous priest of the parish. He was dead, and they had buried him under the flagstones of the church, as they still do sometimes.

The voice went on, "I had sworn on my life that I had not stolen them. I even said I would be happy to be dammed forever if I was not telling the truth. Now I am in hell and know no rest. Do tell the present priest not to pray for me every Sunday, as is the custom, for I suffer more when prayers are said for me."

The next morning the sacristan went into the church to ring the Angelus and found Yann shut in there. Astounded, he went to tell the priest, "There is a robber in the church!"

The priest came along, remembering then where he had left his nephew. "It is my fault," he said. "I shut the boy up in the church yesterday."

Yann told his uncle what the previous parish priest had said, remembering to mention that the things stolen from the church were buried in the priest's garden.

"Let us go and see at once!" said his uncle. They dug and searched in the garden and under the arbor, and they found what they were looking for. The priest kept the golden goblet and gave the stole to the boy. Yann had asked to have it, for the dead man had also said to him, "Keep the stole and you will never be afraid."

One day, when Yann was fifteen or sixteen, he said to himself, "With this stole I am sure of never being afraid. I am going round the world."

On his way he came upon an old house, an ancient castle which was crumbling into ruins, and he asked if he could take shelter there for the night. "Yes," he was told, "if you will sleep in the room up there, but no one dares to go in because no one who does ever comes back."

"I will willingly sleep in that room." So he went in and lay down to rest, but all night long there was noise. It was as if a man were there wailing in great pain. "Why do you wail like that?" said Yann out loud.

"I hid stolen money in this castle. I wanted to give it back, but I died before I could." The dead man also told Yann where the stolen money was. It was in the cellar.

The next morning the landlord went to the room and opened the door. (He had locked Yann in the night before.)

The youth explained what had happened that night and where the dead man had hidden stolen money. The landlord started searching the cellar with Yann. They dug under the castle and brought up a great deal of money. "As you found this money," the landlord said to the youth, "it will be yours. You have freed me at last from this dead man's cries of woe."

"I do not need it," said Yann. He took a little and went off saying, "The rest will be for the poor." So he went on his way.

He reached another house and asked to spend the night there. He was told the same story.

"I have no room to give you except one where noises are heard all night. If you are not afraid, take it!" said the landlord.

"Ah," said Yann, "well, I'll keep an eye open and we'll see."

They gave him something to eat—bread and cider—so that he would stay awake. At midnight as he was warming himself by the fire he heard a noise in the chimney. "Make as much noise as you like! I am not afraid," said Yann. Shortly after he saw a leg fall down the chimney. "Well," said he, "here is a skittle. I will set it up." A moment later he again heard a noise, and there was another leg falling. "Well, well, well, now I have two skittles." Yann placed the two legs upright, one next to the other, and resumed his vigil by the fireplace. As the noise began again, he cried, "Go ahead, make as much noise as you like!" One after the other there fell an arm and a few minutes later another arm, which he set up next to the legs like skittles. Then the body of a man came down the chimney. Yann grabbed the body round the middle and put the legs and arms around the trunk. "Now for the head!" And sure enough a head fell in the fireplace. "Well, well, well! Here is a ball to play skittles with."

Yann sat down again by the fire, eating a piece of bread. Suddenly he turned round and saw to his surprise that the body stood up and was saying as it came back to life, "You are pretty fearless, Yann."

"You are the one who is fearless, as you have stolen my skittles!"

This corpse was a devil who had assumed this form in order to frighten everyone. But Yann calmly went to the table to eat, and said, "Come on and eat with me."

Then another devil arrived, then two, then three. They all went to the side of the table opposite Yann, and pushed the table over on him in order to crush him.

"Cut it out!" Yann said. "I have my grandfather's scarf right here. So you'd better watch out!"

The devils kept on surrounding and threatening him. There was one, a cripple, who was meaner than the others. Yann put the stole around his neck, the devil began to yell, and the others all left.

"Now, before I let you go," Yann said, "you'll have to sign this saying that you won't have any power over anyone in this house for the nine *lignées* (generations)."

But the devil didn't want to sign it at any price. So Yann tightened the stole around his neck, and forced him to sign what he wanted him to.

As he left, the devil shouted at him, "You've gone too far!" and he took a rock from the windowsill and threw it in Yann's face, which turned as black as the chimney, it was so bruised.

"If I ever meet you again, I'll sure make you watch your step!" Yann said in turn.

Once again he had rescued the household with whom he had spent only one night. In acknowledgment, the owner offered him his daughter in marriage.

"No," Yann said, "I don't want to; I'm not going to get married." And once again he left and wandered around aimlessly. One day he heard that large numbers of people were gathering in Paris. In fact, long ago the Devil was promised that he would receive a king's daughter every fifty years; and now it was the turn of the King of France's own daughter to be surrendered to him.

Yann said to himself, "I have to go see the King first." Since traveling wasn't any problem for him, he went to Paris and said to the King, "Everyone is saying that the Devil is demanding your daughter."

"Alas, yes!" the King said.

"Let me stay close by her the night you have to hand her over, and I promise you I'll take care of the Devil. Believe me—if you do as I say, your daughter won't be taken away from you. Have a small vat placed in the middle of the large hall, and have it filled with holy water. You'll send for all the bishops, the archbishops, and even the Pope, and when everyone is gathered around the small vat, you'll have a *balai de cour* (farmyard broom) distributed to each one. When the last one of these important dignitaries enters the large hall, you'll see that he doesn't dare take a broom and go near the vat of holy water."

Yann's suggestions were carried out. Everything was in place on the appointed evening. The Devil appeared at the door of the hall; he immediately saw Yann and recognized him.

"Give me the King's daughter!" he said to him.

"Go get her, if you want her!" Yann answered.

"Throw her over here to me!"

"Come get her over here! If you want her, you'll come in this room to get her."

The Devil finally agreed to cross the threshold. Yann immediately threw the stole around his neck, and shouted to the bishops, the archbishops, and the Pope gathered around the vat:

"Quick! Take your brooms and splash holy water on the Devil. Really give it to him! Don't be afraid."

And they all did as he said. The Devil was caught. Then Yann had him sign an agreement that from then on, for a hundred generations, he wouldn't have any right to any daughter of the King of France, and he added, "Before I release you, and as you blackened my face the last time we met, you're going to make me the most handsome boy there is."

The Devil made him the best-looking boy ever seen in the world. However, as he left, he again grabbed a stone that had fallen out of the palace wall (he had to take something everywhere he went!), but this time he didn't throw it at anyone, and then he disappeared.

When the King's daughter met her rescuer, she fell in love with him, and the King proposed to Yann that he become his son-in-law.

"No," the young man answered, "I won't get married until I've faced another danger; I'm trying to learn what fear is."

Since the Princess very much wanted to marry him, she went and found one of these women who study the stars, to ask her how to frighten Yann.

The fortune teller told her, "You only have to cook a loaf of bread, and when it's done, you dig out the inside and put in a blackbird, leaving it a little air so it won't die. Then you tell this young man to cut into this loaf of bread before leaving the palace, and you'll see: when the blackbird flies out, it'll scare him."

Yann was getting ready to leave the King's palace; the Princess came and said to him, "At least do me the favor of eating some of this bread that I've made for you before you leave."

"That, I won't refuse," he said. And as he cut into the crust, the blackbird suddenly flew out! Yann was so frightened that he fell on his rear.

The King's daughter went over to him and said, "You were scared!"

"Yes," he said.

"Well then, since you now know what fear is, there's nothing to keep us from getting married."

"You're right," said Yann. "I can't ever again take chances, since I've been afraid once in my life."

Remember that he was still wearing his stole in order not to be afraid, but this time he was taken by surprise.

Then Yann consented to marry the King's daughter, and later on he in turn became King.

•2•   Old Fench

• ONCE UPON A TIME there was a King of France who had a son. One day, in looking through his father's papers, the young man found a portrait of Princess Virginia, daughter of the King of Naples. "She is so beautiful! Oh! I must go and find her. Never before in this world has there been such a beautiful woman!"

The King tried to dissuade his son, as he knew he was not very clever. "You will not manage it," he said. "No one has ever seen her in the flesh!"

"Never mind, I dream only of her and I want her so very much to be mine. Father, let me go and try to find her."

The King of France said, "If you go off, my son, take my old servant, Fench Coz (Old Francis), with you; he has known you since you were a child. Go, and obey him in every way. If you follow this advice you may perhaps reach your goal, but if you do not follow it you are a lost man.

One fine morning the young man left, seated in a coach drawn by two horses. Fench Coz, also in the coach, accompanied his master. After a day's travel on the road, just as night was falling, they went into a wood. In a clearing there was fresh grass, and the horses were tired; they put them to graze after unsaddling them.

Fench Coz said to the son of the King of France, "I am going to climb up a tree and spend the night there. You will stay in the coach to sleep, and the horses will eat grass and rest." The young man followed the old servant's advice, and soon he fell fast asleep in the coach where he had lain down. Fench Coz, on the other hand, had climbed a tree and did not sleep a wink before daybreak.

In the middle of the night he heard three characters come and sit at the foot of the tree and start talking. One was saying to the other, "You see the son of the King of France here, hoping one day to find Princess Virginia, but he shall not have her. I know well that at this moment he is asleep in his coach. I will also tell you how he could find her, but if I did not know that he was asleep, I would not speak of it."

"Do tell us then," said one of the others.

"Well, there is a river to cross, not far from here; there is no bridge, but on the bank there is a cluster of willows, and in the middle of the clump is hidden a little wand. All that is needed is to take this wand, hit the bank three times with it, and a bridge will span the river."

The King's son knew nothing of it, but Fench Coz had heard everything.

Another character went on to say, "I know that there is a castle on the other side of the river where Princess Virginia lives. But her father, the King of Naples, does not want anyone to go near her, so he has also given her a governess who watches over her day and night. One would have to signal the princess, who is in a room which has one small window; but if her father or the castle guards saw one signaling to her, they would watch over her even more strictly."

Fench Coz did not miss a word of this.

The third character added, "If, however, the son of the King of France manages to carry off Princess Virginia, which is altogether impossible, he would have the King of Naples and all his guards at his heels. To delay his pursuers it would be necessary to keep the wand found in the clump of willows and to put it back after having crossed the bridge; then the bridge would disappear, and the King of Naples would be delayed in his chase."

Fench Coz did not miss hearing this either.

Next morning, the son of the King of France said to his old servant, "Did you sleep well?"

"Yes, master."

"Me, too," said the Prince. "I did not wake at all."

"Well, our horses are rested; it is time to take to the road again."

It was not long before the Prince's coach stopped at a river;

it was not very wide, but there was no way of crossing it. "Don't worry, master!" said Fench Coz. "I will get out of the coach and see to it that there is a bridge." The old servant found the wand hidden in the clump of willows, hit the bank of the river three times with it, and at once a bridge spanned the river from one bank to the other.

The coach started to cross, and before the end of the morning it stopped before the castle of the King of Naples. Fench Coz then said to the son of the King of France, "Princess Virginia is shut up in that room up there. She has only one little window through which to communicate with the outside world, but if you succeed in seeing her, signal to her and she will be ready to follow you, for she has had enough of living like a recluse in this castle."

Meanwhile, Princess Virginia was in her room alone with her governess. She said to her, "I know that a prince has arrived at the foot of the castle. He has just signaled to me as I showed my head at the window. Let us go down to the garden at once before anyone finds out!"

As she was allowed to walk in the courtyard with her governess, the guard let her pass. They reached the garden gate where the son of the King of France was waiting for them. He made them hurry into his coach while he and Fench Coz leaped onto the two horses. Then they left at full speed. Soon they reached the bank of the river. "Let's quickly cross the bridge," said Fench Coz to his young master, "because it will soon disappear." And as soon as the coach was over, the old servant leaped off his horse and put the wand back in the middle of the clump of willows. The guards of the King of Naples had just reached the bridge when it disappeared, and they were all drowned.

The Prince went on his way up to the little wood where they had stopped the first night. This time he left the coach for Princess Virginia and her governess to rest in, and he said to his old servant, "It is my turn to climb up this tree and sleep there; and you will sleep in the grass in the clearing."

"No, Master, you will sleep there, and I will climb up into this tree again." The Prince let his old servant have his way.

Soon the three characters who had gathered at the foot of the tree the night before came back to it to pick up their conversation. One took over and said, "We have said that the son of the King of France would not succeed in taking away Princess Virginia, and he is over there in this clearing, sleeping at the foot of his coach; but he has not gone back to France, and he will have a good deal of trouble getting back! If, however, he does get there, he will meet a beggar drowning in a pond. This beggar will call for help from him; as the son of the King of France is kindhearted, he will be ready to save him, but if he tries to save him, it is certain that the Prince will come to us to get warm."

Fench Coz was not sleeping any more than the night before, and he missed none of this.

The second character added, "If he stops himself at once and does not rescue the beggar, he will next meet a thief. This thief will ask him to give up all his belongings—his coach, his horses, his money, and even his clothes—and he will put out the Prince and his companions, as naked as worms, to run over the earth; but the son of the King of France, who is proud, will not accept that, and if he rejects the thief's requests, it is then that he will come to us to get warm."

Fench Coz was still listening. It was the third character's turn to speak. "If the Prince accepts the thief's request, they will all, naked and on foot, arrive at an inn which will have as its sign:

Food, drink, and clothes for three days are given here free of charge.

"And if they are foolish enough to go into the inn—well, then they will all come to us to get warm!" Then the conversation between the three characters came to an end. And now all three of them said, "If anyone repeats what we have just said, he will be turned into a marble statue."

Dawn came. Fench Coz woke everyone up, and they set off again. The old servant knew everything, but he did not breathe a word to anyone. They had not gone very far when they had their first encounter. A poor man in rags was thrashing about in

a pond as if about to drown and was yelling, "Help!" The Prince
wanted to get down from his horse to rescue him.

"No," said Fench Coz, "you shall not do it." The King's son
grew angry. "Not only do you want to do everything your own
way, but now you are even turning nasty!"

"Your father, the King, entrusted you to me, and I am telling
you to leave this beggar behind and let us be off!" The young
man, surprised, obeyed against his better judgment.

A little later on, the coach was stopped by a thief who stood
in the way on the road. "If you value your life, you must give
me all that you have on you and with you!"

The son of the King of France wanted to go past him in a
dignified manner. "No, no," said Fench Coz, "we must give him
all we have and he will let us by." The young man was very
put out. As for the Princess and the governess, they did not want
to give into the thief either. "You see," said Fench Coz, "I let it
happen to me!" And he started to take off his clothes. The Prince
could not get over it.

"Your father told you to obey me," Fench Coz said, adding,
"Do as he says, otherwise you're lost!"

Seeing this, Fench Coz's three fellow travelers copied the
servant; and there they were, naked, on foot, walking wearily
along in the hope of finding shelter. They reached an inn where
they saw written:

> Food, drink, and clothes for three days are given here
> free of charge.

The son of the King of France exclaimed, "Let's go in here!"

"No," said Fench Coz.

"Yes, yes."

"Oh no, we must go on. Follow me, all three of you, and you
will soon be home."

The Prince went on in such an angry state that he wanted to
kill his servant. In the end he gave up and obeyed him; and,
guided by Fench Coz, they reached the King of France without
further ado.

His son was proud to come back to his father's castle with

Princess Virginia, but he was angry with Fench Coz, and he told the King all that the old servant had made him do. And so Fench Coz was, at the Prince's request, thrown into prison.

But the King of France, knowing how simple his son was, came and questioned the old servant in prison. Fench Coz explained to him what he had heard up in his tree that first night, and how he had made the most of it; but when he got to the second night, and started to tell about the meeting with the poor drowning man, that very instant his feet changed to marble and his legs also, up to his knees.

As the King insisted on hearing more, the old servant had to tell him how he had heard their meeting with the thief predicted. Then the servant exclaimed, "As I must talk to get out of this prison, ah, well, I shall suffer because of you." Then and there he turned to marble up to his shoulders. The King still insisted, and when the servant told of the predicted meeting at the inn, where what I have told you is written, he concluded, "If he had gone into that inn and had not obeyed me, he would have turned to marble as I am doing." At these words his mouth closed and his whole head turned to marble. When the King and his son saw only a marble statue instead of Fench Coz, they started to weep; but this did no good. So they had the statue placed in the center of the most beautiful hall in the castle, and every day the King's son washed the marble that had been Fench Coz with tears of remorse.

Later the King of France wished his son's wedding to Princess Virginia to take place; and before the end of the year they had a son. But to their utter despair, the child did nothing but cry day and night; there were always three nurses by him, but no one could calm him.

In the end the King's son tired of this. One day he went in secret to a soothsayer to ask her advice. "I don't believe we shall ever know happiness without Fench Coz, my old servant, who has been changed into marble, and I will do anything in order to free him."

The soothsayer replied, "I know. You have a child who cries day and night. He may always have three nurses at his side, but nothing makes him quiet. Well, I will give you some advice.

If you want to set your old servant free, you must first kill your son and spread your son's blood all over the marble image of Fench Coz. When all the stone is washed with it, your old servant will be a man again, and he will bring your child back to life, and he will laugh and run about."

"Fench Coz always told me the truth," said the King's son, "so I shall resign myself to doing as you say."

He went into the King's castle and said to the three nurses, "Leave me alone with my son; I will look after him while you go to Mass with Princess Virginia." The nurses were quite pleased to leave the child for a while, and they gladly accepted the Prince's suggestion.

While all the ladies of the castle attended Mass, the Prince killed his son, spread the child's blood over the marble, and washed it with the blood. Then Fench Coz, very much alive, rose before him and started to weep; but by bathing the child with his tears, he brought him back to life.

When Princess Virginia returned to the castle with the three nurses, she saw her son there before her, toddling about and laughing. Fench Coz was at the Prince's side, and from that day forth he never left him.

·3· *Ugly Yann*

• YANN WAS A BOY who was both very ugly and very poor, hence his surname of Ugly Yann (*Yann Vil*). He had done God a favor, I do not quite know how, and it was because of this that he had received as a reward the power to say, "By the grace of God, may this or that be done." He was so simple, however, that he had never thought of using it.

One day he had gone out to pick up deadwood for his mother, and he made a faggot of it. He came home carrying the wood on his back. Feeling tired, he sat down on the bundle of sticks and had a short rest.

"Ah," he sighed, without having too much faith in his powers, "if only it was the faggot's turn to walk instead of mine! By the grace of God, let this faggot carry me."

To his great surprise he felt himself being lifted and carried along, though he was in fact still sitting on his pile of wood. He was not, however, the only one to be surprised. The King's daughter was at the window of her castle. She was busy watching poor Yann. He was ugly and badly dressed, and to her great surprise she saw him go by carried on the faggot.

"Oh, look at him, that Yann—now his faggot is carrying him along with him sitting on it." Yann was vexed by these words. He decided to use his powers this time to punish the Princess for her teasing.

"By the grace of God, may the King's daughter become pregnant."

And that is what happened. The Princess was amazed and confused. Her father, the King, came to hear of it and asked her many questions to find out who was responsible. The Princess assured him that she had never seen anyone.

"But after all," said the King, "you are the same as anybody else! I want to know who the father is."

In good time the Princess had a little boy. She could say nothing more about how he had come to be.

The King was still just as dissatisfied. He said, "When the child can walk, perhaps there will be a way of recognizing his father."

The King then sent for all his lords and dukes and princes and even the kings of other countries that the Princess might have visited. He had firmly decided to put them to the test. The little boy was beginning to walk. He was given a ball and he was told to put this ball in his father's hat. All the nobles were made to pass in front of the child, but in the end the ball was still in his little hand.

The King did not give up his plan. He ordered that all the poor people, the crippled and the weak, should be brought to him. The same ceremony took place. The poor people filed past the child, but suddenly as it was Yann's turn to go by, the child put his ball into Yann's hat.

The King was dumbfounded, and the Princess was not flattered.

Her father said to her angrily, "Now you can no longer say you do not know your child's father."

"Father, I swear to you that I know as little about it as before."

"How can you expect me to believe you from now on? It is useless for you to protest. You have shamed me in front of everybody, and no one can deny that this ugly Yann has been pointed out by your child's hand. Well, marry this man! I banish you from my court, and I never want to see you again."

The Princess found she had nothing to say. She had to make up her mind to marry this ugly Yann whom she found so wretched and so poor.

So they settled down to live together. One day she thought of asking him how he had made her pregnant, and her husband explained to her that he had been given the power to do anything he wished by the grace of God. He explained that he had only to say, "By the grace of God, let this or that be done."

"Well!" said the Princess, "as you have this power, do ask to become Yann *Vrao* (Handsome Yann)."

Ugly Yann took her advice and at once became as handsome as a prince. He was the best-looking prince on the face of the earth.

And in this way the Princess remained married to Yann.

·4· *The Tailor*

• ONCE UPON A TIME there was a tailor who worked for a farmer by the day. While he was sitting on a bench next to the table where he had placed his piece of fabric, a swarm of flies started buzzing around him. Furious, he pulled off his cap and hit them with it. With one blow he killed a thousand flies!

So once he had reached home he wrote on his cap, "I kill a thousand at one blow!"

And then he went on going to work by the day, cutting clothes now at one place, then at another, but he was careful always to take his cap with him.

People began by looking at him in surprise, then in awe.

"There's a strong man," they said to themselves as they saw him go by.

His reputation for strength reached the ears of a giant who lived with his brothers in a secluded castle, and they came to find the tailor.

"Do come with us! If you can kill a thousand at one blow, you can just as well help us with our jobs."

The tailor did not have to be asked twice. He went to their home, telling himself that he would manage to catch them out somehow.

One day the giant who was boss said to him, "This morning we must fetch water from the fountain. You will come with me." There and then the giant took two barrels to fill.

"Oh, it's not worth carrying all that," said the tailor. "I can bring the fountain here to me."

"Oh, no, no, no!" said the giant. "I do not want that. This fountain is very useful where it is. If you took it home with you, what would we do without water?"

Once again the tailor had won!

Another time they went off into the forest to cut wood. The giant, who was very strong, began to cut down trees one after the other.

"It's your turn now," he said to the tailor.

"No, no, I do not bother to cut down trees. I take the forest with me if I want to!"

"Oh, don't do that!" the giant objected. "Leave the forest where it is; otherwise we shall not have any more wood to cut close by our house."

Not long after, the giant and his brothers were playing au palet. (This is a game rather like bowls but played on the ground with flat stones, the object of which is to find who can get closest to a chosen stone.)

"Well, do you want to play with us?" the giant shouted to the tailor.

But the tailor had sat down on a millstone and he yelled from there, "Look out, because I am going to set all these millstones rolling down the path and send them far, far away from here."

The giant rushed over to him.

"Stop! Don't do that, my friend. My brothers and I need these millstones to play au palet, and if you send them far off, we shall never find them again."

Another time, the giant was walking along with the tailor, thinking as he went that he had really had enough of this man's tricks. "This time," he said to himself, "I shall catch him." He took a stone in his hand.

"You see this stone? Well, I shall reduce it to powder in front of you."

The giant well and truly crushed the stone. There was nothing but a fine powder left in his hand. It was like flour. Then the tailor was so terrified that he wet his pants, and so he put his hand underneath and showed it to the giant.

"Well, you see, I can turn a stone into juice!"

The giant did not know what to do with the tailor.

"We shall never see the end of him," he said to his brothers. "So we must kill him."

One night the giant said to the tailor as he showed him a bed, "You are going to stay and sleep here. Lie down there."

"Yes, yes." But the tailor was more wily than the giant. He soon guessed that they meant him no good, and so he hid under the bed watching to see what might happen.

In the middle of the night the giant came along carrying an iron bar weighing two hundred pounds, and he struck the bed with all his might. "This time," he said to himself, "we have not missed; he must be dead."

The next day he went to see the tailor, to make sure.

"Would you like to come to lunch?" he shouted by way of being polite. But lo and behold, there was the tailor pulling himself up onto his backside in the middle of the bed.

"But how . . . !" said the giant. "But . . . how come! Didn't you hear anything last night? No noise?"

"Oh," said the other, "no, not much, a mere nothing."

The giant could not get over it. "There is no way of getting round this one!" he said.

The tailor did not seem to be worrying very much.

"Listen," said the giant. "Have something to eat and then be off. I do not want you as a friend any more. Go away from here."

You have to face it, you know. The tailor had won every time. Blow by blow, he had beaten the giants.

·5· *The Priest's Pig*

• ONCE UPON A TIME there was a poor family. They were very, very poor. The father had a whole tribe of children to feed, and he could not manage it. One day he said to himself, "What if I went and stole a pig from the priest?"

He had known that the priest had in his pigsty a big fat pig, ready for slaughter. He got hold of it without too much trouble, killed it noiselessly, and cut it into pieces.

The next day, the smallest boy was going off to the fields leading the only cow owned by his family.

He started to hum and sing as he walked along.

> Delicious that meat is, of the pig from the priest.
> T'was my father last night who stole the beast!

The priest happened to be coming along the same path on his way to church. He was quite surprised by these words and shouted, "What are you singing, little boy?" But the child did not want to say any more.

"Sing it again! Repeat what you said a moment ago!"

"Oh, no, I can't say that."

"Well, I am telling you. I want you to say it again, and good and loud!"

"Sir, I was only saying the truth."

"All right, so be it. As it is the truth, you will come to church on Sunday, and you will say it in front of everybody."

"Oh, sir, I shall not be able to go to church like this. I have got only old clothes . . ."

"Well, I will buy you a new suit. Don't fail to come and find me on Sunday before Mass."

And that day the priest gave the little boy some smart new clothes to go to church in. In the middle of Mass he announced to his parishioners who were gathered together, "Listen to this child. You are going to hear the truth." And to the little boy he said, "Here is the pulpit of truth. Climb into it instead of me and say in front of everybody what you were saying on the road the other day."

The small boy was not in the least embarrassed. He climbed into the pulpit and he said very loudly:

> The priest and my mother are lovers,
> And glory be to God, my father knows nothing about it.

The priest was furious. He kept protesting, "This is not true! That wasn't what you were saying."

"Yes, that's it. That's what I said!"

"No, it is not!" said the priest, as he gave him a kick in the backside.

"*Monsieur le recteur,* that's all I can say!"

And everybody started laughing with the small boy.

Part II
Upper Brittany

.6. *The Devil and His Three Daughters*

THE NARRATOR: "Do you remember how the tale about the Devil went? Me, I can't remember it!"

His wife: "Wasn't it about the Devil who had three daughters and about the youngest who used to take food to a lad who was working for her father?"

The narrator: "Lor' yes—lad who ate a bit every six months and drank a gulp every year."

His wife: "That's right. The Devil wanted to poison him! The meal that he was making his daughter take to the lad was poisoned, so she always said to him, 'Don't eat what I bring you. By the magic of my little wand, I will give you something else to eat.'"

The narrator: "That's how it was! But that is not all. The Devil gave this lad a skimmer to empty the pond with. How could you expect him to empty the pond! The Devil had said to him, 'You have from now till this evening to empty this pond. If you can't do it, you are to die.'

'How can I, with a skimmer?'

'You have got to do it or you will be killed.'"

The youngest daughter therefore led him to the edge of the pond. Once the girl had gone, the lad said, "I can't do this job. I am going to lie down and go to sleep."

Every day at noon the Devil sent his daughter to the lad with a meal, as was intended. The girl had said to him—to the lad that is, "Above all, don't touch the pond. I'll come and bring you something to eat."

The young man lay down on the grass hoping this would happen. Well, I would have done the same thing. Think of it— a skimmer, to empty a pond!

Noon came. The youngest daughter appeared with her basket. "You haven't done anything? I'll give you something to eat."

"But the pond has not been emptied."

"I'll see to that at once!"

The girl had a little wand. She struck it three times, saying,

"With the help of my little wand, let the pond dry up!" Lo
and behold, the pond was dry in a flash.

But that evening it was the Devil's turn to be surprised. The
Devil got to the place, and what did he see? The pond was dry.
Did the Devil's mouth ever open wide! He went on looking
around, but he could see only the lad. "So it must be he who did
the job. Well, you are certainly more clever than I am!"

That lad had already surprised the Devil by not eating or
drinking anything that the Devil had had brought to him in a
basket by his daughter. "How do you do this?" said the devil.
"You always send my daughter back with the basket full."

"Oh Lor', I eat once every six months and I take a gulp every
year!"

There was the pond, quite dry. Well, the next day, there's the
Devil saying something like this: "There's a copse of perhaps
about seven acres. The tops must be made into faggots and the
trunks grouped into cords by tonight."

So for the woodcutting the girl led him to the edge of the
copse which was to be cut down. "Don't do a thing. I will bring
you something to eat." (The meal the Devil had prepared was
poison. She would not give it to him. She used to say to him,
"You will eat what I give you." Each time she took the lad's
meal back with her. The Devil could easily see that he was not
eating it.)

With a wooden ax the Devil had given him, how could you
expect the poor lad to cut down the copse? "Ah," he said, "if I
die tonight, never mind, I'm going to lie down by the copse."

At noon she brought him a meal. The same thing happened.
She took her wand and said, "With the help of my little wand,
let there be something for him to eat and drink." And there was
everything you could possibly want. Nothing was lacking, I can
tell you.

The young man said, "What shall I do? Even if I had the
tools, how could I cut down the whole of the copse by tonight?"

The Devil's daughter struck three times. "With the help of my
little wand, let all this wood be cut, made into faggots, and
measured out into cords."

When the Devil saw by evening that his copse had all been

cut down, he was beside himself with rage. "So you cut down the copse?!"

"I chopped it all down."

"Oh, this one is smarter than I am," the Devil said to himself.

Then at night when he went home the lad had other things to do but go to sleep. He had to look after the horses. Ah, good gracious! I remember what the Devil used to say to him.

"If you do not empty the hay from my barn to feed the horses, you are as good as dead!"

So the girl gave him tobacco to smoke so that the Devil would not find him asleep. Otherwise he would have killed him!

When the Devil reached the stables, there was nothing but smoke there. You see, the horses had eaten everything in the hay barn—there wasn't even any food in their mangers!

The Devil's daughter, with the help of her little wand, had emptied all the hay from the barn into the mangers, and the horses had eaten it all. And there was the lad smoking all night so's not to fall asleep!

On the third day, what was it now? Oh, yes, a magpie's nest had to be lifted out from the top of a tree which had no low branches. The Devil said to the lad, "There's a magpie's nest to be lifted out of that tall, tall tree. It's ever so tall, and if you don't get the job done, I'll kill you!"

The girl said to the lad, "This time you have got to kill me. You'll put my bones end to end, and you will make a ladder to climb the tree."

"No, I don't want to kill you. You've done so much for me."

"Well, if you don't want to kill me, then I'll kill myself. Remember carefully, though, how to place my bones. You will put them back when you've got the magpie's nest out. When you are down again, you will put back my bones bit by bit."

Well, there were the girl's bones, end to end, and this made a strong ladder to get to the top of the tree. So the lad lifted out the magpie's nest and then came down again. Then bit by bit he put the girl's bones together again, and she came back to life. "Oh," he said, "a little toe is missing." So there it was. He'd forgotten to put back one of her toes.

Then she said to him, "As you have done all the jobs my

father set you, listen to me. He will get you to marry me or one of my sisters. He will ask, 'How would you like to choose—by their heads or by their feet?' If you choose by the feet, you will be able to recognize me."

When the Devil saw that the lad had lifted out the magpie's nest, he could not get over it. "You're crafty, you are! Now that you have done everything I asked of you, I'll give you one of my daughters to marry."

The Devil led the lad into his daughters' room. They were all three together in a big bed. It was dark. "Choose one. By the head or the feet, just as you like!"

The lad said he would like to choose her by the feet. He felt the feet of each one and found the foot with the missing toe. "You fiend, you," said the Devil, "that's my best one you're taking!" He was angry, but the deed was done. "Well, if that's the one, we'll get you married."

So the boy and the girl stayed with the Devil a couple of days, but the sisters were a bit jealous, so they left with the best horse and carriage.

The Devil, when he saw what had happened, went after them.

When the girl saw that her father was going to catch up with them, she changed the young man into a fountain and changed herself into a frog (in the fountain).

The Devil went to the fountain. "Well, tell me, fountain, have you seen a boy and girl going by here?" There was the frog paddling about in the fountain. "Oh, so it's you who are a fountain and my daughter a frog," said the Devil. But he could not catch them. He went home and then started after them again.

This time the girl turned the boy into a cherry tree and herself into a cherry on the tree. "Well, tell me, cherry tree, have you seen a girl and boy go by here? So you are a cherry tree and my daughter is a cherry," said the Devil, but he could do nothing to them.

The third time that the Devil chased after them, the girl said, "With the help of my little wand, let a river flow between my father and me." And that time it was all over. The Devil could not cross the river, and they were safe.

Now the boy wanted to go back to his part of the country. They left each other, and he went back to his parents. After all, she had said to him: "Go back and see your parents if you like, but don't forget that if you let yourself be kissed by anybody at all, you will forget everything that has happened to you. You will not even know that you are married anymore."

So, what happened? He went home. His mother wanted to kiss him, but he would not let her. An aunt whom he had not seen for a long time arrived, however, and threw her arms round his neck and kissed him. It was all over. He then no longer knew he was married.

One fine day he was with two other boys taking a walk. They met a girl by a Station of the Cross. "Lor', is she pretty!"

"You've never seen her?"

"I don't know her."

The three boys would all three have liked to get to know her better, but all three together were really too much. "Well, do we go over and see her anyway?"

They walked on a bit. "Well, what about going there on our walk?" Then they all got to the house where the girl lived. She gave them a good welcome, all three of them. Eight o'clock went by, nine o'clock, ten o'clock, eleven o'clock! . . . One of them said, "Boys, it's time we were going."

And then as they were about to go, she tapped one of them on the shoulder and said softly, "Don't you want to sleep with me?"

"Yes," he said.

But they went off all the same, all three of them.

A bit farther on, the third one said, "I don't know what's the matter with me. I feel I want to be sick. Go on ahead; I'll catch up with you." And he wheeled round to go back and find the pretty girl.

When he reached her house, she said to him, "Are you glad you have found me?"

"Yes," he said.

"Get undressed then." Then she said, "Oh, there's a bucket of water to fetch from the fountain."

"Well, it's not time we are short of," he said. And off he went, just in his shirt. So he got to the well and shoved the bucket in.

When he pulled it up, there wasn't any water in it. All night it was like that. He went down for water, and the bucket was always empty and there was daybreak coming.

"It really is a disgrace! A man who can't pull up a bucket of water! You don't deserve to spend the night with a woman."

"Oh, well, you will let me warm my feet up by the fire, won't you?"

"No," she said, "I wouldn't dream of it, a man like you."

A little later on, the three boys met once more. "Where did you go last night after you left us?"

"I had a stomachache." He did not tell them what had happened to him.

"You know, she is too good to miss."

The next day one of the other two boys said, "Do we go back tonight?"

"If we feel like it."

So off the three boys went to find her. The girl was pleased, too. Nine o'clock, ten o'clock, eleven o'clock, midnight! . . . "Oh, it's time to go to bed!"

The three boys were about to leave again when the girl tapped one of the other two on the shoulder and said to him, "Don't you want to come tonight?"

"Oh, yes," he said. He left with the other two, and a bit farther on he said, "I've got a stomachache. Go on ahead, and I'll catch up with you."

The first one said to himself, "If you're like me, don't fret."

Well, there was the second lad back with the girl.

"You're happy to sleep with me?"

"Yes."

"You won't have much to do," she said. "You've only got to close the doors before getting into bed."

"Can I undress first?"

"Suit yourself."

He had taken off his shirt, and so went out with his top bare. Whenever he managed to get one door closed, the other opened. He was still trying to close them when morning came.

"You can't even close a door," she said. "You couldn't sleep with a woman if you tried!"

And so there went that varmint.

Now, the third lad was the girl's husband. He didn't recognize her any more, but she recognized him.

The three lads did their day's work. "Oh, she's a lively girl when all's said and done. Let's go and see her again tonight."

The evening drew on. Ten o'clock, eleven o'clock, midnight . . . up to one o'clock in the morning.

"It's time to go to bed. Off with you!"

But this time she tapped on her husband's shoulder. She said to him, "Don't you want to sleep with me?"

"Yes," he said. "I'll take my friends a bit farther on, and then I'll come back."

He hadn't even gone two hundred meters when he said to them, *"Ça ne tourne pas rond là dedans!"* ("There's something fishy about all this.") The two others said to each other, "How did you get caught?"

"I was caught by being made to pull up a bucket all night."

"And I got caught having to close the two doors!"

So, what do you know, the third one went back to find the girl.

"You are quite happy about spending the night with me?"

"Yes."

"You won't have much to do. Just damp down the fire in the fireplace. You know how."

Well, the same thing happened! The more ash he piled on, the more the fire kindled. He spent all night looking after that fire.

The next day she said to him, "You can't even damp down a fire."

"Oh, but even so you let me warm up my feet!"

"Well, well," she said, "you don't recognize me!"

You see he'd been kissed by his aunt, so he didn't know he was married any more, but she did. She knew he was her husband.

There and then he recognized her and never left her ever again.

---

[1] Expression used in connection with a cart wheel turning unevenly.

·7· The Boy Whose Mother Wanted to Throw Him in Boiling Water

• He was a wretched little lad whose mother could not bear him. One day she asked him, "Which would you prefer, to be cooked in boiling water or stabbed to death with a knife?"

The little lad saw he would rather be thrown into boiling water. However, while his mother was putting the water on to heat in a huge kettle, the boy ran away.

He ran and ran along the road to get away, far, far away. In the end he didn't know where he was anymore. At night he took shelter in a kind of grotto, and there he met a fairy. "I don't know where to go," he said. "My mother wanted to throw me into boiling water, so I left home.

"Go and ask at the castle over there whether they need a swineherd on their farm, and if ever you need me again you say, 'Come to me, little old woman, come to me!' and I shall come and help you."

The boy thanked her and then he got himself hired at the farm, where they just happened to need a swineherd. It was the King's farm.

Every day they sent the little lad to the heath. Sometimes he had to run after one pig and sometimes another, so much so that he got quite exhausted looking after them. Then he thought of the old woman's words and he called her, "Come to me, little old woman, come to me!"

"What do you want, little boy?"

"I cannot go on looking after the swine from now on, for I am tired out."

"I'll give you a coach to save you from getting tired running after the swine. Wherever your swine go, your coach will go, too, and all you have to do is remain sitting inside it." And the fairy made him a coach out of a turnip, and it was drawn by four white rats who had been harnessed.

The little lad was very pleased. Wherever his animals wandered, the coach was sure to follow.

The next thing was that he became fed up with always having to look after the swine. "Come to me little, old woman, come to me!"

"What do you want, little boy?"

"I don't want to look after the swine any more. I would rather look after the sheep."

"Well then, go back to the farm. They will put you in charge of the sheep, as you wish; and don't worry. Wherever the sheep go, your coach will go, too."

And off went the little lad to the heathland to look after the sheep. You should have seen how he used his turnip coach with the four white rats harnessed to it, and how fast it went.

But again he grew tired of looking after sheep. "Come to me, little old woman, come to me!" he said.

"What do you want, little boy?"

"I am tired of looking after the sheep. Now I would like to look after the turkeys."

"Well, then, don't worry and go back to the farm. Tomorrow they will put you in charge of the turkeys, and your coach will go wherever the turkeys go." He was lucky, wasn't he? But even then that was not enough for him.

One fine day he said again, "Come to me, little old woman, come to me!"

"What do you want, little boy?"

"I would like new clothes to put on and to walk about in when it is a fine day."

So the old fairy gave him three fine suits. One was colored like the sun, one colored like the moon, and one colored like the stars. The little boy, who had grown up a great deal, was very proud at the thought that he could go about dressed like that in his turnip coach drawn by four white rats.

The first day he put on his sun-colored suit and he climbed into his coach to go for a drive on the heathland. The King's daughter, who was at the window of her room, saw him dressed in his sun-colored suit and found him very pleasing.

The next day the little boy put on his moon-colored suit and again went off driving over the heathland in his coach. The King's daughter, who had been watching out for him since the day before, saw him again and could not believe her eyes, he was so magnificently dressed.

The third day it was time to put on his star-colored suit. It sparkled with gold. From her window the Princess saw the little boy go by. He was a young man now and he went by in his coach dressed in this way. She could not take her eye off him.

A few days later she saw a lovely glowing light on the heathland. She went and found him there, and he asked her to get into his coach.

From then on, it was like that nearly every day. He put on his fine clothes to be seen by her; she went to find his coach; and they went for walks together.

When her father, the King, heard about this he soon grew very angry. "You, my daughter, going with a turkey boy?"

"But I love him, Father, and I wish to marry him."

"Marry him, daughter? No, I will never agree to that."

The King had two other daughters who were already married, but to noblemen, and they were rich in the bargain. He, so help him, did not want a son-in-law of this sort. However, the young girl's two brothers-in-law kept saying jokingly, "Come on, turkey boy, you'll get there in good time!"

Some time later, as the King was getting old, he decided to make those who had claims to the throne draw for it, in order to hand it over to the winner of the contest.

Naturally his two sons-in-law were the first contenders. The test was to last three days in succession. The first to get to the goal with his horse would be the winner. But the young Princess said to the turkey boy: "There is an old mule in the stable. If you tried to mount it, perhaps you might win and then we could get married."

They went to the stable together. The mule was so old that he could no longer make her stand up on her feet to be ridden.

The young girl went on, "I know there is an old sword in the hearth. What if you took it? Perhaps it might come in useful to you." But when they saw the sword, it was too old and too rusty. So the young man said, "Come to me, little old woman, come to me!"

"What do you want, my little son of the King?" answered the fairy.

"A horse, a sword, let me have the lot, and by getting these, let me win the fight!"

The fairy gave him a horse and a sword and said to him, "Off you go, little King's son, by you the battle will be won!"

Three times the young man asked the fairy for the same things, and so the race was run three times on three successive days. All three times the young man won against the King's two sons-in-law. Sometimes he left half an hour after them, sometimes one hour, sometimes two. Each time he overtook them and got there before them.

The third time was the test which would decide who was to get the crown.

To their great disappointment, the two brothers-in-law were beaten, but they went and said to the young man, "If you want to live, you must agree to tell the King that it is we who won the fight, or else we shall kill you."

"I am not afraid of you," said the young man, "but I agree to let it be believed that you are the winners on condition that you give up to me the two orange apples that the first two daughters of the King gave to you when they chose each of you for a husband."

The two brothers-in-law gave up their orange apples to the young man. It was in this way that they sort of sold their wives so as not to seem to have lost the fight.

Shortly after, the King was rejoicing with his sons-in-law, saying, "I am so glad, children, that you won the contest."

Suddenly who should turn up before him but the turkey boy, who said, "Sire, you think that it was your two sons-in-law who won the contest, but ask them to show their orange apples they were given by their wives. They sold them to me."

The King had to find out about this from his sons-in-law. They could not deny it, as they did not have the orange apples anymore. So the turkey boy took from his pocket three orange apples.

"Sire, here are the two orange apples belonging to your eldest daughters. Your sons-in-law gave them up to me because I beat them in the contest. Now they have to give up all claims to the crown resulting from their marriage to your eldest daughters. And here is a third orange apple. Your youngest daughter has given it to me because she wishes me to be her husband."

The King was extremely angry with his sons-in-law, who had behaved as if they had sold their wives. After this he really had to choose the turkey boy as heir to the crown.

Thus the young Princess was able to marry him. Later they had a very fine castle built for them in which they then lived happily together.

· 8 ·   *The Seven-Headed Monster*

· ONCE UPON A TIME there was a small boy all crippled and hunched. His brothers could not bear him. In the end his parents said to him, "Go and earn your daily bread elsewhere! You are one too many here, and you can see that your brothers can no longer stomach you. Off with you!"

"No," said the small boy. "I do not want to leave the house until you have had a suit of thirty-six colors and a small white stick made for me."

His parents looked high and low before finding a suit of thirty-six colors. At last they found one, and they gave him the suit and the stick saying, "Off you go now and never come back here."

The poor little boy started walking and walking. On and on he went. He got himself hired at a farm, one of the King's farms, as a cowman.

One day as he was looking after the animals there, he let the little black cow go into a field belonging to the giants who had a castle in that neighborhood. This did not go by unnoticed. Before long the first of the giants appeared before him.

"What are you doing there, you wretch. You let your little black cow graze in my fields. Watch out or I shall punish you in no uncertain manner."

"Oh, you may well be a giant, but I am not afraid of you,"

said the little cowman. Thanks to his suit of thirty-six colors
and his little white stick, he was afraid of nothing, for they were
the secret of his strength.

The fight started, and when the giant was about to defeat
him, the little cowman hit him with his stick and soon finished
him off. "Oh," said the giant, feeling he was mortally wounded,
"if I die, what will become of my black horse of which I am
so fond?"

"Don't worry about your black horse. I'll look after it at the
stable."

The next day he again let the little black cow eat the grass in
the giant's field. The second giant appeared in a fury. "Wretched
cowman, you have again allowed your black cow to steal my
grass. Now you'll see how I'll deal with you."

The second giant was even stronger than the first, but the
little cowman did the same as the day before. He put on his
suit of thirty-six colors and hit the giant with his little white
stick and the giant crumbled. Knowing the end was near, he
shouted, "And my chestnut horse, of which I am so fond, who
will look after it now?"

"Don't worry about your chestnut horse. I shall go into your
stable and groom it."

The third day the cowman again let his little black cow graze
in the giant's field, and so then appeared the third and strongest
of the three giants.

"Oh, you unlucky little devil! You steal my grass every day
and you have killed my two brothers, but you will not get me!"

The little cowman put on his suit of thirty-six colors and took
his little white stick. Once more he gave a mortal wound, this
time to the third giant. "Ah," shouted the last of the giants, "and
what will happen to my white horse that I loved so much if I
die now?"

"Do not worry about your white horse. I shall go and look after
it at the castle stable," said the cowman.

There were no more giants. From then on, the little cowman
spent half his time in the fields looking after the cows from the
King's farm and the other half in the giant's stable, where he
cared for the horses and had fun riding them. They were all

three magnificent horses. They were very strong and could go anywhere, but the chestnut horse was stronger than the black horse, and the white horse was even stronger than the chestnut.

One fine day news spread throughout the district that the seven-headed monster, who every year demanded that a young girl be given to him, was soon going to come along and fetch her. Every year all the girls in the district drew lots to find out which one of them would be handed over. That year the King's daughter was the ill-fated one. Her father was most upset, but he could not save her from her fate. He was to lead her into the forest at nightfall in order to hand her over to the monster.

Then the cowman who was working on one of the King's farms appeared before him clothed in his suit of thirty-six colors, his white stick in his hand, and seated on a magnificent black horse. It was the one that belonged to the first giant. "Sire, I believe that I am strong enough to fight the seven-headed monster if you will allow me to accompany your daughter this evening."

The King did not recognize him, of course, and, seeing no other way open, he took this proud knight at his word. He put the Princess behind him on the saddle, and soon they reached the part of the forest where the seven-headed monster was supposed to come and take her. There the young man made the Princess get down, and he led her to a clearing. Then he stayed on his black horse to await the monster.

The monster arrived in a fury. Raising his seven heads in a menacing manner, he faced the young knight, but the latter's horse was so strong that he attacked the monster, and the youth, with his suit of thirty-six colors, feared nothing. He managed that evening, thanks to his white stick, to cut off two of the monster's heads. But that was all for that evening. The monster withdrew foaming at the mouth with rage. The youth took the two heads, cut out their tongues and wrapped them both in a handkerchief given to him by the Princess, who was overcome with gratitude.

The monster had agreed to meet him again the following evening. The youth, after having spent the day looking after the cows, this time took the chestnut horse from the giant's stable and appeared before the King in his suit of thirty-six colors. Once again he put the Princess in the saddle and left for the forest. The monster did not take long in coming to the scene of the fight.

This time was harder than the day before. The more heads the monster lost, the more difficult it became to cut off the remaining ones. But the chestnut horse was stronger than the black horse, and he attacked the monster even more fiercely than before.

At last the youth, with the help of his white stick, managed to knock off two more heads. "Tomorrow at the same time!" shouted the monster, who was even angrier than the day before.

The youth cut out the two tongues again, leaving the two heads on the ground. He brought the tongues to the Princess, who gave him yet another handkerchief in which he wrapped them.

The third day he went back to the farm to look after the cows, and that evening he went and fetched the girl from her father's house to take her to the forest to the monster's meeting place. This time he had taken the third giant's horse, the white one, the strongest of all. He intended to have done with the monster even though it still had three heads.

The monster arrived shortly after the young people and seemed to be particularly threatening during the fight, but the horse closed in on it so much that it could not stand up to the blows of the youth, who again managed to cut off two of its heads.

"Let there be a truce!" cried the monster.

"There shall be no truce," said the youth. "This is your last day to draw breath." Though he was exhausted by the previous fight, he at last managed to cut off its seventh head.

The monster was dead. The youth picked up the three tongues, threw back the last three heads, and came and found the Princess, who gave him yet another handkerchief to wrap the tongues in and threw her arms round him to kiss him. "You have saved my life," she said to him.

"Now I will take you back to your father," he said.

He lifted her into the saddle and led her to the castle. There, as soon as the Princess got down from the white horse, the youth ran off and took his horse back to the giant's stable. As the only remembrance of his victory, he took with him the monster's seven tongues wrapped in the King's daughter's handkerchiefs.

Dressed once more as a cowman, he took up his job at the stable in the evening and went back to looking after the cows in the fields during the day. But nevertheless he could not forget the black horse, or the chestnut horse, or the white horse. Not only did he groom them every day, but he also enjoyed himself riding them, jumping hedges with them, and he became a past master in the art of managing them.

One fine day, without putting on his suit of thirty-six colors, he had the idea of cantering round the King's castle on the black horse, and he also had fun crossing the gardens. He made no pretense of stopping but disappeared by leaping over a fence.

The next day he began all over again with the chestnut horse, and then with the white horse, and soon he would do his tricks every day in the King's courtyard, and nothing could be done to stop him.

The King had fences put up everywhere. These were fences so high that neither the black horse nor the chestnut horse was able to leap over them. But the young man came back with the white horse, and nothing would stop that one. He jumped over the highest fence and came to a halt in the King's courtyard in front of his castle. Quickly everybody surrounded him and made the youth dismount. He was soon recognized as being the cowman from one of the King's farms. But the youth had chosen that day for the Princess to recognize him.

It must be stated that all this time the King had tried in vain to have the man who saved his daughter found. As no one showed up, one of his gardeners had the idea of going to pick up the monster's seven heads which had been left in the forest. He took them to the King, saying, "It is I who killed the monster. Here are the heads."

But the King had his daughter brought to him, and the Princess said that the gardener was not the one who had saved her. From then on, she refused all the advances made to her by the noblemen of the court who hoped to marry her, saying always, "I will only marry the man who saved me."

So then the youth presented himself before the King and said to him, "It is I who killed the seven-headed monster, and as proof here are the seven tongues that I have kept wrapped in the handkerchiefs given to me by the Princess."

The King had the seven heads which the gardener fetched from the forest brought to him in the castle, and everyone could see that the tongues fitted exactly into their places in the seven heads.

Then it was the Princess's turn to be led before the youth, and she recognized him at once as her rescuer.

The King gave his daughter to the cowman to marry, as she liked him better than any of the others, and the wedding feast was to take place. But that afternoon he said to his wife, "I would like to go and see my old parents so that they can join a little in the festivities, as it is going to be my wedding day."

They took a carriage and they stopped at his parents' house. "Stay there and wait for me," her fiancé said to her, "I shall just pop in and say hello." Before going into the house, he slipped on his old clothes and appeared before his parents as a cowman. His father and mother and his brothers were not too happy to see him. Without telling them anything, he put his fingers into the dishes and started picking up bacon and potatoes without a fork, by the handful, as a tramp would do in one's house. His family was revolted to have him back. Oh, how he roared with laughter to find himself at home with his family in this way!

In the end he told them his story. "And as I am getting married to the King's daughter," he said, "I shall go and live in her father's house." He put his suit on again and took his fiancée in to see his parents. Everybody was really happy then. So both of them went off to the King's castle.

·9· *The Beast*

• ONCE UPON A TIME there was a Prince who was making a long journey. He met a fairy on his way. The fairy liked the Prince very much and asked whether she could marry him, but he would not agree to it, and so she changed him into a beast, saying, "You will always remain a beast until a woman agrees to marry you."

The Prince owned a castle, and he stayed on there, living mostly in the gardens. In the house there was always a well-laden table. Those who went into the castle found dinner all ready for them.

Now one day three girls happened to be walking around out there. The youngest, who was tired of squabbling with her two sisters, ran away and found herself opposite this gorgeous dwelling. She went in and saw a meal there all ready made. Seeing no one about, and as night was falling, she ate the dinner and stayed on in the castle.

One day she was strolling in the gardens when she heard sighs coming from a bush. She went nearer, and what did she see?—a beast who spoke to her in the following manner: "Do go on living in the castle, if you wish. All your meals will be served to you. Your housework will be done, and you will have nothing to worry about."

The girl accepted. Every day she strolled in the garden and saw the beast there. But one fine day, what did she hear once more?—the sighs and groans of an ailing beast about to die. She ran to him and said: "Oh my poor little beast. If you do not die, I shall marry you!" Hearing these words, the Prince stood up and took off his beast's skin. He was a handsome youth.

The young girl was so happy. They became engaged, but the Prince did not stay with her for long. "Now I must go and find my old parents," he said to her. "I'll soon be back. I give you my animal skin. Lock it up carefully in a wardrobe and be especially careful that no drop of water falls on it."

And so the Prince left. As for the young girl, she had a visit from her two sisters, who were filled with jealousy when they saw her so happy. As she had told them her story, they decided to destroy the beast's skin. The elder said to her junior, "Listen, go and fetch a basin of water, and we shall throw it on his beast's skin."

No sooner had they done this than the Prince came home. He was greatly dismayed. "What have you done? My skin is lost and I can no longer stay here. As for you, I cannot even take you with me, but you can live here in comfort as before. Your two sisters will stay here as doorjambs, so in that way you will have company after all."

But the young girl was absolutely determined to go with her betrothed, and she decided to follow him by hook or by crook.

As the Prince was getting ready to leave by carriage, he said to her also, "I am going to leave you three things to remember me by: a golden spinning wheel, a golden distaff, and a golden spindle. In that way, when you spin you will still be thinking of me."

The young girl began to cry. As he kissed her, she let three drops of blood from her finger fall onto his shirt saying, "No one except me will be able to get these three drops of blood off your shirt."

After this they parted. The Prince left in a carriage to go and see his old parents, and there he stayed. His father begged him to take a wife, but the youth would not hear of it. By going on and on about it, his father managed to overcome his opposition, and the Prince accepted his father's plan.

Meanwhile, the young girl had started off on foot to follow her betrothed, taking with her as tokens of his esteem her golden spinning wheel, her golden distaff, and her golden spindle. By walking like this she reached his father's farm looking all disheveled, and there she was hired as a turkey maid.

A few days later the Prince's wedding was supposed to take place. The girl knew about it. She had certainly recognized him even if he had not recognized her, and she tried to find a way of making herself known to him.

As she led her turkeys along, she went to find the washerwomen who were bleaching the house linen for the wedding. "Lord in Heaven!" one of the washerwomen was saying, "these spots can't be removed."

"No, I agree. There is no way of getting them out," said another.

The turkey maid stopped in front of them. "If you gave me that shirt, I could perhaps remove them."

One of the washerwomen laughingly started to object. "Do you really think that you who watch the turkeys know more than we do about washing clothes?" Another said, "Dear God! here is the shirt—you certainly can't do worse than we have done!"

I must tell you that the Prince wanted to wear that shirt and no other on his wedding day.

The turkey maid took it, rubbed it once, and then again before the spots disappeared.

When the maids returned the Prince's laundry he was amazed to see his shirt was without spots. "Who managed to take these spots out?" he asked.

"The turkey maid."

"Ah," thought he, "it must be she. I was not able to recognize her in her rags."

However, his wedding to the other girl had been arranged, and the wedding feast took place.

Yet the turkey girl had managed to get in to see the young bride, and she showed her the golden spindle on the evening of the wedding. "Oh, what a beautiful spindle! I have not had anything like it as a present."

"I'll give it to you if you like, on one condition, and that is that you let me go to your husband's bedroom to stay with him all night."

The young woman wanted the golden spindle so much that she agreed, but she, too, had some tricks up her sleeve. She gave the Prince *de l'ean d'endormie* (a sleeping draught) so that he slept all night long and the turkey girl was not able to talk to him. However much she kissed him, he would not wake up.

The next evening the same thing happened. One seeing the golden distaff, the young woman agreed to let the turkey girl go up to husband's room, but she had again given him a sleeping draught so that he did not wake until the following morning.

However, the castle maids had heard the sighs and the words the turkey girl let slip during the two nights she spent at the foot of the Prince's bed. They went and found the Prince and said to him, "Didn't you have another wife in the part of the country where you lived before?"

"No, but my betrothed was there whom I was to marry."

"Prince, for two nights now we have heard a woman moaning

in your room and calling you husband, yet you were never awakened by her cries. Did you drink something from a glass?"

"Yes, every night."

"Well, do not drink it tonight. She is sure to come, and you will be able to answer her."

The third night the turkey girl showed her golden spinning wheel to the young woman. Again the girl agreed to let her go up to the Prince's room, in exchange for the golden spinning wheel. But the Prince, taking the maids' advice, poured away the contents of the glass next to his bed. Trembling, the young girl said to herself, "Oh dear, this is the last night I can speak to him, and perhaps he will be asleep again."

But the Prince was not asleep this time. They recognized each other, and they talked together all night.

The next day the young man said to his father, "Father, I still have something to ask you."

"Then what is it you wish, my son?"

"Order a great meal to be made to which all the castle servants will come. I want my wife next to me on one side and on the other the turkey girl."

The father agreed to this odd idea, and that day the turkey girl put on her best dress to appear at the Prince's side. In the middle of the meal the Prince spoke to the host, "Father."

"What is it you wish there?"

"If you lost the keys to your castle, would you have more made?"

"Yes."

"But if you found the old keys, which worked far better than the new ones, which would you take?"

"Well, the old ones, of course!"

"Ah well, it's the same with women. I was betrothed to a girl in another part of the country, and now I have found her again. From now on, I wish to live with her."

And the Prince took the turkey girl with him.

· 10 · *John of Calais*

· JOHN OF CALAIS' FATHER was a shipowner of some importance. He had ships, and he loaded them with cargo in order to go and sell the merchandise in other ports. Now this man's wife said to him (when John was still quite young), "Find a ship for your son so that he may learn to work."

The father would not hear of it. "No, John is too young. If I give him a ship and the goods, he will spend everything and eat everything there is in the hold."

The wife insisted, and in the end the father looked for a ship for his son and loaded it with cargo for him to sell. He said to him, "You will go to such and such a port. You will sell your goods, and as soon as you have sold them, you will unfurl your sails and go off again."

So John of Calais left on his ship, and he reached the port mentioned by his father. He sold all his goods, but after that he went ashore in spite of his father's forbidding him and went and strolled about on land. He had not been given permission to do it, but he did it anyway.

While walking, what did he find but a corpse which had been thrown onto a heap of manure. "How did this happen? Don't they bury people round here?"

They answered him, "When people have debts, they have to be paid off first and then the burial must be paid for."

"Oh, did he owe very much?"

Then the voices started to shout, "He owes me so much!"

"And he owes me so much!"

"And to me he owes even more!"

There were some yelling around the corpse, and there were perhaps some to whom the dead man owed nothing, but there they all were, some yelling louder than others.

John spent all his money paying off the dead man's debts and also for his burial. By the time he reached his parents, at midday, he had spent all the money he had received for his father's goods. His father was not proud of him!

So another day his mother said to her husband, "You ought to get your son another ship so that he can learn to live by the clock to earn his living."

His father did not want to, but in the end he gave in.

There was John off again with a ship and goods to sell. He had got right out to sea when he heard frightful screams. "Who goes there?"

They were girls who were screaming, "Want to buy some?"

"Yes, I'll buy quite a lot of girls, I will!"

So then two girls appeared on the bridge of the ship, and John took one as his wife and one as his cousin Isabella. (Those voices were those girls yelling for someone to set them free.) So John had again spent all his money to buy himself a wife and a cousin Isabella. (The wife—can't remember what her name was—this girl he'd picked up there was the King's daughter).

He went home. On seeing his parents, he said, "I spent all the money again, this time to buy myself a wife and a cousin Isabella.

John's parents were not at all pleased, so they gave John and his wife the pigsty to sleep in. And so they were married there and they had a little boy.

John's mother never stopped saying to her husband, "Now in spite of everything he has done, give your son another load and let him go and sell it."

There was John of Calais off to sea again. His father had said to him, "You will drop anchor in such and such a port without permission. You will not ask anything of anybody."

He left with his wife. When they reached the port his father had told him to go to, someone yelled, "You are not allowed to disembark here."

So John of Calais was forced to go on farther. He started up the river. Now on the ship there was not only his wife but a friend of his, Don Jean, who wanted him out of the way because of his wife. And so this Don Jean gave John of Calais a shove with his elbow and threw him into the river. He drifted out to the open sea and found himself hanging onto a large rock, where he stayed seven years eating nothing but shellfish.

Well, by the time seven years had gone by, the corpse had appeared once before him in ghost form on the rock, saying to him, "You are not in love just now, but your wife is much more in love than you. She is going to marry again tomorrow!"

"If she is more in love than I am, I am not surprised. Look at me. I have been on this rock all the time—for seven years!"

"What are you doing there?"

"Well, you see I am awaiting death!"

"You did me a good turn by burying my body. It is my turn to do something for you. If you like, I will take you where your wife lives."

"Ah!"

"However," he said, "what would you give me if you wanted to be taken where your wife lives?"

"That which I hold most dear in this world, but are you going to be able to take me there?"

"If you give me what is most dear in the world to you, I will take you to your wife's dwelling place."

"Well," he said, "I have a child . . ."

"If you give me half of it, I will take you to your wife's dwelling place."

And to think that his wife was getting married the next day!

So his wife was still on the ship with Don Jean. She could go on until she was blue in the face saying, "What have you done, Don Jean? You have thrown my husband into the river," but Don Jean had threatened to kill her if she spoke of what he had done. He had come back on board with John of Calais' wife, and then she had gone to her father the King. Don Jean would not leave her alone. He courted her, but she did not want to have anything to do with him.

So in the end the King said, "As your John of Calais has fallen into the river (she could not say more, for otherwise Don Jean would have killed her), "you ought to marry Don Jean."

The wedding was nigh. The corpse carried John of Calais to the King's castle. He carried him from the island where he was marooned to the castle, and then he said to him, "You have only to ask if the King needs a woodcutter."

But for seven years John of Calais had neither shaved nor cut his hair, and it goes without saying that he was still wearing

the same shirt. As they reached the castle, the guard stopped
them, saying, "Where are you off to, *guenillu* (ragbag)?"

"Let him through. The King has said so."

The wedding was to be the next day. There was wood to
chop before the feast. So John of Calais tried to split the logs,
but he hadn't the strength. For seven years all he had eaten was
shellfish. While he was trying to split the logs, he saw his wife,
the King's daughter. She could no longer recognize him. It was
seven years since he had fallen into the river, but he of course
recognized her.

Now he saw his wife going by in the courtyard, and for
seven years he had kept the embroidered handkerchief she had
given him. So in front of her he drew out the handkerchief, and
she recognized it.

The King's daughter went upstairs and asked her father,
"Daddy, John of Calais is downstairs splitting logs—"

"John of Calais! It is seven years now since he fell in the
river! How can you mean him?"

"I tell you it is."

She went down into the courtyard again. He was still trying to
split wood, but he was tired. He could not manage it, and so he
mopped himself with the handkerchief. The King's daughter
hesitated no longer. She went upstairs again to her father.

"I told you John of Calais is downstairs."

"Well, if it is he, tell him to come up to my room with an
armful of wood."

The servants would not let him through. "Hey there, you
barbu, peillu guenillu (hairy, lousy ragbag)! What are you doing
there?"

"I am going up to get to the King's room."

"Eh, what's that you're saying?" But the order was given.
"Since the King has said so, let him through!" On each step
of the staircase there were guards who shouted: "Hey there, you
hairy, lousy ragbag! What are you doing there?"

"Let him through! The King has asked that he go up to his
room." John of Calais reached the top. He put his armful of
wood in a corner of the King's room. He was about to leave

without saying a word when the King said to him, "How is it that you are here?"

He pulled out the embroidered handkerchief that she had given him. She threw her arms about him, saying to her father, "This is my husband, John of Calais."

The father could not get over it.

"So then you fell into the river and you survived?"

The daughter said to him, "No, Daddy. It was Don Jean who pushed him into the river."

"How is it that you never told me?"

"I could not tell you. I was not allowed to; otherwise Don Jean would have killed me."

And there you had Don Jean getting ready to marry the King's daughter. The wedding took place, at least the wedding feast as it had already been made, but it was not for Don Jean. The King said to the stokers, "Heat the oven. Let Don Jean be put inside!"

And so they had the banquet. John of Calais was by his wife, but the ghost interrupted the middle of the meal. The ghost had certainly told him when he was on his rock, "I will be next to you during the wedding feast but I shall not eat. Don't let anyone bother about me!"

So in the middle of the meal the ghost appeared. John of Calais remembered that he had promised him half his child.

The ghost said to him, "What did you promise me, John of Calais? What was most dear to you in the whole world if I carried you back to your wife's dwelling place. Will you give him to me?"

John of Calais said, "Yes, I promised you what is most dear to me in the whole world. Well, here he is!"

Then he took his child. He put him with his head down and his two legs apart, and he took a huge knife in his hand and said to the ghost, "I promised you half my child. Take one leg, and I will take the other."

"No, you did me a good turn. I did you one. Do you remember the dead body which was in the heap of manure? You had it buried. Well, I have brought you to your wife's dwelling place, and I shall let you keep your child!"

. 11 . Gold Feather

• THERE WAS a poor young lad who was one of many children of a large family. The others had put his eyes out so that he would go and be a beggar and they could collect the money he was given. For a few years they lived like this, making him hold out his hat, and as people were sorry for the blind boy, they put something in the hat.

Soon as he grew older the others decided to get rid of him and lose him in the forest. So they took him into the woods, and there they left him. The poor young lad might well walk along feeling the trees as he went, saying, "Where are my brothers? I want to find my brothers again!" The trees of the forest were not his brothers, and he had to get used to the idea that he had been abandoned there all alone. So he climbed to the top of a tree and stayed there to spend the night under shelter.

Well, now, some giants—three giants—came and sat under this great tree to eat their dinner and enjoy each other's company in comfort. Soon the young lad, who was still sitting in the branches, wanted to pee. He did. It fell in the giants' dish. One of them exclaimed, "Oh, how good the Lord is! He sends us vinegar."

A little later the young lad wanted to shit, and he did. Again it fell in the giant's dish, and this time one of them said, "Oh, now the good Lord sends us mustard!"

When they had finished they saw the young lad and told him to come down. "What are you doing there?"

"My eyes have been put out, and I have been left all alone in the forest."

The giants were sorry for him, and each one decided to make a wish for him. The first giant said, "I would like you to see again." The second giant said, "And I wish that you should soon meet a mule on your way." And the third giant said, "As for me, I wish that you should then find a golden feather on your way."

"No No! Don't wish that on him," said the two other giants to their brother. "It will bring him too much unhappiness."

"Yes," said the third giant, "I make that wish all the same."

After that the three giants left the young lad in the forest. But now he could see, and, oh, how straight he walked! Soon, just as the second giant had wished, he met a mule on the road and he mounted her. That was much better than walking! Suddenly at the edge of the road he saw a gold feather. "Stop," he said to the mule. "I want to pick up this gold feather."

"No, no," said the mule, "why ask for more worries?"

"Yes, yes. I want to pick it up." Anyway the spell cast by the first giant forced him to pick it up.

Shortly after, he got to the door of the King's farm and he was hired as a cowman.

The King became friendly with the young lad—with Golden Feather, if you like. The people around the King—the peers of France, you know what I mean—were soon jealous of his presence at court and decided to harm him in every possible way.

The King wished to gain the farms of the Queen of a neighboring country whom he had kidnapped and kept in his castle without, however, managing to make himself liked by her. He often begged her to accept him as a husband, but she always refused.

One day as he persisted in his advances, the Queen said to him, "I will not marry you unless you have my own castle, which is still in my part of the country, brought here opposite your castle." This was quite impossible. "Oh, I cannot have it brought here," said the King, "but, if you wish, I can have one built just like it."

"No, no," said the Queen. "It's my castle I want, not one just like it." The King was very put out.

Making the most of these circumstances, Gold Feather's enemies said to him, "Sire, Gold Feather, who is a friend of yours, has said that he could bring the Queen's castle here."

The King had the young lad brought to him. "You have said that you are able to bring the Queen's castle here. You shall do this."

"Oh, Sire, I did not say that."

"You said it and you shall do it."

Gold Feather was very downcast. When he went and found his mule, she said to him: "Ask the King to give you four ships loaded with bulls and cows and sheep, and you will take yourself off with these ships to the giants' island. They have lusty appetites. When they have eaten everything, they will give you a hand in getting the Queen's castle onto the four ships, and you will take it to the King."

The King had four ships full of cattle made ready for Gold Feather, and the young lad soon reached the giants' island. You should have seen how they swallowed all these animals that were being landed on their island. In the end their leader said, "Stop! We have eaten enough." High time, too, for there was nothing left to throw to them but a quarter of beef!

"You have done us a good turn, for we were famished, and we are ready to do you one like it."

"Well, then, carry the Queen of England's castle to my ships!" said Gold Feather.

The giants immediately did as he asked, and soon the castle sailed for home, placed on the four ships, and the King was somewhat surprised to see it. Gold Feather had managed to save his own skin, but as for the Queen, she was very sorry for herself, for she still would have nothing to do with the King.

As he still pressed his suit, she said, "I will not marry until the keys of my castle have been found. I threw them overboard when you brought me as a prisoner to your land." The King said, "But why, when it is impossible to find them again, and it is so easy to have some made just like them?"

"No, no," said the Queen. "I want the keys that I threw into the sea to be found."

So the peers of France, more and more jealous of Gold Feather's success, decided once more to get rid of him. They went to the King. "Sire, Gold Feather has said that he could find the castle keys which the Queen let fall into the sea." The King had him brought before him. "You said that you could find the castle keys which the Queen let fall into the sea. You shall do it."

"But, Sire, I never said anything of the sort." However much Gold Feather went on protesting his innocence, he had to obey the King. And so he went again to his mule. She said to him, "Do just as I say and you will find the keys. Ask the King to

give you four ships loaded with bread, and you will go right out
to sea. You will distribute it to all the fish, and one of them will
bring you the keys." So off went Gold Feather with his four
ships loaded with bread, and he started throwing the bread into
the water, and then more bread, so much and so well that all
the fish came and surrounded the ships. The King of the fish
even started to round them up so that each one could have his
share of the banquet, but when the roll call was over there was
still one missing, a little fish who was gallivanting heaven knows
where. At last he was seen, arriving long after the others.

"Ah, I have caught you, you little ne'er-do-well," said the King
of the fish. "What were you doing gadding about in the sea
when I called upon you all to rally?"

"Well, I have found a rather odd thingumajig on the sea bed.
I tried to pick it up to carry it, but it was too heavy. I didn't
succeed." (These were the keys to the Queen's castle.)

All the fish gathered around, and all together they lifted the
keys and carried them to Gold Feather's ships as a way of
thanking him for the bread which he had given them so generously.

Thus the young lad came back triumphantly, bringing the
castle keys to the King. The King was very happy, but the
Queen of England was most vexed and still refused to marry
the King.

The peers of France, more jealous than ever, managed to
persuade the King that the Queen of England had set her cap
for Gold Feather, whose success had gilded him in her eyes. The
King decided to have Gold Feather burned in a pile of faggots
set up in the square.

The poor young lad, who was really afraid this time, went to
see his mule again. "Don't worry," she said. "I will save you
again. Do everything I tell you to do. You will go and fetch
seven *aunes* [1] of worsted, and you will cut out of it a piece of
fabric folded over seven times—that is to say, you will need a
piece which is seven times the thickness of one piece of fabric.
Then you will take this piece and put it on my back as a saddle,
and you will mount me and make me walk until the first six

[1] The measure used here is *aunes*. One aune = 118.3 cm. = 46.5 inches.

folds are worn through. Then you will take the seventh cloth and wrap yourself up in it on the day they want to burn you in the middle of the faggots."

Gold Feather did what the mule advised him to do. He put the seven *aunes* of fabric on her back, mounted her, and made her walk and walk so much that he took pity on her because he was crushing her under him as she toiled on and on.

But the mule went ahead, saying, "Go on! Keep walking. Don't take any notice of my weariness, for the fabric must be worn down to the seventh fold." At last there was only the seventh thickness left.

This was on the day the King had decided to burn Gold Feather alive in the square. The faggots were already piled up there. Wrapping himself in the fabric, he put all his faith in the words of his mule. And soon the fire was lit, the flames consumed the wood, but the higher they reached and the nearer they got to him, the more handsome Gold Feather seemed, and not one of the flames hurt him.

The King was stunned to see him not only survive the flames but grow more handsome. Giving up all thought of killing him, he asked him how he had managed to escape the flames, which had even made him better-looking than any other living man; for the King wished to become even more handsome than Gold Feather to please the Queen of England.

Gold Feather said to him, "Sire, I did not use any extraordinary means. I simply wrapped myself in seven *aunes* of fabric that I soaked in water first in order to resist the flames at the stake."

The King said to himself, "I shall buy fourteen *aunes* of fabric, as I can afford it, and I shall then be even better protected, and I shall become twice as handsome as Gold Feather. Then I shall have no rival to fear for the Queen's favors."

The faggots which were going to be set fire to and which were intended to surround the King with flames were soon seen piling up in the square. And soon the burning took place. Though the King had soaked his fourteen *aunes* of fabric in water, the fire did not take long to dry the stuff, and the King was soon turned to ashes.

And so there was an end to the misfortunes of Gold Feather. The Queen of England was at last rid of the King, whom she had always rejected, and as Gold Feather had become the most handsome man alive, it was he who married the Queen.

·12· *The Orange Tree*

• ONCE UPON A TIME there was a lord, a Marquis, who had three sons. In their garden there was an orange tree all covered with oranges. There came a time when, every morning as the Marquis was doing his round of the garden, he noticed that an orange had been pilfered.

Day by day and one by one the orange tree was losing all its oranges. "Soon there will be none left," said the Marquis to his sons. "One of you should go and keep guard at night at the foot of the orange tree so as to catch the thief."

The first evening the eldest went, but although he kept watch all around him, the night wore on without his seeing anyone coming. In the end he got tired of waiting and went home without having found out anything.

The next evening it . was the second son's turn to go and watch, but he also became bored and went home to bed without having caught the thief.

The third day it was the youngest son's turn. He went off to the garden with a pack of cards, quite determined to spend the whole night at the foot of the orange tree and to play cards to while away the time while waiting for the thief.

He had played several card games all by himself when, in the middle of the night, he heard a rustling in the branches and he saw a bird. "Ah, there's the one who steals our oranges!" He immediately aimed at it with his gun, but the bird started to talk to him. "Don't kill me," it said. "If you like, we will play cards together." The bird then took on his human form again.

He played several games of cards with the young man, and then he said to him, "We'll bet like this, if you like. If you win, I will make you a castle all of ivory, and if it is I who win, you will come and join me without fail where I live."

The young man accepted the challenge. At the first go it was he who won. "You shall have your ivory castle," said the bird. "And now let's have another go." The second go was won by the bird. "Goodbye," he said to him. "I am counting on your coming to find me where I live. Ask everyone for the road that leads to the Bird King, and they will show it to you. You can bank on seeing the ivory castle rise in front of your house."

In fact, as soon as he awoke the next day, the young man could see that an ivory castle was rising opposite his home. So, as the bird had kept his promise, the youth really was obliged to keep his.

He set off, and wherever he asked for the way to the Bird King, he was answered, "Oh, you poor soul, don't go there. No one who has gone there has ever come back!" Anyway, in spite of everything, he went on walking. Soon he met a poor old woman who really looked most wretched. "Here, my poor old soul," he said, "here are two pennies. I can't bear to see you so wretched."

"Thank you, my lad," she said to him. "Good luck to you on your way but—where are you going?"

"I am going to the Bird King."

"It is here," said the old crone, "and I'll show you how to go about getting the upper hand with him. You'll see that near here there is a pond, and the King's three daughters just happen to be swimming there now. Creep closer to them, but very quietly. They have left their three girdles on the bank. There are two blue ones. Don't take them, but take the one that is green. It belongs to his youngest daughter, and it is she who will rescue you from her father. But listen carefully. You will take the boat which seems to have the largest hole in the bottom by the pond and you will row toward the three girls. They will be surprised to see you, and the one who sees her green girdle in your hands will claim it from you. Don't give it back to her before she has promised to be faithful to you. When she has sworn it, you will be sure of her and you can give it back to her. From then on, it will be her job to advise you on how to escape from her father."

The young man thanked the old crone and obeyed her to the letter. When he had taken the boat and rowed toward the three girls, showing the green girdle, one of them came toward him. "That's my belt. Give it back to me."

"Not until you have promised to be faithful," answered the young man. The girl was obliged then to swear she would be faithful. Then he gave the green girdle back to her. After she had come out of the pond, she took her things and accompanied the young man up to her father's house. "I am going to give you a piece of advice," she said to him. "My father is a very demanding man, and you'll have to put up a good fight if you want to gain the upper hand with him. When you go into his house, he will offer you bread saying, 'Be first to cut the loaf.' You will answer, 'In my part of the world it is the custom for the host to cut the bread first.'"

The young man took her advice. The old woman who was the wife of the host said to her husband, "You will have your work cut out with that one!" The host hired the young man anyway to work for him.

The next morning he led the young man into a grove and said: "You see this? It must all be cut down and made into faggots by seven o'clock tonight." And all he left him as a tool was an axe made of glass. The poor lad was very discouraged. How could he cut down a forest in one day with a glass ax? He broke his ax at the first blow, and so he sat under a tree feeling very despondent.

At noon the youngest of the King's daughters came to him with his dinner. "Well," she said to him, "aren't you doing anything?"

"What do you want me to do? I broke the ax your father gave me as soon as I started."

"Here," said the girl, "take this little knife. You will stick it into the largest tree you can find in all the forest and you will say, 'Through the magic of my little knife, let the whole forest be cut down and made into faggots by seven o'clock this evening.'" And she left him there.

The young man did what the girl had told him to do, and

that evening all his work was completed. When his boss came to see him, he could not get over it. When he told his wife about this, she said: "Ah! There you are! We haven't seen the last of him!"

The next day the boss said to his hired hand, "You see that bank over there? Well, it must be completely flattened and leveled by seven o'clock this evening." He gave the lad a pick made of glass. The youth did try hard to hack at the bank, but a glass pick, as you know, is easily broken. There he was, discouraged once again, and he sat by the bank not doing anything more.

At noon the girl arrived with his dinner. "Well," she said to him, "that's your job, is it. Don't worry. I know what my father has given you to do. Take this little shovel and dig it into the bank and say, 'With the help of my little shovel, let the whole bank be brought down and leveled by seven o'clock this evening.'" The same thing happened as the day before.

The boss no longer knew how to deal with this lad. It was all becoming more and more peculiar. His wife again said, "That workman is going to be hard to keep!"

The next day the King said to his workman, "I would like all the grains of sand on the sea bed counted, to know how many there are of each size, whether small, medium, or large." The poor lad kept asking himself what he was going to do, but the girl had not forgotten him. As she brought him his dinner, she said to him, "I shall give you a bowl [*roquille*] to empty the sea and sort out the grains of sand by size and to count how many there are of each size. You will simply say, 'With the help of my little bowl, let the sea be emptied, and let all the grains of sand that are therein be sorted and counted.' But be very careful to remember the number of grains of sand, whether small, medium, or large, that there are in the sea while the sea is emptied, for when it is full again it will be too late to find out."

Step by step the young man followed the girl's instructions. By evening the whole job was finished and he was able to tell his boss how many grains of sand there were of each size in the sea.

The boss was more than a little surprised!

"I'll tell you, you haven't seen the last of that one," his wife said to him.

The next day the boss led his workman to the foot of a glass mountain and said to him, "You must go and fetch three crow's eggs which are at the top of this glass mountain." He gave him a paper ladder. The poor lad was not able to climb very high with his paper ladder! He sat at the foot of the mountain feeling even more dejected than he had been on the other days.

This time the girl was at her window and she saw a crow fly by her. "Come this way, crow, and listen to me. You go off and fetch the three eggs you put on top of the glass mountain and give them to the one you find crying at the bottom of the mountain."

This was done.

"Aha," said the boss's wife, "I told you you would have trouble with that workman." The boss did not know how to get rid of such a man, and he tried to find some task he could still make him do.

The next day he said to the young man, "We are both going to have a drink, and we shall see who can drink the most without falling down drunk."

The girl again came to the rescue of her father's workman.

"Listen carefully," she said to him. "It takes three barrels of wine to get my father drunk. Be very careful, because he will pour you as much as he'll pour for himself. For each glass he fills for himself, he will fill yours, too. You will accept—this goes without saying—but you must not drink. When he takes a glassful, take one, too. Empty it into a flask that you'll have hidden in your ruffle, and while he's getting drunk, you will throw away the contents of the flask."

And so this took place. The barrels of wine were soon emptied, and the father fell down drunk. Then the young man went to find the girl to tell her. "Your father has now drunk the lot, and he has just fallen asleep."

"Let us leave together while my father is asleep," she said. "We will make the most of his slumbers to get away, for I know his plans against you. You will reach the stable. There are three horses there, Little Wind, Medium Wind, and Great

Wind. You will take the one who looks most worn out, and we shall ride on it."

The young man went to the stable. He saw the three horses, but one of them looked so tired out that he could not make up his mind to take him, and so he took the second one, who looked less tired.

The King's daughter arrived and said, "I'll mount the horse first. You get on behind." They left immediately. "What have you done!" said the girl. "You have taken Medium Wind. Now we are done for, as Daddy will rush after us, and he will take Great Wind." A few seconds later she said to the young man, "Don't you hear him coming?"

"I see a cloud of dust rising."

"It is he," she said. "And now let the horse turn into a mill, you into a mill's sails, and I shall be the miller."

The boss soon arrived on Great Wind, and he found the mill in front of him. The sails were turning so fast he could, however, find no way of approaching it. Furious, as he had by now lost all trace of the fugitives, he went back home and told his wife of his failure.

She said to him, "But haven't you understood? The mill was the horse, the sail was your workman, and the miller was your daughter." So off went the boss chasing them once more. But the mill was no longer there.

The young people had mounted Medium Wind again, and he was going full speed ahead. However, they heard something like a storm brewing behind them. It was Great Wind at their heels. So the girl said, "Let the horse become a chapel, you the altar, and I shall say Mass."

And then along came the boss, and he stopped in front of the chapel. "Haven't you seen anybody?"

"Amen," said the priest without turning round. That is all the boss could find out. Once home again he told his wife of his adventure.

"But you don't understand. The chapel was the horse, the altar was your hired hand, and the priest was your daughter."

This time the boss decided to take his wife with him, and both of them threw themselves into the chase after the young people.

When they saw them, they made a kind of barrier in front of them, an enormous fire, which was gaining in their direction. So the girl said, "Let the horse become a pond, and you shall be a drake, and I shall be a duck. But be very careful. When Mummy and Daddy reach the edge of the pond, they will have fun throwing us bread crumbs in order to trap us. Above all, don't eat any!"

There they both were, changed into duck and drake, on the pond. On seeing this, the people stopped making their fire and came to a halt at the edge of the pond. The old woman began to crumble bread to attract them, and the drake was tempted to catch it, but each time the duck stopped him by pecking [*pigossait*] at him.

In the end the old woman said to the old man, "Jump into the pond and catch him!"

"Oh, no, I would drown." And he wouldn't jump into the pond.

"Well, that's that," said the old woman. "You've lost your daughter now."

So the two young people were then free, and they went to the youth's parents' home. But soon the girl said to him, "I am leaving you to go and save my father, because otherwise he will be damned forever. You must be very careful that your parents do not kiss you, as then you shall remember nothing at all."

The young man was very careful about allowing anybody to approach him, but during the night his parents kissed him. When he woke up, he could not remember a thing, and when the girl came back he did not recognize her.

Now wasn't she clever! It was she who kissed him, and then they both recognized each other. After all this they were married, and they lived in the ivory castle which the youth had earned.

I was at their wedding feast. They gave me a piece of bread, butter and jam, and a kick in the arse, and after that I left.

·13· *March and April*

• ONCE UPON A TIME there were two brothers. The elder one was called March, and the younger one was called April. As they could no longer live with their old father, one of them had to get himself hired out on a farm. "Don't leave. You're too hotheaded," said April to his elder brother. "You will never stay with your master."

"It is my duty to leave," said March, "as I am the elder one." He went to work on a farm. The gentleman promised him three hundred francs a year as wages. That was good pay at the time. March was pleased. "Ah," said the boss," I must tell you something else. Here I hire my workers in this fashion. Whoever gets angry first, whether man or master, will have a strip of skin torn from his back by the other."

Anyway, that was what was said.

The next day the farm owner sent March to scythe the furze on the heath. When the lad reached the place, he began scything. As he went on and on working he became fed up with it, but there was not much chance of a rest. Every time he stood up, the dog from the farm went for him and bit him. Well, March was not very patient. In the end he left his work and went back to the farm in a fit of temper. "Boss, I cannot work under these conditions. Your dog keeps on trying to bite me!"

"And so you are angry?"

"Yes."

So, as was agreed, the boss tore from him a strip of skin. Much saddened, poor March went back to his brother.

"Ah, I knew you would not stay there long," said April on seeing him. "It is my turn. This time I'll go, and we shall see what happens."

"Listen," said March, and he told him about the business he had had with the farm owner.

"All right. You've told me all about it. I am going to your boss," said April, "and this won't happen again."

The farm owner imposed the same conditions on April, who accepted them.

The next day he was also sent out to scythe the heath, and the farm dog was with him. April worked all morning, and then the dog lay down to sleep. April then took advantage of this opportunity and cut his head off with his scythe.

At noon the hired man went back to the farm to have his dinner. The farm owner was very surprised to see him come back without the dog. "Hey, you have not brought back my dog!"

"Why should I bring back a mad dog? He bites everybody. I cut his head off with my scythe."

"What do you mean? You killed my dog?"

"Oh, are you angry?"

"No, I am not."

The next morning the fields were under heavy dew. The farm owner said, "You will take the mare out to graze in the field without disturbing the dew or knocking down the gate."

April went off with his ax on his shoulder, and he climbed onto the mare and cut off her head. Then he began chopping up the carcass and throwing the pieces into the field.

At noon the farm owner questioned him. "Have you done what I asked you to do?"

"Yes, don't worry. She will not be too glutted with grass tonight." The farm owner went and had a look. "What have you done, you wretch!"

"Well, you forbade me to disturb the dew and to open the gate, so I had to cut your mare to pieces to send her into the field."

The farm owner controlled his temper, because he was afraid of having a strip of skin torn from him.

The next day he said to his hired hand, "You will take the swine to the fair. You will drive them before you on the road. Later I will join you at the fair."

Now, on the way April met a swine dealer.

"Do you want some pigs to sell?" suggested April.

"If you like. Yes, certainly I would."

"Well, then, all right. I shall keep the tail of each one, and I shall keep the smallest pig as well. Look, you'll see. We shall bury him in the bog over there."

April sold the pigs, stuck all the tails in the mud, and he buried the smallest pig so that none of it was sticking out, but he made certain where it was.

Now then the farm owner came along the road. He was looking everywhere to see where his pigs could have got to. "Where are the pigs?" he cried.

"How do you expect me to herd them along? They are covered in mud. You see, only their tails are left."

The farm owner began to tug at the first tail. He pulled it up like a blade of grass. "Well, that's funny," he said.

"Then come here," shouted his hired hand; "the little pig is here, but I cannot catch hold of him." The farm owner raced up to him and helped him to free the only pig which was buried.

In the end he was red with anger. "You will ruin me, you will," he said.

"Are you angry?"

"No, no."

Sunday morning came. "As you killed my mare," said the farm owner, "you will carry us to Mass, my wife and me, on your back."

"Oh, well, we'll find a way. You will each sit in a basket, your wife in the front and you behind."

The hired hand started on his journey. As it was a long one, he got fed up with it. He stopped to kiss the woman in the basket.

"Oh, you wretch," shouted the farm owner, "you dare to kiss my wife?"

"Are you angry, boss?"

This made the farm owner well and truly angry, and he jumped out of the rear basket.

"If you are angry," said April, "give me my hundred francs, and I will tear a strip of skin from your back."

He got what he wanted, even the master's strip of skin. Then, later, he joined his brother.

Part III
Pays de Retz

·14· *The Tale of La Ramée*

• THERE WAS A KING with a daughter (I don't know her name.) He had a daughter, and she had never laughed in her life.

So the King said, "If a woman makes her laugh, I will give her a reward. If it is a man, I will get him to marry my daughter."

Now there was an old man called La Ramée who used to tramp across the fields with his bag on his back, earning a living as best he could.

One day he found a mouse.

"Where are you going, mouse?"

"I am going this way to make a life for myself."

"Climb into my bag. You'll come in useful. There is bread in there, and you can eat some of it."

So the mouse climbed into his bag.

After this he went a little farther and came across a small cricket, you know, the kind that goes "Cri-cri-cri." The old man said to him, "Cricket, where are you going?"

"I am going this way to make a life for myself."

"Jump into my bag. You'll come in useful."

So he went farther on, and he came across a beetle, you know, one of those little beetles you place on a stone saying (as you spit on your palm): "St. John's beetle, I give you white wine! You give me red."

"Where are you going, beetle?"

"I am going this way to make a life for myself."

"Jump into my bag. You'll come in useful."

Off he went with his three little creatures in his bag. He reached the King's door. In order to get his daughter to laugh, the King had lots of people trying all sorts of ways, such as putting little men up one way and then knocking them over the other way. They did all sorts of tricks. Suddenly La Ramée picked up his three little creatures in his hand and presented them to the King's daughter, whereupon she roared with laughter. "Oh, what pretty little creatures, all three of them!"

So, upon my soul, that was that. La Ramée was a poor old

codger, and it was not exactly an easy situation, as the King had promised to give his daughter to the first man who would make her laugh.

The others did not want it to happen. Then the King said, "Never will I have those two get married."

Now, there happened to be a huge elephant about. It was a fierce animal. Everybody said, "Give the old codger to him to eat, and we will marry the Princess to a handsome gentleman. (The King's daughter said nothing. She was not taking part in any of this.)

So they put the old codger La Ramée together with the elephant. But he popped the little cricket into the animal's ear, and it went, "Ti-ti-ti" in the elephant's ear and sent him to sleep.

So the others, they married the King's daughter to a handsome gentleman. Lord, I should say he was! When La Ramée saw what had happened, he took the beetle and shoved it up the gentleman's arse on the Princess's wedding night. Then the beetle (you know jolly well where it goes) scratched so much that the bed became all covered with diarrhea. The gentleman was unwell all night long. At the same time, the little mouse went and fed the cricket and the beetle where La Ramée had put them.

The King's daughter no longer wanted to be with the handsome gentleman, and as his discomfort went on for so long, they had to go and find La Ramée in order that he should take back his three little creatures.

What could be done with La Ramée? They had to let him marry the Princess. Then they put the handsome gentleman with the fierce animal, and this time the cricket didn't go, "Ti-ti-ti" to send the animal to sleep, so the elephant ate the handsome gentleman, and La Ramée married the King's daughter.

Part IV
Lower Poitou

.15. *The Goat Who Lied*

• ONCE UPON A TIME there was a man who used to send his little boy out every day with his goat so that she should graze. He had to take her grazing by Bois-Breton.

Every morning the little beggar used to leave with the goat, and he led her along, saying:

> Graze, my goat, graze
> By the Bois-Breton.
> Eat up the thistles,
> And when you're quite full up,
> You'll have milk
> For your little kid.

But this little goat would not behave herself. She refused to graze when the little beggar led her. In the evening when the little beggar came home to his father's house with his goat, she hadn't any milk.

"What have you done?" his father asked the little beggar.

"I really did take her to graze, and I really did say to her:

> Graze, my goat, graze
> By the Bois-Breton.
> Eat up the thistles,
> And when you're quite full up,
> You'll have milk
> For your little kid.

"Well done, my little beggar. That is just what you had to say to that goat."

The next day the little beggar led his goat to Bois-Breton to graze and said once more:

> Graze my goat graze, etc. . . ."

However, that naughty goat would not eat thistles. When she came back that night to suckle her little kid, her master asked her:

> Have you good milk
> In your udder
> To feed your little kid?

The father was very surprised. "Where did you take her?" he asked his little boy.

"I really did take her to Bois-Breton," answered the little beggar.

Oh dear! that goat just would not eat thistles. After a while, the goat's master was angry when he saw she had no milk, at least that she had barely enough to let her kid suckle even a little. What did he do? He broke the goat's leg and left her all alone in the Bois-Breton with her broken leg. The goat stayed there. She made herself a nook, or, better still, a little shelter, if you prefer to call it that, and then she would go and graze wherever she felt like. However, she had to go to the bonesetter to have her leg seen to. She carefully told her little kid:

> I'm off to St. Jacques
> To set my leg,
> To set my hammy ham.
> When I come back,
> I'll show you my white paw.

The goat went off to see the bonesetter, but a wolf who had heard her go, went into the goat's shelter and managed to slip his paw under the door, saying:

> I'm off to St. Jacques
> To set my leg,
> To set my hammy ham.
> When I come back,
> I'll show you my white paw.

The little kid answered, "You have a black paw. You are not my mother."

So the wolf went away and dipped his paw in flour to whiten it. This time when the little kid saw the white paw, well of

course he opened the door of the shelter. Thereupon the wolf
leaped on the kid and ate it. Then he went to sleep right there.
When the goat came back after having had her leg set, she said
at the door:

> I've come back from St. Jacques,
> Where I had my leg set,
> Where I had my hammy ham set;
> When I come back,
> I'll show you my white paw.

In the end the goat pushed open the door and went in. Alack!
She saw that the wolf had eaten her kid. So she put a kettle of
water to boil on the fire, saying:

> Boil, boil kettle mine,
> So that I may scald my wolf!

When the wolf woke up, the water was hot. The goat un-
hooked the kettle from the pot hook and placed it on the floor.
Then the wolf said to the goat, "Will you jump over this kettle
of water?"

The goat answered, "Where I come from, it is not the women
who jump first." So the wolf was the first to jump over the kettle, but as he was made heavy by the kid being in his belly, he
missed and fell into the kettle and was scalded to death.

·16·   *Boudin-Boudine*

· ONCE UPON A TIME there was a little boy. His father and
mother had killed a sow. The mother had sent the child out to
take some black pudding and *fristure* (pork stew) to some of
their neighbors, and then he was to go on to his grandmother's.

The little beggar left with his basket on his back. This was a
basket in which his mother had put black puddings and pork
stew. First he went to their neighbor, saying:

Good day to you, my neighbor and your wife,
I bring to you some black puddings-puddeous
From our sow Courtine
And a little bone from a trotter.
But if you do not want it,
I shall take it back.

The neighbor accepted it, as you can well imagine! And so
off went the boy to his grandmother's, but it wasn't exactly next
door. He had to go this way and that. His mother had said,
"Make quite sure that you go by the Grand Veurdé so as not to
fall in the ditch."

Now it so happened that the child was followed by a wolf, who
asked him what he was carrying. "I am going to my grandmother's to take her some black puddings."

"Which way are you going?"

"I'll take the path through the woods."

The wolf went through the woods the shortest way possible,
that is to say, by the short cut, in order to be the first to get
there, and then he waited for the child.

When the little lad reached the old woman, he shouted
through the door:

Good morning, grandmother, godmother.
I have brought you black puddings-puddeous
From our sow Courtine,
And a little bone from a trotter.
But if you do not want it,
I shall take it back.

The grandmother, however, was not listening.

"Knock! Knock! Open up, Granny. It's your grandson bringing you black puddings."

"Show your white paw."

The child slipped his little hand through the peephole in the
door, and then the old woman said, "Draw the wooden bolt,
and then the latch will fall."

Oh, what enormous white teeth that wolf had! He was all
ready to catch the little beggar by the calves. And do you know
he had great big ears that stood straight up!

"Open up as quickly as you can, Granny, because the wolf is right next to me!"

"You mustn't be afraid, boy. The door will be open for you before the wolf reaches it."

At last the boy drew the bolt and let fall the latch.

So the wolf hid near the door and waited until the little beggar had gone in.

Then it was his turn to knock on the door.

"Knock! Knock!"

"Don't open the door, Granny. It's the wolf."

"Where did you pick him up?"

"At the corner of Bois-Bené. That's where he caught up with me. He asked me where you lived, so I told him."

Now the grandmother was better-hinged than the little lad. As the wolf was knocking at the door, knock, knock, she answered, "Show your white paw!"

The wolf slipped his paw through the peephole. But the wolf showed her a black paw, and the old woman did not open the door. The wolf went away. He then dipped his paw in a dish of *bouillie bordelaise* (white semolina), which had been placed outside to cool, and he even upset the dish. Anyway, he buried his paw in it and went back to show it through the peephole.

The grandmother was still not very sure. Supposing it was the wolf? As she stood there wringing her bonnet in her hands, while the wolf waited, her grandson said to her: "Granny, you're afraid. You are wringing your bonnet." The old woman looked through the peephole, and then she saw the porridge on the ground.

> That's pork stew which has spilled.
>   Then the wolf has lapped it up.
> I'll take up my broom.

The wolf was near the door. The old girl closed the door behind her and went after the wolf with a broom. She sent him flying, whisking him away with her broom.

After all that the little beggar was really very frightened and he did not want to go back to his parents. He was hiding in his grandmother's petticoats. Meanwhile his parents found that it was all taking a very long time and that their boy was still not back. The father went off to the grandmother's house, but he stumbled in the ruts on the road to Bas-Galioux, where they lived, and he fell down.

Well, the little lad had left his grandmother's to go home, hoping to reach it before nightfall, and the wolf made him run fast. But the boy met his father on the way, and they went back together. Then the father took a cleft stick, hit the wolf with it, and killed him.

They made a coat for the boy out of the wolf skin, and he was so happy after all that to have that wolf skin on his back. Lord, he had been so terribly frightened when he was taking his Granny those black puddings-puddeous!

•17• *The Iron Pot*

• ONCE THERE WAS a fairy who put a girl in an iron pot. Would you believe it! In an iron pot! So there the girl was, shut up in an iron pot under a rosebush.

Along came a gentleman out hunting with his dog. He saw the castle where the fairy lived and went in, hoping to be able to ask for food and drink. However, this house was somewhat unusual.

The gentleman met an eagle there. It was a great big bird. What on earth was it? Then he said to himself, "What shall I do?" The eagle said he liked him and that he would become the gentleman's master. Then the eagle went on to say, "In this castle lives a fairy who has shut a girl up in an iron pot." (The eagle must surely have been a man changed by magic. Perhaps he was a relative of the girl's whom the fairy had turned into an eagle.)

The gentleman found the fairy. When she saw how things stood, she said, "You've got work to do. There's a girl to set free."

By trying again and again, he finally set her free, but it took all of a month. The girl was buried under the earth, and she appeared only between eleven in the morning and noon, so the gentleman had to work hard during that hour to see her and set her free.

The fairy had said to him, "If you set her free, you will have won her and you may even marry her."

The gentleman had a little dog who went hunting with him every day. One day he met a woman on the road (I suppose it was the Blessed Virgin), and she said to him, "Would you like me to give your little dog a piece of bread?"

"Yes."

"Be on your way. Wherever you go, luck will follow!"

So luck followed him, and he rid the girl of the iron pot where she was imprisoned. He worked and worked every day between eleven and twelve to set her free. During the last days she could talk to him a little. Lor', when he began to work to set her free she was so far underground! To lift the girl up and the dog and the gentleman was the eagle's job. He said, "I'll lift all three of you, but you must feed me; otherwise, I'll never have the strength to reach the top."

The gentleman went hunting with his little dog. He killed some animals to feed to the eagle, and the first time the girl was lifted up to the top. The second time it was the little dog's turn to be lifted. But the third time the gentleman was still down there. The eagle said to him, "Go out hunting and kill some bulls and some sheep to feed me." The gentleman killed these animals and fed them to the eagle. The eagle then lifted him up. When he reached daylight, he said to the gentleman, "I'm all in. I'm going to let you drop." The eagle dropped him, but the gentleman had a box with all the necessary ointments in it, and he rubbed himself and recovered from his fall.

The next day he went back to his hunting and he killed animals to feed the eagle. That time the eagle lifted him to the top.

The girl and the little dog were waiting for him in the castle. They stayed there together, and the gentleman married the girl whom he had freed from the iron pot.

18 • The Little Lad Who Became a Bishop

• He was a very intelligent little lad. His parents had only the one child, but his father did not understand a thing about the boy. He was sent to school, and his father asked the schoolmaster if his son was doing well. The master always replied, "There is nothing one can teach your son."

So the father began to beat the little lad, thinking that the boy did not want to learn anything at school, but of course the boy hadn't anything to learn from the master, because he understood everything. The father went on beating his son. When his father beat him, the boy would say, "One day, Father, you shall pour water over my hands." The father then beat him even harder, saying, "You miserable failure, there is nothing one can do with you except beat you and then kill you."

One evening he took him to the forest to lose him. He had tied him to the foot of a tree. Then the little lad saw some priests going by on the road. They were on their way to a town where a bishop was being ordained. So the little lad called out, so that they would set him free, "Brothers, Reverend Fathers, save my life!"

Well, the first one did not hear him. Then another group went by, and they heard him. They set him free and took him with them. After that they went into an inn to eat, I expect. There was a girl there who was very ill. The little lad said to the innkeeper's wife, "If you will make me robes like the priests have, I'll save your daughter."

In the doorway was a large stone. Well, then the little lad said to the lady, "Get a good fire going." Next he lifted up the large stone in the doorway. There was a big toad underneath. At once the toad was placed in the fire, and the girl found herself cured. She said, "I feel a millstone has been taken off my shoulders!"

In this way the boy had the robes he wanted, as it was just, and he left with the priests to go to the town where a bishop was being ordained. When they reached the door of the church, the boy began playing marbles with some urchins who were around the church.

When it was time, he went into the church and up to the altar. Actually there was a dove in the church and she was supposed to land on the head of the future bishop. The boy was wearing his robes like the priests, and the dove made its way toward the little lad's head. Then all the priests shouted, "Hail, Monseigneur!"

Later the Bishop (by now the little lad had become a bishop) wrote a letter to his parents without saying who he was. He let them know that the Bishop asked them to come to such and such a place. The mother said to the father, "You know what the Bishop is going to say to you. You went and abandoned our little lad in the forest. We shall certainly be reprimanded."

And so the parents came to the said place, but they wore the costumes of that particular spot so as not to show the clothes of their own village. When the Bishop saw them, he said to them, "Those are not your clothes you are wearing. Go back home and fetch your own clothes before you appear before me."

The mother and father went back to their village to fetch their clothes. The mother said, "You see, you abandoned our boy. What will the Monseigneur say to us?"

They came back to the place and went to bed in the Bishop's house. The Bishop said to the fellow, "Tomorrow morning you will serve the Mass, which I will say." He said to the old girl, "Tomorrow you will assist with the Mass."

So he said the Mass, and when it was time for Communion and the father had poured out the bottles, the Bishop said, "I told you, Father, that one day you would pour water over my hands."

At that the fellow was so overcome that he died! He fell down stone dead! As for the old girl, she lived happily ever after with "her" Bishop.

·19· Tom Thumb

• TOM THUMB was so very very small that he could turn up anywhere.

One day he went to his aunt's house. As she wasn't there, he climbed into the cheese basket. In those days it was hung from a beam in a storeroom. He tasted several of the cheeses, and then he ate the best ones. After that, he hid in the straw under them.

When his aunt came back she brought down the basket to take out the cheeses.

"Oh," she said, "who has been tasting my cheeses?" Tom Thumb, who was in the straw in the basket, kept quiet.

Off went the aunt to the cow barn. She put the straw from the basket into the manger. At that moment Tom Thumb's uncle came along. He put a cabbage on top of the straw in the manger. Tom Thumb hid in the leaves. The cow ate a leaf and swallowed Tom Thumb whole.

Then the aunt came in to milk the cow, and what should she hear but the cow talking!

"What on earth am I doing in here!" shouted Tom Thumb (imprisoned in the cow's belly).

The aunt was afraid. "Is this cow under a spell?"

Whereupon the cow raised a leg and pushed the aunt over.

"All is lost!" cried the aunt.

The cow wanted to shit. She produced Tom Thumb in a cowpat, and as there was a bucket of water quite close, he jumped in and washed himself.

In the end the aunt believed that the cow was under a spell good and proper, and she told everyone about it.

·20· The Tale of Jean-le-Sot

• JEAN-LE-SOT was the son of a poor woman from near here. He wasn't very bright.

One day his mother said to him, "You will go to market and take this pot of butter to sell."

"Oh yes, Mom."

"Then you will go to the dealer. You will sell the butter to him and bring the money back to me."

"Yes, Mother, I'll do that."

So off he went with his pot of butter. He had to cross the fields of our Vendee marsh. As it was summer, the earth there was dried up. (You know in these parts the marshlands are under water in winter, and then in the summer the water withdraws and the earth splits into little cracks.)

Jean-le-Sot noticed how the earth had great cracks in it, so he said out loud, "Oh, poor earth, when I have cracked skin on my fingers it is very sore." Then he took his pot of butter and he put some in the cracks in the earth to make them better. He soon used up his pot of butter in this way. So home he went with an empty pot.

"Home already, Jean?"

"Yes, Mom."

"Ah! You sold the butter?"

"Oh, no. I did not sell it." he said, "I saw that the poor earth there in the marsh was so split up with cracks that I put butter in them to make them better."

"Ah, poor Jean! You'll always be Jean-le-Sot."

"Oh, well, Mother. I couldn't leave that earth all split up like that . . ."

Another time his mother said to him, "I can't go to market. You will go and sell the eggs there. Take them to the egg seller and bring back the money."

"Yes, Mother."

So once again he went over the marsh. It was the time of year when there are frogs. They were going, "coâ, coâ" in the ditches.

Jean-le-Sot soon had enough of this.

"Ah, there you are!" he said (he saw some frogs looking up at him). "This is the way you make fun of me, is it?" He picked up his eggs to throw them at the frogs. Soon his whole basket of eggs had been used up, and so he had to go home empty-handed.

"Well, Jean, you managed to sell the eggs?"

"Oh, Mother, don't talk about it. The ditches were full of

frogs, and they were making fun of me, so I threw the eggs at them."

Well, that was another of Jean-le-Sot's mishaps.

Then one day Jean-le-Sot was wandering along when he met a priest, and he said to him, "Oh, Monsieur le Curé, you are a happier man than I, for I have to work."

"You are happier than I, Jean!"

"Shall we exchange our clothes, Monsieur le Curé?"

"I don't mind if I do."

They exchanged clothes. Jean wore the priest's habit and let the other have his suit.

"Well. Tomorrow there is a burial to look after. How will you cope, Jean?"

"I'll get through." However, he said to himself, "What shall I do? I don't know any Latin. And here I go trying to speak Latin."

He saw an old girl going to market with a jug of milk on her head. She started to dance about, and the jug fell and the milk was spilled on the ground.

Jean-le-Sot started with his Latin there and then:

> Milk is spoiled! Jug broken! Amen!
> I've seen your arse? Amen!

(The old girl had fallen over and was showing her buttocks.)

Later Jean saw a magpie at the top of a tree, and at the foot of the tree, a quail sang.

> The magpie has her nest high!
> The quail has her nest low! Amen!

Following this he met a dead she donkey under a bridge. It didn't smell good, and Jean was soon started on a psalm:

> Under the bridge stinks the she donkey! Amen!

After that, as he went back to his parish, he stopped to spend the night at an inn. He went into the dining room and saw a dresser with plates on it, so he started to count, "Ten glasses!

Six cups!" That night he slept in a square bed without curtains or canopy, and he said, "Bed without a canopy!" Next to the bed there was a little table. Jean-le-Sot had a look at it. There was nothing on it.

So he started to sing, "Bed without a canopy and without a pisspot!"

Jean reached the church. The people had come to receive their new priest with all the pomp at their disposal. Came the time for a burial.

One man said to him, "You see, my father is dead . . ."

"We shall bury him. What was his name?"

"Well, his name was Pierre."

"Shall we bury him tomorrow? You may be a little surprised by my Latin but it is the Latin spoken nowadays."

"Yes, Monsieur le Curé."

The next day Jean-le-Sot put on his vestments and went up to the altar.

He began singing slowly, "Pierrot, Pierrot! Poor Pierrot!"

The chorister answered in spite of this, "Amen!"

The curé started up again, "Bed without a canopy and without a pisspot?"

The chorister answered, "Amen!"

The curé: Ten glasses, six cups."

The chorister: "Amen!"

The curé: "Under the bridge stinks the she donkey!"

The chorister: "Amen!"

The curé: "The magpie builds her nest high. The quail builds her nest low."

The chorister: "Amen!"

The curé: "Milk is spoiled! Jug broken! Arse seen!"

The chorister: "Amen!"

The burial ended like that. People asked each other what sort of priest this was.

After two or three burials, the parishoners were really worked up. "What a strange kind of priest! We must catch him out."

"One of us will pretend to be dead and get into a coffin. We'll soon see what happens. That will soon rid him of this whim."

They did as they had planned. One of them hid in a coffin.

(He was perhaps hard put not to laugh.) Now Jean-le-Sot started up his burial service singing. At a given moment the "deceased" lifted the lid of the coffin. The parishioners burst out laughing and they all came out of the church.

"What is happening?" asked the priest.

The "deceased" also popped his head out to see what was going on.

"Aren't you dead?" said the priest. "And here you are now wanting to get up!" Jean-le-Sot grabbed the candle snuffer and bashed the so-called dead man with it.

"Ah, so you don't want to die?" Then he took the cross from the choir boy's hands and he killed the "deceased" with it.

"Come, come!" he shouted to his parishioners. "He wasn't quite dead, but now he really is!"

And so the burial was over.

In the end Jean-le-Sot said to himself, "I really was better off at my old job. I shall give back my priests' robes and take back my clothes, and I'll be a sight more happy!"

Part V
Upper Poitou

The Wolf and the Soldier

• THERE ONCE WAS a wolf around here near the Fontaine-blanche. This wolf had heard it said that no one could compete with a creature called man.

This wolf was roaming along just off the road to Areney. He was going by there when he reached the Croix-cassee and met an old woman. This wolf stopped and told the old woman what he had heard. "I would like to fight a creature called man."

The old lady answered, "You will go to the Fontaine-blanche, where you will see a soldier. You will ask him if he wishes to fight."

So this wolf went off. Having reached the Fontaine-blanche, he found a soldier who was returning from the wars with his uniform, saber, and musket.

The wolf stopped. He had only just met the old woman when he caught sight of the soldier and said, "Well, it's really happened!" And all at once he said to the soldier, "So there you are. Well, if you wish to fight, I am ready."

"Ah," said the soldier, "all right, if you wish it, just the two of us."

The wolf said, "Throw something in my eyes to make me angry."

The soldier had a loaded musket. He said to him, "Stand back a bit!" Then the soldier shot him in the eyes.

"How badly you spit!" said the wolf.

The wolf turned round, and that second the soldier drew his sword and sliced off his thigh.

Another wolf, who was only a few steps away at La Chausse-en-l'air, saw him coming back limping and asked him, "What has happened?"

The wolf who had wanted to fight the creature called man came along holding his severed thigh in his paws.

"What happened to you?"

"Oh, my poor old friend, I wanted to fight with a creature called man. He spat in my face. After that he hit my body with a stick. Oh, my friend, what will become of me now?"

"Well," said the other, "you would have been far better off if you had kept quiet."

•22• *The Little Elves of La Chausse-en-l'Air*

• At La Chausse-en-l'Air there lived an old man and an old woman. In the winter when the old woman had a moment to spare, she would spin in front of the fire. She wore a cape—you know what I mean, with a kind of hood—which she drew over her head when it was too cold.

During the winter evenings the old woman would do her spinning by the light of a resin candle, which smoked. It smoked so much that one could hardly see the people in the room. When the old man was in bed, she drew the flax off her distaff to make thread from it.

Now one evening a *fadet* (elf) came down the chimney and started laughing. He came right up to her, saying:

> You spin and you spin,
> To your spindle roll it in!

This old woman complained to her old man after she had had this visit. (The elf used to come back every evening.)

"Oh, well, don't worry. It won't be long before I rid you of him," he said, and he added, "This evening I will change into your clothes, and I will sit and spin in your usual place.

The old man took his wife's cape and sat in her place by the fire with the distaff and spindle, which he started turning. Almost at once the elf came down and settled next to him. Then he said:

> Ah, but you spin and you spin,
> To your spindle nothing roll it in!
> This is not yesterday's lady.
> The spindle it turned,
> And onto that spindle she rolled it.

Then what did the old man do? Well, he had been careful to place a poker in the fire in order to make it red hot. As the elf's call was over and he was going up the chimney, the old man slammed the poker on his backside.

The elf, who was busy going up, began to scream, "Burned buttocks! Burned buttocks!"

The other elves said to him, "Who did that to you? Who did that to you?"

The old man, who was busy spinning, replied, "Me. I did it."

The other elves, thinking it was the scorched elf answering them, all said, "Oh, so it is you who did it. Well, then, keep it to yourself."

•23• The Piece of Cloth

• THERE WAS a Prince with three children who also had a niece whom he cared for as well. Now the three brothers came to love their cousin as they grew older. All three wanted to marry her, so there wasn't a moment's peace between them. The two eldest brothers were always teasing the younger one, who was a bit simple and whom the father looked upon as a fool.

One fine day their father said to them, "He who brings me the largest piece of cloth shall be the one to have my niece."

The two elder boys left at once to find carriages and horses and attendants—the whole lot—and then off they went!

The father said to his youngest son, "You're not budging, I suppose?" As I have already told you, the boy was a bit simple.

Well, he went. He went, too, but on foot. After a long walk he reached a ruined castle. He could not see the actual castle, but he noticed a fenced-in paddock where a horse was grazing. Meanwhile, his brothers in their carriages were already miles ahead. "What can I do?" the poor devil said to himself, and he went toward the horse. The horse looked at him. The youth was about to stroke it when the animal said, "Get up on me." He had never mounted a horse and there he was climbing onto it. The horse cantered off, but the young fellow was not afraid and did not fall off.

The horse took him before the ruined castle. Just an ordinary cat lived there. The poor devil went into this castle, and then the cat led him through several rooms. She made him twist and turn in that castle of hers. There was nothing but gilt and mirrors everywhere. Then she gave him a meal with her claws. He was having rather a good time, what with the cat being on his knees and her bringing food to him.

Just then he heard his brothers going home with their carriages filled with pieces of cloth.

"My brothers are going home, and I have nothing to take back there!" Well, then the cat gave him a tailor's box.

"Off you go with that box!" she said.

The youth unfastened the lid of the box. There was a little piece of cloth showing at the top.

"Someone must pull on that end, and the whole cloth will come out," said the cat. "Above all, don't show it to anyone. Put your hand in your pocket and the box also."

The poor devil climbed back onto the horse which had led him to the cat's castle, but he was the last to reach his father's house. His brothers had brought back magnificent pieces of cloth. They were very long but they had seams.

Their father was watching them. He caught sight of his third son and said to him, "Well, boy, what have you brought back?"

"A tailor's box."

Now, without showing them the box, he called his nurse.

"Nurse, I want you to pull on that."

The nurse began to pull on the little piece of cloth which was only just showing. She pulled and pulled. The cloth came out of the box. There was not a seam in it, and the more the nurse pulled, the more cloth came out.

Their father crossed his arms. "Where did he get that?" He was not at all pleased, and he was saying to himself, "There I was treating him so badly, and it is he who has won!"

The other two were dumbfounded to see what had happened to their brother. Then the father said, "That's not all, you know. You have brought back fine pieces of cloth, but that's not all." And to the youngest he said: "It is impossible for me to give you my niece. You are the youngest. Your brothers have the right of seniority."

Then the father thought this over, and at last he said, "You are all three going to go off once more. He who brings me the finest hunting dog will be the bridegroom." (The father was probably master of the hunt.)

And so they hit the road once again. The three brothers were searching for hunting dogs. The two eldest left with their horses, and that same evening they came back with dogs of all sizes, enormous ones and tiny ones.

The youngest? Well he went back to the cat, riding the horse he had found near the castle. He heard his brothers on their way back to their father with all their dogs. "Oh," he said, "my brothers will soon be home."

The cat gave him an egg.

"Here," she said, "here's an egg for you. You are not going to say a word about it. You will keep it in your pocket and hold your hand over it, but don't let anyone know."

The boy stroked the cat before leaving.

"See you a week from today," said the cat.

He went home to his father. When he got there, there were all kinds of dogs in the courtyard.

"Come on," he said (that was the father talking to the youngest son), "my boy, what have you brought home?"

The lad pulled the egg out of his pocket. The cat had also said to him, "When it's your turn, put your thumb on the egg, and you shall see what will come out."

He put his thumb on it. Out of the egg popped a little green dog who yapped and ran ahead of the others. He outran all the other dogs and, better still, he jumped back into the egg when the fellow placed his thumb on it. You should have seen how that dog obeyed!

"Ah," said the father, "it is the youngest there who has brought me the best hunting dog."

The father did not know what to do. In the end, he said, "I have had enough of this. All right, off you go, all three of you. The one who brings me the prettiest wench shall be the one to have my niece."

Once again the three brothers were off. The two eldest were

in the lead, and they brought back all the girls they could find. There were girls with raw, red hands who milked the goats, and old cooks—a hodgepodge of women of all kinds.

The lad went to the cat.

She said to him, "You must do me a favor and do as I say. You will get a good fire going. Now listen to me carefully. This is the last trick."

"Yes," said the fellow.

"You'll get a chopping block ready near the fire."

The fellow looked at her. He was scared stiff.

"Go on. Do as I say," she said.

He was so afraid that he was whimpering.

"This is your last trick, and don't bungle it. I shall put my neck on the block. You must cut through it with one blow." (How he shook, the poor fellow!)

That cat put her neck on the block, and her head flew into the flames in the hearth. The lad turned his head and saw a lovely maiden dressed in gold and silver who asked him to take her to his father's home, to the Prince's castle in fact.

When they had gone (there was no more cat; her head had been chopped off), the lad took the girl by the arm.

The horse was still grazing in the meadow. They went and found him, both of them together, and they rode on him and they got there in that way to the courtyard of the castle. There were ladies and maidens of all kinds brought there by the two elder brothers. The lad arrived on his horse with the beautiful young girl dressed in white satin trimmed with precious stones and diamonds.

The father could not get over it. In the end he said, "Well, you can marry my niece, if you wish."

"I don't want her," said the lad. "One is enough for me."

"Well then," the lovely girl said, "Come on, let's go! Off to my castle!"

And so the fellow married the cat. The horse was waiting for them. They mounted him and went back to the castle.

The cat was a fairy. She helped that fellow because his father and his two elder brothers had always despised him.

·24· The Three Gold Hairs from the Devil

• ONCE THERE WAS a little boy born of poor folk. There was also a King who was jealous of this little boy. He did not want him to live, for he had heard said, "That child shall one day become king."

So what did the King do? One night he went and knocked on the door of the poor people's house and asked, "Could you take me in to live in your house?" There was not much room in the house. "I shall sleep near the cradle," said the King. But during the night he jumped out of the window with the basket in which the little boy was sleeping, and he put it on the river. The little boy floated along until he reached an old house where some kind folk lived. They rescued him and brought him up until he was twenty years old.

The King who had placed the little boy on the water heard he had been rescued. He went to the old house where the boy had been taken in and said to the young man, "I am going to give you a letter. You will go to my country with this letter for my wife."

"I'll go there and take it to her," replied the young man.

So off he went taking the King's letter with him. The evening closed in. He did not know where to spend the night. In the end he landed in a house where there were three girls. They agreed to put him up, and then he said to them, "Above all, do not touch this letter."

He left the letter on the table and went to bed. But the three girls were inquisitive. They wondered what was in the letter. In the end, they unsealed it. In the letter it was stated that the young man, the bearer of the letter, should be killed.

"Oh," said the girls to themselves, "this young man is so kind and polite. We must not let him take this letter."

They rewrote the letter saying at the end of it that the young man should marry the King's daughter. (This letter was intended for the Queen.) Then the three girls tore up the King's letter after having forged the writing, and they then put in the envelope the letter which they had written.

The next day the young man picked up his letter from the table and took it with him. He was to take it to the Queen.

He walked for a long time and showed up in front of the castle. The Queen opened the letter and read it. Thinking that this was a message from her husband, the King, she did her best to make the young man welcome. Shortly after, she said, "Well, as you are to marry my daughter, we shall have the wedding at once."

The wedding took place, or at least the preparations for the marriage ceremony went ahead. Then the King arrived and was very astonished to find all this going on.

He asked, "Why? For whom are all these preparations being made?"

"Why, this is for your daughter's wedding to the young man you sent with a letter to the Queen."

The King exploded in a frightful rage.

"This is impossible. In the letter it was stated that he should be killed."

"No, no. In the letter it said that your daughter should marry the young man."

The King could contain himself no longer. So the young man toyed with the idea of running away alone, and then he thought of his betrothed and came back. The King said to him, "You shall marry my daughter on one condition only. You must first go and fetch three gold hairs from off the Devil."

Then the young man wondered what to do to please the King. Off he went walking and walking and walking. He crossed great forests, and one morning he reached the shore. There was a man there who took people from one side of the river to the other, and he was very fed up with his job. He asked the young man, "Have you any idea what to do in order not to carry on with this job?"

"Take me over first. I shall give you an answer when I return."

The young man crossed the river. He walked and walked and walked and arrived in front of the Devil's house. The door was guarded by an old woman. The young man introduced himself

to her, saying, "I have come to take three of the Devil's gold
hairs."

The old girl answered, "That is going to be very hard, but
to help you, I shall turn you into an ant, and you will put yourself in my apron so as not to be seen by the Devil."

At that time the Devil was asleep. The old woman plucked one
hair from him.

"Ouch! Why have you woken me up?"

"I was looking for a louse on you. I have killed it."

"If you start that again, watch out, or I'll give you something
you didn't bargain for."

The old girl gave the gold hair to the ant hidden in her apron.
A moment later the Devil was asleep once more. The old girl
plucked another hair from him.

"Ouch! What are you doing to me?"

"Oh, I've squashed a great big flea!"

"Any more of this and you'll get the stick a hundred times
over."

The old girl gave the gold hair to the ant. Not long after, the
Devil fell asleep again. The woman plucked yet another hair
from him.

"Ouch!" said the Devil, waking up. "I smell fresh flesh here."

"No, no, no. No one can come in here."

The old girl slipped the third gold hair to the ant. They left
the room where the Devil was asleep, and the old girl turned
the ant back into a young man.

So there he was on his way again and very pleased with himself, as he had the three gold hairs from the Devil to take to
the King. He went along to find the ferry man on the river
bank.

"Have you found out what to do so as not to go on with this
job of mine?"

"Take me over, and then I shall tell you."

Having reached the other side of the river, the young
man said, "Well, now, to get out of this job, you will hand over
the boat to the first man who comes to you to cross the
river."

The young man went off and hastened to take the Devil's
three gold hairs to the King.

The King showed great surprise. He took the three gold hairs saying, "Fine, fine! This is well done."

He, too, had the idea of going to the Devil's house. "I shall try and get in there," he said.

The King went the same way as the young man, and he met the ferry man, who was still there on the river bank with his boat.

"Would you take me over?" The ferry man took the King aboard his craft and leaped onto the bank, leaving the King alone on the river.

Since then the King has been the ferry man, going endlessly back and forth.

One fine day a hurricane swept by. The waves toppled the King into the water, and he fought there in vain and was drowned.

Since these days the young man who married the King's daughter became king of that country.

•25• *Puss in Boots*

• A MILLER HAD three boys. When he died he gave the mill to the first boy, the donkey (who carried the sacks) to the second boy, and to the third boy he gave the cat (who used to catch the mice). The third boy was very downhearted. He said, "What shall I do when I have eaten my cat?"

But the cat said, "I am very intelligent. Ask of me what you will, and it will be granted to you." The boy had nothing to eat. He said to the cat, "I am hungry."

The cat went and stole four or five fat sausages and black puddings and a roast from a butcher's shop. Then he ran and took them back to his master.

"Which do you like best?" the boy asked the cat.

"Black puddings," said the cat, putting his paw over his tummy.

The boy gave him the black puddings and ate the sausages and the roast himself. "Now I am thirsty," he said.

"All right, I'm off," answered the cat.

He took a bowl and went to find some Anjou wine from a hotel and brought it back to his master. The boy drank the wine and gave some of it to the cat. "Now I want some work," said the boy. "I should like to be placed with a rich man. I'll work hard and then I shall be satisfied."

What did the cat do? He went to the King and asked him, "Would you be needing a fairly capable young man to help you?"

"Why do you ask me this?"

"Well, because I have a master who is out of work, and he would like to have something to do."

"All right, I'll take him on. He shall serve all the dishes and he shall eat a quarter of what he serves. Off with you! Your master shall be rich."

Oh, how happy the cat was!

"Will I, too, live with my master?"

The King said, "Yes, yes, yes."

So the cat went and found his master and told him what had happened. "I have found just what you need. You will be rich. You will eat well. You are to serve the King, and a quarter of the dishes served shall be yours."

Then the boy said to the cat, "And where will you live?"

"Well," he said, "I asked the King, and he said that I could go with you."

The cat and the boy went straight to the King at once.

The King had three daughters. The boy served at table, and the King was very pleased with him.

Somewhat later the King said to the boy, "If you wish to marry, you will have to choose one of my three daughters."

There was the eldest, the next one, and the last. The boy wasn't quite sure what he should say. "Well," said he, "I'll choose the eldest . . . Oh, no, I'll choose the next one . . . No, the third! Oh, I don't know!" he said, throwing up his arms.

"Choose whichever one you wish," said the King.

The boy said to the three girls, "Well, all three of you shall dance. The one who dances the best shall be mine."

At once the three girls danced before him, and it was the

second one who was the best dancer. The boy said to the King, "Right! I'll take your second daughter."

So the following Saturday the wedding celebrations took place. Now the two sisters were jealous, and they did not want to be present at the wedding. The King was very angry. He had people looking for them everywhere.

"If they are found," he said, "I'll chop their heads off!"

So the boy said, "Oh, no! This cannot happen today, nor can it happen tomorrow or the day after that, as the wedding celebrations will not yet be over." And then of course the bride was very fond of her sisters. She said, "Never shall they have their heads chopped off!"

Then the King said, "All right, all right. In order to please you, I shall not have their heads chopped off."

Now the cat was still with his master, even at the wedding. He, too, went and found one of the girls, and as he looked for her he thought, "Why shouldn't I get married, too?" At that moment he saw a big rat (at least it was a large female rat). "Oh ho!" said he, "I'll get married to that one, I will!" Then at the same time he took the female rat in his arms and started running about everywhere, under the tables and over the guests' feet and all over the place. Oh! If the King had seen this! (But he was still busy looking for his two other daughters.) Then the cat and the female rat went to the place where the cat was eating at the banquet table.

The cat said to the rat, "You will eat from my plate."

But the rat was too small. She had to climb up onto the table, and the King saw her. Ah, well, he killed the rat.

So the cat said, "Now I have lost my wife, but why shouldn't I marry a young girl?"

There and then he turned into a young man, and he went and found a young girl at the wedding and asked her, "Where is the King's youngest daughter?"

"No one knows where she has gone."

"I shall run after her." And he ran after her (as a young man still) and found her crying and crying and crying.

"What is the matter, Mamôselle?"

"Oh, I have lost my elder sister."

"Oh, poor Mamôselle. Perhaps you would like to get married, too?"

"Oh, yes," said the girl.

"Well, then," he said, "take my arm."

The cat (still as a young man) and the youngest of the three sisters both went and found the King.

"Who is this newcomer?" said the King, looking at the young man (who was none other than the cat!).

"Oh, well," said he, "I want to marry the youngest of your daughters."

The King was perhaps a little encumbered with his three daughters. Anyway he then said, "Well, while we are at it, we shall go on and have another wedding after this one."

Meanwhile the eldest of the King's daughters was listening at the doors and said, "What a handsome youth! Why shouldn't he take two wives. I shall go and ask him."

At the same time, the young man came out. The eldest daughter asked him, "Would you like two wives?"

"All the girls in the world!" said the young man.

"Well, will you have me?"

The cat (that is to say, the young man) took the two girls by the arm. That made three weddings at one go, or at least two, but the cat had taken two wives.

Now, it happened that the eldest noticed that the young man stopped looking after her and did not talk to her anymore. Then she said, "I would be better off dead." (Well, I would have thought so, too, if I had been in her place, I can tell you that.) So she hanged herself.

Then the cat stayed with the youngest of the King's daughters while his master had the second one (the one who danced best of all).

Well, that is about all I know!

·26· *The Pea*

• THERE WERE a fellow and his wife who were so poor that all they owned was one pea, and so they planted it in the earth, and the pea started growing. It grew so tall that it looked like a tree.

So the woman said to her husband, "Climb up this pea plant there. Climb up, right up high, and go tell St. Peter we have nothing more to eat!"

The man climbed from branch to branch and reached the top of the pea stalk. There he knocked at the gates of paradise.

St. Peter opened them and said, "What have you come to look for here?"

"I would give anything to have something to eat."

"Well, listen to me carefully. You will go back to earth, and then, when you are home, you will say to your table, 'Table, table, lay yourself!' and you will see on your table everything you could wish to eat."

The fellow came down from the top of the pea stalk and explained to his good wife what St. Peter had said to him.

At once they said, "Table, table, lay yourself," and they saw on the table all sorts of good things to eat.

The fellow and his wife now had enough to eat their fill, and they spent some time in this way.

Then the old girl said to her husband, "If we had a few crowns, we'd be a lot happier."

"Well, yes."

"Then up the pea plant you go, and ask St. Peter to give us some crowns."

The fellow climbed back up the pea stalk from branch to branch, and he reached the top, and there was paradise. St. Peter opened up for him.

"Now what do you want, my good fellow?"

"My old woman would like you to give us some crowns."

"Go right down again, and as soon as you get home, you will say to your chest, 'Chest, chest, be filled,' and the chest will fill itself with crowns."

The fellow came down from the pea stalk.

"What did he say to you?" said the old woman. "Did he give you anything?"

"I have to say to our chest, 'Chest, chest, be filled,' and we shall have plenty of money."

"Then go ahead. Try at once," said the old woman.

Immediately the fellow went to his chest and said, "Chest, chest, be filled." And when they opened the lid of the chest, it was full of crowns.

Well, by now this fellow and his wife were rich. They spent some time with their chest full of crowns. Then the old woman said to her husband, "Now we have plenty to eat and lots of crowns, but we ought to have a house, too. Go on up our pea plant and ask St. Peter."

The fellow climbed up the pea plant again from branch to branch, and he reached the top. He knocked on the door. St. Peter opened up for him.

"Well, now," said the fellow, "we have plenty to eat and lots of crowns. We should now like a lovely house."

"Go down again," said St. Peter. "You will find that by tomorrow you and your wife will be living in a lovely house."

The fellow went down to the ground.

"What did he say to you?" asked the old woman.

"He said that by tomorrow we would have a lovely house."

"How?" she said.

"You'll see right enough."

The next day when they awoke they were in a lovely house with all sorts of furniture and what have you and servants to look after them.

"Madam desires something?" said the maid.

"Would you like to go out, Sir?" said the coachman.

And so on. The fellow and his wife lacked nothing, but as a result of living in a beautiful house and being served like a king, they became arrogant and despised the world about them.

One day a beggar came and asked for a piece of bread at the door of their house. The old woman was there. "I shall give you nothing," she said, "and even if you don't ask, I'll send the dog after you."

As the beggar asked again for a piece of bread, the old woman set the dog on him, and that was the end of it.

But the next day when the fellow and his wife awoke there was neither a fine house nor any servants left. They were in their hovel as poor as they had been before planting their pea.

Part VI
Lower Marche

.27. The Black Hen

• ONCE UPON A TIME there was a beggar who was at the crossroads, at the spot they nowadays call the Crêpe-au-lait. It was nightfall and very dark. Our beggar had pulled down his hood so as not to feel the cold, and he could see nothing but the hedges ahead of him. Just then the man heard something rummaging around in the night. He looked around, of course, but saw nothing except the hedges along the path. Midnight drew closer, but our man was not afraid to be there. Then he saw a black hen scratching and scratching at the soil. He went a little nearer and saw that she was unearthing gold, lots of gold coins with her claws.

Our beggar did try and pick up a few gold coins, but then the hen beat her wings three times. Next she sang, "Cocorico!" three times. She had looked at our man straight in the eye, and he was so frightened that he fled without having been able to pick up the gold—that is, apart from a few coins. He ran off as fast as he could and only stopped when he reached the castle of a squire, perhaps the castle of Barres. As soon as he saw this castle, he went into it to hide. Then he dropped to the floor of the grange and fell fast asleep.

The next day the squire asked him what had happened. Our beggar told his story, but the squire said, "This isn't true."

However, the next day the squire went to the crossroads of the Crêpe-au-lait. It was winter and the moon was full. The same thing took place as had happened to the beggar. At midnight the black hen appeared, and she started scratching at the soil, and the squire saw that she was bringing out gold.

Perhaps the squire loved gold more than our beggar did, for when he saw the gold coins on the earth, he stretched out his hand to pick them up. He picked up as many as he could, and there and then the coins turned to soot. They were nothing but little burned out embers.

The squire just saw the black hen beating her wings three times and he heard her sing out, "Cocorico! Cocorico! Cocorico!" The black hen gave him such a look that he was terrified. He fled as fast as he could to the castle, and there he fell fainting to the ground.

He lay there like a corpse all night long and all the next day. No one could bring him back to life. When midnight struck, the iron gates of the castle were heard to squeak. The walls creaked. The shutters banged, and then something in the earth could be heard rummaging around. It was the black hen, who had appeared in front of the squire's castle. She could not be seen, but everyone heard her sing out, "Cocorico!"

Well, then, the squire gave a sigh and sat up in bed and asked for a drink, and then he said to them, "When the old beggar told me he had found a black hen at the crossroads stirring up some gold, I wanted to go there and pick some of it up, but the gold coins turned into embers as I was about to carry them off. I tell you that black hen is the Devil!"

At that the men made the sign of the Cross, and the old women took to their rosaries.

Since that night time went by, but the black hen came every night and sang out before the squire's castle as midnight struck. She was seen by no one, but everybody heard her. From midnight on, the village could no longer get any sleep. The squire of the castle realized that he had sinned in wanting to pick up that gold.

He said, "I must go barefoot to the Holy Land as a penance."

So off he went on foot to the Holy Land. He was dressed in rags and took no money with him. Winter went by. Everybody in the village was waiting in the hope that the squire would soon reach the Holy Land. But the black hen still came and sang at midnight before the squire's castle, and no one around there could sleep. The master sent no news to the castle.

When spring came, it so happened that the whole village awoke to a morning of sunshine after having slept right through the night for the first time. That black hen had not come to sing at midnight before the castle.

"This means our squire has reached the Holy Land!" said an old woman.

It was true. The squire had entered Jerusalem at midnight.

Since then no one has ever heard the black hen of the Crêpe-au-lait sing again.

·28· *Jean of Bordeaux*

• JEAN OF BORDEAUX WAS a poor boy who used to go out to the fields in his wooden clogs to mind the hogs. He was a wretched lad and not very bright.

One fine day he went off. He left his parents and went to start a new life. He reached a country where everyone seemed melancholy. It was England. The King of that country had a daughter who was held prisoner by the Devil in a crypt below the altar of the church. The King of England had proclaimed, "He who frees my daughter shall be her husband." Many had tried to set her free, but none had come out of the church, because the Devil had eaten them.

Jean of Bordeaux said, "I shall try and set her free."

The King gave him a gun and a bayonet. He also had a cake brought to him for him to eat and a bottle of white wine to drink during the night he was to spend in the church. He was not to touch it until midnight. In actual fact, every night toward midnight something made a most frightful noise, but no one was any the wiser, for no one had ever come out of there.

Thereupon, one night Jean of Bordeaux went round the church and met an old woman there. She addressed him.

"Well, what do you know? So you are here, Jean of Bordeaux?"

The boy answered her, "How is it that you know me, old lady?"

The old woman replied, "I am going to give you some advice. If you go into the church tonight, the Devil will eat you, but here is what you have to do so as not to be eaten like the others. You will hide by climbing into the priest's pulpit. He won't find you there before midnight, and when midnight strikes, the Devil will be powerless against you."

Jean of Bordeaux took the old woman's advice. He hid in the

pulpit and waited. Eleven o'clock, half past eleven—there was the Devil beginning his round.

"Where are you, Jean of Bordeaux? I am so hungry tonight, and I haven't eaten yet."

The Devil went all over the place. He broke a chair, then another; he even lifted the pews. Nothing stood up to him. In the end he caught sight of Jean of Bordeaux in the priest's pulpit, but the first stroke of midnight rang out.

Then Jean of Bordeaux left the pulpit and ate his cake and drank his wine. Then he walked about the church awaiting daybreak.

The next morning the King had the door reopened for him to find out how he had protected himself with his gun and his bayonet. When he saw Jean of Bordeaux coming out of the church alive, he said to himself, "This lad is worth something more than the others. I shall trust him."

All day long Jean of Bordeaux lived as a free man. He ate and drank at the King's expense and did exactly as he pleased.

That night he had to go into the church again to face the Devil. The King of England gave another cake and another bottle of wine to Jean of Bordeaux.

That night the lad went in front of the church and met the old woman, who said to him, "Ah, you know, Jean of Bordeaux, tonight you will have to hide inside the statue of a saint. You will saw off the head of the statue, then you will slip into the body of the statue, and you will not move your head or even look around. When the Devil sees you, it will be too late for him."

Jean hid there. Eleven o'clock, half past eleven—there was the Devil coming out, and he climbed into the pulpit where he had seen him the day before, but this time he was nowhere to be seen. The Devil in a fit of temper shook and broke everything he came across, shouting, "Where are you then, Jean of Bordeaux? I tell you I am so hungry. This is the second night I have not eaten."

Midnight struck just when the Devil saw Jean's head sticking out of the statue. The lad came out of his hiding place and ate his cake and drank his bottle. Then he waited for daybreak.

The King was delighted with him. He said to himself, "This lad will manage to rescue my daughter from the Devil's clutches." And during that day again Jean drank and ate anything he wished at the King's expense.

The third night the old woman said to Jean, "This time the Devil will find you, but midnight will strike and he will not be able to eat you. Hide behind the altar in such a way that only your feet are showing. As after midnight the doors of the crypt will remain open, the King's daughter will say, 'Give me your hand, Jean of Bordeaux.' You will say to her, 'If you wish to take the end of my bayonet take it, but if you do, do not let it go.'"

Eleven o'clock, half past eleven—the Devil appeared in a frightful rage.

"Where are you, Jean of Bordeaux? For three nights now I have had nothing to eat. This time I shall find you." But then he saw the tip of Jean's foot which was sticking out from under the altar. Midnight struck. Ah, the Devil had not been able to eat him like the others.

This time Jean got up, but, instead of eating the cake and drinking the bottle of wine, he opened the door of the crypt where the girl was closeted. She was there, but she could not get out by herself.

"Give me your hand, Jean of Bordeaux," she said.

"If you wish to take my bayonet, take it, but if you do not wish to, leave it." (Actually Jean of Bordeaux could not draw her out by taking her hand.)

In the end the girl touched his bayonet and she was safe. She came slowly out of the crypt. So then Jean of Bordeaux took the cake and the bottle. They both had something to eat and drink, and then they began talking of love.

The next morning the King of England was there to open the door of the church. The King had to marry his daughter to Jean of Bordeaux, and really king though he was, the match delighted him. The wedding festivities lasted some time. Then one fine day Jean felt he wanted to go and see his parents in Bordeaux.

His wife gave him one hundred horsemen as an escort. They

were all mounted on fine horses, and she also gave him one hundred thousand francs to make the journey. As for him, he was dressed as marshal of England. What gorgeous clothes he had!

He was off. One night he reached an inn, which was in fact run by the old woman who had given Jean such good advice. He asked for rooms for himself and all his following.

"Ah, so there you are, Jean of Bordeaux! We shall give your escort something to eat. As for you, you shall sup with me, and we shall play cards."

Jean of Bordeaux stayed and played with the old woman, and then she won the lot. The hundred horses, the horsemen, the gold, and even his uniform of marshal of England went to her. He had nothing left. The next day the old woman sent him away dressed only in his old clothes.

So he went off feeling foolish and sheepish ¬with his two wooden clogs on his feet. He reached his parents in Bordeaux in this state. There, in spite of his telling them all that had happened to him, no one would believe him.

His wife, who was anxious, as he did not seem to be coming back, left to search for him. She took with her two hundred horsemen and two hundred thousand francs, and she started on her journey.

That evening she drew up in front of the inn run by the old woman, and she asked for rooms. She received the same welcome.

"Let's play cards," said the old woman.

"You will give back my hundred horses, my hundred horsemen, my money, and my husband's uniform, which you stole from me, or else I shall kill you."

In the end the old woman did have to give back everything to her, but they killed her just the same.

There was an escort, therefore, of three hundred horsemen to lead the daughter of the King of England to Bordeaux. To everybody's surprise, she asked where the little inn owned by Jean's parents was. She then had her escort lodged at the large hotel, and she made for the little hotel.

"Oh, Madam, you cannot stay there—it's just a little inn."

"I wish to go there."

Anyway, she went into the inn and asked, "Madam, would you give me something to eat?"

"We haven't much to offer you . . ."

The King of England's daughter sat down at a table.

"Is it your son who serves the meals?"

"Oh, not on your life! With his wooden clogs on, he is so clumsy he might break the dishes."

"I wish him to serve me at my table."

Jean was sitting in a corner in his old clothes looking very unhappy. Anyway, he brought in the first dish and slipped on the waxed floor by mistake. He fell to the floor and broke the dish.

"It doesn't matter," said the Princess. "I would like him to bring me another."

Jean of Bordeaux stood up and went to fetch another dish. He had to be very careful in order to carry it without falling.

Just then the King's daughter said to him, "Don't you recognize me, Jean of Bordeaux?"

"Oh, yes, I recognize you."

So then the King's daughter took him to the barber to have his hair cut, for it was that long. She had him put on his gorgeous uniform of marshal of England. Then they went strolling round the town of Bordeaux in their fine wedding clothes, and after that they went back home and lived very happily.

•29• *Golden Hair, or The Little Frog*

• ONCE UPON A TIME there was a little girl. She was so pretty that she was called Golden Hair. The Holy Virgin was godmother to this pretty girl, and she often came to see her. Now she had given her a parrot, and this parrot talked sometimes and had his little say.

One fine day the Holy Virgin went off to visit her godchild, but by now of course Golden Hair had grown up and was a young girl, and she had a suitor, a good-looking young man who was very much in love with her and came to see her in secret. (He may well have been a king's son.)

The Holy Virgin knocked on the door, so Golden Hair quickly made her lover hide in the space between the bed and the wall. After that she said out loud, "Come in." The Holy Virgin opened the door. Then the parrot started to say out loud, "Madam, the gentleman is hiding behind the bed."

"Oh!" said Golden Hair, "the naughty little devil! It was my broom that I put there this morning."

The Holy Virgin left. She often came to visit her godchild, but this time she did not stay long.

Two or three days later she came back to see her godchild. This time Golden Hair saw her through the window.

"Let's get out of here," she said, and ran off through the garden with her lover.

Then the parrot began to screech, "Madam, the gentleman is taking her very far off into those woods!"

The Holy Virgin took the path through the woods to find her godchild. She went faster than the girl, and she found her all right. Golden Hair was on the bank of a small stream, and she could not cross it.

Her godmother said, "Golden Hair, where are you off to?"

But Golden Hair wanted to leap over the stream to follow her lover, who had already set off on the other side.

The Holy Virgin really scolded her. "Don't say another word. You shall become as ugly as you are pretty now."

And so in this way Golden Hair turned into a frog. She was a little frog in this stream.

This did not stop her lover from coming to see her every day. Then he would talk to his little frog.

This young man was the third son of a king, and his brothers, who went out a lot with girls, said to him to tease him, "Go on, go and see your little frog!"

The Holy Virgin also went to see her on the bank of this stream, but Golden Hair remained a frog all the same.

Now then the King said to his three sons, "I shall give my castle to the one who brings me back the finest horse."

Off went the two eldest to look for horses at the fairs. Now, then, the youngest went to find his little frog, and then he told her what the King had promised his sons.

"Go on, ask your godmother whether I can have the finest horse, for then I shall have the castle."

When the Holy Virgin came to call on Golden Hair, the latter made a point of asking her, and then a fine horse was discovered on the banks of the stream.

Now, then, the brothers reached the castle with the horses which they had bought, but they were nothing compared with the fine horse which the Holy Virgin had found.

The brothers were terribly jealous. They said, "Go on! Keep on going to see your little frog!"

So the King said, "I shall give my castle to the one who brings me the finest dog." (I think it was a dog this time.)

Off went the two eldest looking for dogs. The youngest left again to find his little frog, and the same thing happened. The Holy Virgin found the finest dog in the whole world for him, but the eldest were still teasing the youngest, saying, "Go and see your frog!"

Now then the King said, "I shall give my castle to the one who brings me the prettiest girl."

The elder brothers went off to see the girls they knew, but the youngest went to the bank of this stream and said to his little frog, "Go on and ask your godmother to make you as pretty as you were before!"

This King's son could not forget his Golden Hair, and he had never left her after she had been turned into a frog.

Now, then, the Holy Virgin forgave her godchild, and the little frog turned into Golden Hair again.

Along came her lover. He reached the bank of the stream. "Come on, Golden Hair. My brothers are arriving in the court-yard of the castle with their girls. You should see how ugly they are. I shall certainly be the one to win my father's castle."

Then the King's son took Golden Hair by the hand, and they left the little stream to go to the King's castle.

The King said to the others, "There can be no doubt about this. It really is your young brother who has won my castle. He deserves it more this time than the two other times."

The young man married Golden Hair, and then he was given his father's castle.

· A FAT GENTLEMAN had found a louse. He put it in a pot of fat. He then said, "When this louse is big enough and fat enough I shall skin it, and I shall have gloves made for my daughter from its skin. I shall wed my daughter to the man who guesses what kind of skin these gloves are made from."

There was a Prince round there who was much loved by this fat gentleman's daughter. He was called the Comte de mes Comtes. And so the girl whispered in his ear that the gloves were made of louse skin.

Sunday came. The gentleman was to give his daughter to the one who guessed what skin the gloves were made from. It would have been a poor man who would have said it; it would have been a poor man who would have seen it if he had found out what kind of skin it was!

A lot of people came to see those gloves, and many hoped to win the girl—but nobody guessed correctly!

Now, then, a little coalman appeared. (He was the Comte des mes Comtes, who had changed into a coalman).

He said to the fat gentleman, "It isn't a flea skin?"

"No."

"It isn't louse skin?"

"Yes."

This little coalman had won, and the daughter of the fat gentleman was awarded to him. Then, believe me, he took her by the hand and led her away with him, as was to be expected. It wasn't yet marriage, but the girl was his!

The little coalman made the girl climb onto his donkey, and left with her for the countryside. The poor girl kept saying, "Oh, I can see the farms owned by the Comte de mes Comtes.

"Keep the donkey moving, Mademoiselle," said the coalman. She could well grieve at the Comtes de mes Comtes! Then he took her into his little house or, that is, his barn. There was nothing but straw to sleep on.

The next day he said to her, "Guess what? Tomorrow they are doing the big *bugée* (annual wash) at the castle, the house of the Comte de mes Comtes. You will go there to help. We have no linen, nothing at all for our home. You will try to steal a few napkins to set us up."

When the washing was done, it was time for some fun in the evening. The little coalwoman was asked to dance, but she had put some napkins in her pocket. She had to dance with everyone from the farms, and soon the napkins fell out on the floor, and the people shouted, "The little coalwoman is a thief!"

She ran off home covered in shame and said to her coalman, "You know I had taken some napkins, and they fell out of my pocket, and it has put me to shame. I shall not steal any more."

"Oh, that's nothing," said the little coalman.

A few days later he said to her, "Ah, tomorrow at last they are making black puddings because it is the day they *firent boucherie* (slaughter the pig) at the castle. They will not count the black puddings, so you'll take a dozen and slip them into your pocket."

"Oh!" said the little coalwoman.

"Well, now, do you really think they are going to count the black puddings? That will give us both something to eat," said the coalman.

The next day the little coalwoman again went to the castle to help. She managed to get hold of a few black puddings, and she slipped them into her pocket. But in the evening there was merrymaking. She had to dance again. She skipped and skipped about so much that the black puddings fell out of her pocket.

"Oh, the little coalwoman is a thief! Now she has pinched the black puddings!" you could hear them saying loudly.

Once again she left, quite ashamed of herself, and she did not take the black puddings with her.

"Oh! Oh!" she said to the little coalman, "I was so ashamed of what I had done."

A little later the coalman said to her, "Guess what? The Comte de mes Comtes you are always talking about is getting married tomorrow, but the bride comes from far away. They need someone with a good figure up at the castle to try on the bridal gown. Well, go on up there. They need you."

"What do you mean?" said the little coalwoman.

"Don't you see? Your Comte de mes Comtes is getting married. He is having his bride's dress fitted for her. You try it on and keep it. Then you shall be the bride."

The little coalwoman went to the castle to try on the bride's dress. Her Comte de mes Comtes was there. They dressed her in the bridal gown and led her to the owner of the castle. Well, now she was the bride!

However, the little coalwoman did not want this.

"Oh, no, I do not want him. My daddy gave me to my little coalman. I shall not go as bride to the wedding of my Comte de mes Comtes."

So then the Comte de mes Comtes had to change back into a little coalman in order that she should agree to be his bride.

•31• *The Woman with Her Hands Cut Off*

• ONCE UPON A TIME there were a brother and a sister left living alone together. They loved each other very much. They had promised each other that they would never marry, neither one nor the other, so as not to leave each other.

Now the brother found someone to marry. One fine day he said to his sister, "Guess what, sister? I have found someone to marry."

"If she is right for you, this is marvelous. Get married, brother."

However, this woman was spiteful.

The sister went and lived in a house farther away, and the brother and his wife lived in the father's house.

Now the woman said to her husband, "You've no idea what's happened. Tonight I dreamed of your wicked sister. She had strangled your mares."

Her husband got up and went to look in the stables. The mares were dead. "Oh," he said, "it's really true."

The next night his wife said to him, "You've no idea what's happened. I dreamed again that your wicked sister had knocked over your wine barrels and that all the wine was spilled on the floor."

The husband got up and went to look in the cellar. All the barrels were knocked over, and the wine was spilled on the ground and in the cellar. But the brother said nothing of this to his sister. Every day he went to see her at her house.

"Good day, sister!"

"Good day, brother!"

Five or six days went by.

The woman said to her husband, "I dreamed tonight that your wicked sister had come here. She had killed our child. The knife was under the door."

The husband got up.

"You have only to look at the knife," said his wife.

The husband went up to the door and found the knife. It was covered with blood.

He went and found his sister. Anger forced him to speak. "Ah, you spiteful wretch! So you want me dead. You have killed my mares. You have knocked over my barrels, and I have said nothing. Now you have killed our child with this knife. Look! I have brought you the knife."

The sister said nothing. Then her brother grabbed his sister and cut her hand off at the wrist to punish her. So she said to him, "Don't say anything, wicked brother. When you jump over the hedge with the help of a ladder, you will get a splinter in your knee. Only I will be able to take it out."

Her brother, who was on his way home, lost his temper and cut off her other hand at the wrist. So the poor girl was walking around like that. She could no longer eat, as she had no hands. It so happened that as she walked she found herself in the King's garden. In it there were beautiful apples and pears. She hid herself, and then during the night she tried to catch them in her mouth as best she could, to eat them. The next day she hid in the garden during the daytime. This happened several times running.

The King said to his mother, "I am going to hide in order to see the creature who is eating my apples and pears."

So the King hid in the garden. At midnight he saw the young

girl who had come to catch the pears and apples in her mouth. She was all in rags. Her clothes barely covered her. The King went off without making any noise.

The next day he said to his mother, "Do you know? I have found the creature who is eating my apples and pears. You will give me dresses to clothe her in. She has no hands."

The King brought the clothes the Queen had given him to her, and then he took the young girl home with him.

A few days later he said to his mother, "I want to marry her." The mother did not wish this at all, but her son wanted the girl so much! In the end they got married.

Not long after, a great war took place. The King went off with his armies to make war and do battle. The King's wicked mother still refused to see her daughter-in-law, so she had her led into the woods by servants, and when the poor girl found herself there alone, it was only to give birth to two little boys.

At that moment the Holy Virgin and St. John and St. Paul appeared at her side to help with the birth.

Later the Holy Virgin was godmother to the two little twins, and each one had a godfather. Then St. John and St. Paul christened the two children.

The Holy Virgin said to St. John, "What are you offering your godchild?"

St. John said, "I, well, I offer him a fine castle in these woods."

The Holy Virgin said to St. Paul, "What are you offering your godchild?"

"Ah, well, that the castle should lack nothing, neither furniture, personal belongings, nor even servants," said St. Paul.

So the Holy Virgin said, "Well, then, I ask that the mother be given back her two hands."

The mother's hands were restored. In front of her was a fine castle, and nothing was lacking in this castle, and so she stayed there with her two children.

Seven years later the war was over. The King went home. He asked to see his wife. His mother answered, "She went off into the woods and has never been seen since."

The King left to find his wife in the woods. He reached the woods near the castle, of which he knew nothing. He saw two little boys playing there. (They had grown tall, those twins.) He asked them, "Where is your father?"

"We have never known a father."

"And Mummy?"

The twins' mother appeared. Naturally the King found himself staring at her. He asked her whether she had seen a woman (his poor wife, of course) who had no hands. She answered, "No."

"You look like her," said the King.

"You say she has no hands," she said. "I have some."

The young woman talked to the King for a while, and then she made herself known to him. The King was very happy.

Then she remembered that she had promised her brother she would go and look after him once she had her hands back. She had a horse saddled, and then the two of them, she and her husband, were led to her brother in their finest coach.

There must have been at least ten children in the courtyard, each dirtier and more ragged than the other. Even the threshhold of his house was filthy. A woman who was all dirty and in rags came and asked them what this coach was, stopping at his house.

The sister got out of it and said to her, "How do you do, Madam?"

"Ah, how do you do, Madam?"

"Is your husband here?"

"Oh yes, Madam. It is seven years today that he is lying in bed. He is still in bed, and no one can cure him."

"May I see him?"

"Yes, Madam." Then she went into the wretched room where her brother was in bed.

"Can you get up, Sir?"

"I cannot get up."

"Just a little, that's all. Let me see your leg."

There was a splinter imbedded in his knee, which was all swollen up.

The sister put her hand on the knee. The splinter flew up into the air, and so the brother recognized his sister. He started to cry and beg her forgiveness, and then he explained to her,

"My wife is to blame for my cutting off your hands. It is she who made me think you were the cause of all my misadventures."

His sister told him her story, and in the end they burned the spiteful sister-in-law.

· 32 · Souillon

• THERE WAS a mother with two little girls. This mother loved one of them and made the other one do all the unpleasant jobs. They called this one Souillon, because she always wore a big apron to do household chores and farm work.

The other one, the mother's favorite had nothing to do. She acted as lady's companion to her mother. Her mother always approved of what she said or what she did, and yet I assure you the girl did not work at all.

Souillon had to feed the poultry and sweep out the hen coops. She had to take away their droppings and give them fresh litter. Not satisfied with making her into a farmyard servant, her mother made her do the washing every week and wash the dishes every day.

Then came a time when both girls were grown up. Souillon was proposed to by a potter. She left with her husband, who plied his trade in another village.

The other one married, too, but her husband did nothing but drink and lead the gay life, squandering all his money.

A few years later the mother went to visit her two daughters, who lived with their husbands in different villages.

Souillon's husband was a potter, as I have told you. Every day he worked shaping his pots of clay, and every morning he prayed to God and asked him, "Lord, give me fine weather so that my pots can dry out and I can sell them and be able to feed my children."

When their mother reached Souillon's home, she saw a bunch of children clustered round their mother like a brood of newborn chicks. Then she noticed that her daughter had a lot of poultry in her backyard and that in the pigsty she had some very fine young pigs.

Souillon asked her into her house, which was spick and span. There was nothing missing, because she knew how to do every kind of work, as she had had to do all the most menial tasks ever since she was a child.

After having spent a few days with Souillon, who had welcomed her and given her everything she could possibly want, the mother said, "Now I shall go and see your sister, and I hope that she is as happy as you are."

"My sister, Mummy? Do you mean to say that you don't know how unhappy she is?"

"I thought as much," said the mother.

Souillon said to her, "My sister came here the other day to beg from me, saying she hadn't any money left to buy food."

The mother went to her favorite daughter's house. Before going in, she noticed that the house looked neglected. There was no poultry in the courtyard. The pigsty had fallen to pieces (perhaps that was why the hogs were dead!).

That woman was not surrounded by children but was alone and sad because her husband had abandoned her, preferring to lead a merry life with other girls.

When her mother went in to see her, the poor girl was crying. There wasn't even a chair in her house to give to her mother to sit in, not even a piece of dry bread to make her some soup.

The mother understood then that she had not helped to make her daughter happy by letting her do nothing. She went back to Souillon, who lived in comfort, and said to her: "Now I understand how I behaved toward my two daughters. Stay happy with your husband and promise me never to have favorites among your children as I had with you and your sister."

·33· *The Devil and the Good Lord*

• THIS HAPPENED when the earth had not yet been cultivated. The Devil and God were both there, so they set out to sow some wheat.

The Devil was a man who seemed as strong as a donkey, and

God looked like a weak man, but you'll see that he was one up on the Devil every time!

And so the wheat was sown.

"Which will you take? That which grows in the earth or that which grows in the air?"

"I want what grows in the earth."

So at harvest time the Devil had the roots, and God had the grain.

The following year they planted potatoes. "Which would you like to have?" God asked the Devil.

"I want what grows in the air."

This time when they were harvesting, the Devil had only the old leaves from the potato plants, because God had taken the roots.

The third time they sowed maize. God said to the Devil, "Come on now, I do not want to trick you. Which will you take this time?"

"I'll have both ends of this maize."

When the maize was ripe, God picked off the corncobs (you know how the cobs grow in the middle of the maize plant), and the Devil had only the stalks and the tassels of the maize.

So the Devil went away. Winter had come, and the Devil built himself a castle of stone, but God built himself a castle of ice.

The Devil thought this ice castle was so beautiful that he wanted to exchange his stone castle for the castle of ice.

So God made the ice castle melt in the sun. Then the Devil had no castle at all and he had to go elsewhere.

·34· *The Rat and the She Rat*

• ONCE THERE WAS a rat who used to go and work in the woods cutting furze. (In the old days furze was used as litter and cut with a scythe.) Now at soup time—that is to say, at noon—this rat did not see his she rat bringing him his food. In the end he started home. And when he got there, what did he find? No she rat. He looked in the soup tureen. The she rat had fallen into it and had drowned.

So then he began to weep. He bumped himself on the bench. The bench said to him, "You poor rat, why are you weeping so much this morning?"

"Oh, my she rat has drowned, and I am all alone!" So then the bench started to leap around. It bumped against the table.

The table said to it, "Oh, you poor bench, why are you leaping around so much this morning?"

> Oh, if you knew, you'd be dancing!
> The she rat has drowned!
> The rat is weeping!
> And I leap because of it!

And the table began to dance. It bumped into the door.

The door said to it, "Oh, you poor table, why do you dance so much?"

> Ah, if only you knew, you'd fall to pieces!
> The she rat has drowned!
> The rat is weeping!
> The bench is leaping!
> And I am dancing because of it!

And so the door began falling to pieces, and as it did so, it bumped into a cart which was standing in the courtyard, and the cart said, "Oh, you poor door, what are you doing, falling to pieces this morning?"

> Ah, if only you knew, you'd roll!
> The she rat has drowned!
> The rat is weeping!
> The bench is leaping!
> The table is dancing!
> And I am falling to pieces because of it!

And so this cart, rolling away, bumped into an oak. And the oak said, "Oh you poor cart, what are you doing, rolling away this morning?"

Ah, if only you knew, you'd uproot yourself!
The she rat has drowned!
The rat is weeping!
The bench is leaping!
The table is dancing!
The door is falling to pieces!
And I am rolling away because of it!

Now on this oak there was a magpie who had made her nest,
and this magpie said very angrily to the oak, "Oh, you wretched
oak, why did you uproot yourself like that?"

Ah, poor magpie, if you knew, you'd molt!
The she rat has drowned!
The rat is weeping!
The bench is leaping!
The table is dancing!
The door is falling to pieces!
The cart is rolling away!
And I am uprooting myself because of it!

The magpie molted near a fountain, and the fountain said,
"Oh, poor magpie, what are you doing molting this morning?"

Ah, if you only knew, you'd flow because of it!
The she rat has drowned!
The rat is weeping!
The bench is leaping!
The table is dancing!
The door is falling to pieces!
The cart is rolling away!
The oak is uprooting itself!
And I am molting because of it!

Yes, but just as the fountain began flowing, a woman who was
about to make her bread came along with two pitchers to fetch
water, but the water was running on the ground.

"Oh, poor fountain, why are you flowing like that when I
am so much in need of water?"

Oh, if you knew, you'd break both your pitchers!
The she rat has drowned!
The rat is weeping!
The bench is leaping!
The table is dancing!
The door is falling to pieces!
The cart is rolling away!
The oak is uprooting itself!
The magpie is molting!
And I am flowing on the ground because of it!

And so the woman broke her two pitchers. As she did not seem to be coming back, her husband went to see what had happened to her, and of course he said to her, "Oh, my poor wife, what have you done?"

Ah, if only you knew, you'd bash the oven to pieces!
The she rat has drowned!
The rat is weeping!
The bench is leaping!
The table is dancing!
The door is falling to pieces!
The cart is rolling away!
The oak is uprooting itself!
The magpie is molting!
The fountain is overflowing!
And I have broken my two pitchers because of it!

Then the man bashed his oven in. A man went by taking a horse to drink at the pond, and he said, "Oh, what are you doing to your oven, you poor man?"

Ah, if you knew, you'd slash your horse's belly!
The she rat has drowned!
The rat is weeping!
The bench is leaping!
The table is dancing!
The door is falling to pieces!
The cart is rolling away!
The oak is uprooting itself!

The magpie is molting!
The fountain is overflowing!
My wife broke her two pitchers!
And I bashed in my oven because of it!"

Thereupon the pond spread over everything, over the dead as well as everything else.

The child asked his grandmother, "And then?"

"And then? The dogs are off! Run after them!" answered the grandmother.

·35· *The Little Hen*

• IT WAS harvest time, and there were a little rooster and a little hen who had gone to glean in a freshly harvested field of wheat. Now, then, the little hen was always forging ahead of the little cockerel. In the end the little cockerel said: "Don't eat the lot, little hen. If you go in front of me again, I'll pierce your ruffle." However, the little hen went on gleaning in front of him, so the little cockerel leaped on her little ruffle with one blow from his beak. How could she get her ruffle to heal?

The little hen, who was very put out, went and found the tailor and asked him, "Poor tailor, would you sew my little ruffle, which the cockerel has pierced?"

Then the tailor said, "I'll sew on your ruffle, all right, but you must bring me a nice piece of bacon."

How was she to find bacon?

The little hen went and found the sow. "My poor sow, will you give me a piece of bacon, so that I can take it to the tailor, and he can then sew my little ruffle, which the little cock has pierced."

The sow said, "I cannot give you any bacon until I have eaten acorns."

"How shall I find acorns?" asked the little hen.

"It has to be windy," replied the sow.

The little hen went under the oaks and said, "Let there be wind. Let there be wind to make the acorns fall, so that I can take them to the sow, so that she can give me bacon, so that I can give some to the tailor and he can mend my little ruffle."

Now the wind began to blow through the oaks. Loads of acorns fell down.

The little hen picked up the acorns. She carried them to our sow, who fattened into bacon. She took the bacon to the tailor, and the tailor then sewed the little hen's ruffle, which the little cockerel had pierced.

Part VII
Angoumois and Ruffecois

The Goat, the Kids, and the Wolf

• THERE WAS a nanny goat who had broken her leg. She had to go and have it set at Saint Jard. She had to leave her little kids behind, and she said to them, "I am going off to have my leg set at Saint Jard. Don't open the door to anyone. When I come back I shall say to you:

> Little kid and she kid,
> Open the door for your mother,
> Who comes from St. Jard,
> Where she's had her leg and ankle set.
> Up you get, as if straw tickled your bottoms!

And then I shall show you my white leg. You'll know it's your mother, and you will open the door."

The kids knew quite well that they mustn't open that door. However, the wolf heard what the nanny goat said to her kids. He came to their door and said to them:

> Little kid and little she kid,
> Open the door for your mother,
> Who comes from St. Jard,
> Where she's had her leg and ankle set.
> Up you get, as if straw tickled your bottoms!

But the nanny goat had said to her kids that a white leg must be shown.

The little kids shouted through the door, "Show your white leg!"

The wolf put his leg through a hole, perhaps it was through the cat hole. (You know, of course, that there were cat holes in the doors in the old days.)

The kids saw that he had a black leg. "Oh," they said, "you have a black leg! You are not our mother."

The wolf went and dipped his leg in flour, which was nice and white, and he came back and knocked on the little kids' door, saying once again:

> Little kid and little she kid,
> Open the door for your mother,
> Who comes from St. Jard,
> Where she's had her leg and ankle set.
> Up you get, as if straw tickled your bottoms!

The kids said, "Show your leg!"

So then he had a beautiful white leg. The little kids opened the door, and the wolf was in their home.

"If you have something to eat, give it to me at once, or else I shall eat you."

The kids were so frightened that they did not know what to do. The wolf asked them if they had any *froumajhé* (cheese-cake) in the dough bin to give him to eat.

Now it so happened that the nanny goat had just made cheesecake, which she had put into the dough bin next to the cheeses so that the cakes would keep cool. Well, now, you won't believe this. The wolf leaped into the dough bin, the greedy thing, intent on eating the cheesecake. So then the little kids had closed the lid of the dough bin, and the wolf was so busy eating that he took no notice.

When the nanny goat arrived, she knocked at the door, saying:

> Little kid and little she kid,
> Open the door for your mother,
> Who comes from St. Jard,
> Where she's had her leg and ankle set.
> Up you get, as if straw tickled your bottoms!

The kids ran to open the door for her.

"Do you know, the wolf came. He showed us a white leg, so we opened the door, and then he wanted to eat cheesecake. He went into the dough bin, so we closed the lid on top of him."

The nanny goat said they had done the right thing. "Wait a minute! We must put some water on to boil in the stew-pot."

The wolf began yelling, "Open the lid of the dough bin!"

"Make some holes in the dough bin," said the nanny goat to her kids.

The little kids pierced the lid, and the wolf was able to breathe more easily. As soon as the holes were finished, the water began to boil over the fire. Then the nanny goat took the handle of the kettle and poured water through the holes in the lid.

The wolf tried to get out of the way, first one side then the other, but he could not escape. Try as he might, in the end he was scalded by the nanny goat.

When they had poured out the whole kettle, the nanny goat lifted the lid of the dough bin and the wolf hurled himself out.

Then the nanny goat stood on the threshhold and shouted:

> The running wolf is on his way!
> Watch out, shepherdesses in the hay!
> The scalded wolf is on the run!
> Watch out, shepherdesses every one!

·37· *The Sleeping Beauty*

• WHILE HUNTING with his guests one day, the King's son, who was after a stag, went astray in the forest. Dusk was approaching, and he was wondering what the night would be like out in the very heart of the woods, when he saw a light shining in the distance.

He followed it and saw a great castle surrounded by high walls. He pulled the doorbell, and the gate opened at once, but he nearly swooned with fright when he saw who was watchman at the gate. It was a monster with seven heads and as many paws, with claws like a lion. She did not harm him. On the contrary, she said to him, "Go to the castle. They are waiting for you. The fairy who made you lose your way did it on purpose so that you would come here."

He went on into the castle and entered a fine banqueting hall, where his place was laid. Footmen holding torches stood behind the chairs. At the end of the table was a girl as fair as the dawn, who said to him, "Come on, it's about time. A hundred years have gone by since my dear godmother promised me that a king's son would come and take me out of this castle and marry me. Is it you?"

The King's son looked at this girl who was so pretty and said to himself, "If she has been here one hundred years, how old must she be?"

He went up to bed, and every day he would eat at her table, as she was mistress of the castle. Afterward he would walk in the great park.

One day as he was thinking how anxious his father, the King, must be not to have seen him again, he saw, coming toward him, a woman with a crown on her head. She said to him, "I am the godmother of the pretty girl you see every day and I know that you love her, but to take her away, you will have to kill the monster who guards the gate. There is no other way out. You must go through the gate; all those who have tried to go through it have been eaten by the monster. I know that you are called the brave Prince, and tonight I shall bring you a sword. You must cut all seven heads off at once, for as soon as a head is cut off, another will grow in its place."

The King's son went up to the monster, whose seven heads rose ready to devour him as she saw him approaching. However, the fairy who had given him the sword was Queen of the fairies, and she made the sword lengthen by at least two meters when the King's son stretched out his arm to protect himself. This allowed him to reap all seven heads with one blow.

At the same time a rook, a very black one, came down from a great oak and squawked, "Long live King Arthur's son, who has set our Princess Yolande free and who shall have her as his bride!"

It took over a month to get the dresses ready. Never had there been such a gorgeous wedding. All the fairies were there, and after the banquet they brought in the monster's seven heads set on a great dish. Ah, yes, but now they were all of gold, and they said that seven children would be born and each of these children would have a ball of gold as a christening present.

That is what happened, and when the seven balls had been given, no other boys or girls were born, but the King and the Queen died in time surrounded by many grandchildren.

The castle of the seven-headed monster still stands in the middle of a great forest, but one can see only part of the high wall, all ruined and crumbling.

.38. *The Three Innocents*

• THERE WERE a girl and a youth who were about to get married. The girl's mother and father had invited the youth to a meal. They were about to eat when they saw that there was no wine on the table. They sent their daughter to draw off enough to drink from the barrel. A few minutes went by and she did not come back. All three wondered what she was doing.

The wife sent her husband off. "Go and see what our daughter is doing since she left to draw the wine from the barrel."

When the father reached his daughter, he found her standing in front of the barrel dreaming.

"What are you doing, Daughter?"

"Oh, Father! I have been thinking,

If I marry, how do I do it?
If I have children, how shall I have them?
And what names shall I give them?
All the names have been used!"

And the wine went on running out of the barrel.

Then the father said, "Well, you are right, Daughter. We shall both think this out together."

Then the mother, who had been alone with the youth all this time, said, "I do not know what those two innocents are up to. They aren't coming back. I, too, am going to go and fetch them."

Off she went, and when she reached them she saw them both standing in front of the barrel.

She said to them, "What were you up to, you two fools, while we have been waiting for you all this time?"

The fellow said to his wife, "Our daughter is far more clever than we are! She is thinking that if she gets married, how does she do it? If she has children, how does she have them? And what names shall she give them? All the names have been used."

"You are quite right, my poor dear. She is far more clever than we are."

And still the barrel flowed.

So then the youth, who was at the table all alone, stood up, saying to himself, "What are those three innocents up to? Aren't they going to come back? I had better go off and see."

Then when he reached them he found them all three standing like that, thinking.

He said, "What are you up to, you three silly fools?"

Then they told him their stories. They began their chorus, "Our daughter is far more clever than we are. She said to us, 'If I marry, how do I do it? If I have children, how shall I have them? And what names shall I give them? All the names have been used!'"

And the barrel still flowed. The youth bunged the barrel, and then he said to them: "I'm off. If I find three people as crazy as you are, I'll come back to fetch your daughter and marry her."

· *39* · *Coué or Couette*

· ONCE UPON A TIME there was a ram called Coué (or, if you prefer, a goat called Couette). When his mistress wanted to lead him to the fields, Coué did only as he wished. Coué ate as much grass as he could, but in the evening he did not want to go back into the pen.

"No, no. My mistress has done nothing but make me run all day long. I shall not go into the pen."

So the mistress called the dog.

"Coué does not want to go into the pen. Dog, go and yap at Coué!"

The dog said he did not want to yap at Coué.

The mistress said to him, "Well, Coué does not want to go into the pen. The dog does not want to yap at Coué. Stick, go and beat the dog!"

She stick said that it did not wish to beat the dog.

"All right," she said to him. "Coué does not want to go into the pen. The dog does not want to yap at Coué. The stick does not want to beat the dog. Fire, come and burn the stick!"

The fire said it did not wish to burn the stick.

"Well," she said to him, "Coué does not want to go into the pen. The dog does not want to yap at Coué. The stick does not want to beat the dog. The fire does not want to burn the stick. I shall tell the water to come and put out the fire!"

The water said it did not want to put out the fire.

"All right!" she said to it, "Coué does not want to go into the pen. The dog does not want to yap at Coué. The stick does not want to beat the dog. The fire does not want to burn the stick. The water does not want to put out the fire. I shall tell the ox to come and drink the water. Ox, go and drink the water!"

The ox said, "I'll go and drink the water."

The water said, "Well, I'll go and put out the fire."

The fire said, "All right, I'll go and burn the stick."

The stick said, "All right, I'll beat the dog!"

The dog said, "All right, I'll yap at Coué."

And Coué said, "Oh, well, I'll go into the pen!"

> The ox goes and drinks the water.
> Water goes and puts out the fire.
> Fire goes and burns the stick.
> Stick goes and beats the dog.
> Dog goes and yaps at Coué.
> Coué goes willingly into his pen.

Part VIII
Limousin

The Gold Ball

· I AM GOING to tell you the story of the gold ball.

Once there was a girl who lived all alone in a castle. A young man came to see her every day with the idea of marrying her later on. Every evening the old women came to spend the evening with the girl. They said to her, "Oh, Mademoiselle, when you are married we'll come and see you in bed."

On the wedding night these old women wanted to go and see the young woman in bed. Yes, but this did not please the bridegroom. So he left the castle, going by the crossroads. Away went the husband—far away! And she, the poor girl, was very upset and sad about it all. She also left to find her husband, but she did not know where to find him.

Now on the way she met the Holy Virgin, who was her godmother.

She said to her, "Where are you going, Goddaughter?"

"Ah, Godmother, I am most upset. My husband left on our wedding night. He went by the crossroads, and I do not know where he has gone."

"Right. You'll see. I am going to give you something that will enable you to find your husband. I am going to give you a golden ball, and you will throw it. This ball will lead you straight to the place where your husband is. And then I shall also give you a hen with her chicks, all of gold, and finally I shall give you a skein winder made of gold. That will be very useful to you."

The young woman was on her way. She had thrown the ball, and it took her straight to a castle where her husband had settled. Her husband had remarried a certain lady.

The young woman with the gold ball thought of using the things given to her by the Holy Virgin. She brought out her golden skein winder.

The second wife was thrilled with it.

"Madam, if you allow me to spend a night with your husband, I shall give you the golden winder."

And in the end the second wife said, "Yes." However, as she

was cunning, she gave her husband a draught of opium. This drink put him to sleep. The next day he was not able to leave with his first wife. The following morning, as soon as he was awake, they had a talk, he and his first wife.

She said to him, "Tomorrow you will not drink any opium, and we shall both go away together."

So what did the young woman with the gold ball do? She went and stood once again under the castle windows, and this time she brought out her gold hen with its little gold chicks.

The second wife was even more thrilled.

"Oh, Madam, if you allow me to spend the night with your husband again, I will give you my gold hen and all the little chicks."

So once again the lady ended up by saying, "Yes." This time the husband did not drink any opium! Neither of them slept at all, but they left in secret. They took with them the gold skein winder and the gold hen and her gold chicks.

They were careful not to forget the gold ball. They gave it one blow so that it would direct them, and the ball led them to their castle.

And the next morning when the lady found nobody—neither husband nor gold hen nor gold chicks nor gold skein winder —she was most upset, but it was too late.

And now my story is over.

> I passed through a rat hole,
> And my story is whole.

•41• *The Brother Who Was a Lamb*

• ONCE THERE WERE three children, two brothers and a sister. They had lost their parents. They left home and walked and walked in the woods without ever coming to a fountain. In the end they were thirsty.

Then they met a man, and they asked him, "Where can we find water?"

He said to them, "There are three fountains over there. Do not drink from the first or the second but drink from the third."

When they reached the first fountain, the little girl tried to stop one of her brothers from drinking, but she was unable to and so he disappeared.

She brought her other brother there, but the boy drank from the second fountain and he was turned into a lamb.

As for the little girl, she drank only from the third fountain and she was turned into a beautiful princess who was well dressed.

Every day this little girl went to the fields to watch over her brother, the lamb. One day the King's son went by and found her so attractive he saw a lot of her. And then he asked her to marry him.

"No. I do not want to leave my little brother, the lamb."

"If you come with me, he will not be unhappy at home. He will have the courtyard and the room in which to play and run about in."

In the end she accepted, and both of them came to live in the King's castle. War broke out and her husband had to go off and fight. Now the mother-in-law was not very fond of her daughter-in-law, nor was she fond of the little lamb, who ran about everywhere. She wanted to kill them.

So she had the idea of drowning them in the well. The young woman was pregnant. She caught hold of her and threw her down the well. That is where her baby was born, on a fine white bed which happened to be there.

As for the lamb, even though they made every effort to catch him, he went on running round the well.

As for the King, the mother-in-law wrote to him that his wife was a flirt and that she was now pregnant.

Now the husband came back from the war. The mother-in-law was in bed. She was making herself ill saying, "The only thing that will make me well is to kill the lamb."

The husband said to his servants, "Catch the lamb."

But the little lamb began saying as he jumped about:

> Therèse, Therèse, my friend,
> Here are your husband's servants
> Coming to kill me.

The young woman's voice answered him from the depths of the well:

> Jump and skip, my friend,
> Make them run hard!

The servants had to withdraw without having caught the lamb.

Then the husband sent his maids, but the same thing happened. The little lamb ran to the well and said to his sister:

> Therèse, Therèse, my friend,
> Here are your husband's maids
> Coming to kill me.

And the sister's voice answered again from the depths of the well:

> Jump and skip, my friend,
> Make them run hard!

And the lamb escaped again. Neither valet nor maid was able to catch him.

The husband said, "I'll go myself."

The lamb again ran to the top of the well and screamed:

> Therèse, Therèse, my friend,
> Now here's your husband
> Coming to kill me.

But this time the young woman did not answer, and the lamb stayed on the edge of the well.

The husband came nearer, and then the child, who had been born at the bottom of the well, cried out, "Papa!"

The King saw his wife at the bottom of the well sitting on a beautiful white bed. He pulled her out of the well and the child also.

To end off, instead of burning the lamb, they burned the mother-in-law.

• ONCE THERE WERE two little boys. Their mother was just about to have another baby. They said, "We do not want a sister. If our mother has a girl, we shall take off for the woods."

The mother died after her little girl was born, and the father married again.

The stepmother did not like the poor little thing. The little girl got to hear from neighbors that she had two brothers much older than she was. The Holy Virgin was her godmother. One day she thought that she would try and find her two brothers; then she started to cry, so the Holy Virgin appeared.

"Why are you crying, Godchild?"

"I want to go away and find my two brothers."

The Holy Virgin gave her a little ball. Perhaps it was even a nut. Then she said to her, "I am going to give you this little ball. You will throw it down in front of you on your way. It will lead you to the place where your brothers are."

The little girl walked along for a while in the woods. Then she ate her bread and walked a little farther. It was beginning to get dark. Now, the Holy Virgin had told her, "You will give your ball a tap, and it will bring you a *ponne* (laundry vat). You will sleep under that laundry vat for the night."

The next day, as soon as she came out from under the laundry vat, the ball was once again there to show her the way.

She tapped the ball again. This time she found herself in front of a *gabiote* (little shack). Her two brothers had built this shack, and they would go out all day to cut wood in the forest.

The Holy Virgin had said to the girl, "You will do the housework for your two brothers. You will sweep the floor and make some soup for them."

So when the girl had finished the housework, the soup was ready to eat. From her ball came a laundry vat so that she could lie under it and sleep there.

That evening her two brothers had come back from the forest. They found the soup ready and everything nice and tidy in their house. They were most astonished.

The first one said, "I am going to have a good look and see if anyone has been here." (He could not see the laundry vat.)

But the boy who was keeping watch fell asleep.

The second one said, "Now I'll watch, and I will not go to sleep."

Then the girl came out from under the laundry vat and she began sweeping the floor. The boy woke up his brother. Then he said to the girl, "What are you doing in our shack?"

She said, "I am your little sister. I have come here to live with you."

The two boys were very glad to see their little sister. They said to her, "You shall stay at home to do the work, but be careful. We have a neighbor and he's the *malbrou* (ogre). Be sure not to go into his home. Be very careful of the fire. If the dog peed on the fire, you wouldn't have one any more and you wouldn't know where to go for one other than going to the ogre's house."

One day the little girl did not want to share her bread with the dog, so the dog peed on the fire. Then the fire died out. How was she to cook the soup? The girl went to the ogre's house. The ogre's wife was there.

"What have you come to fetch, you poor little wretch?"

"I come to ask you for some fire."

"I would willingly give you some, but my husband will come along and he will eat you up."

In the end she gave her some fire. Then the ogre arrived. He could smell fresh flesh. Then he was in front of the shack. He said at the door, "I let you have some fire. You shall give me your little finger to suck every day at such and such a time."

So the girl had to put her little finger under the door, and then the ogre would suck it.

In the end she was getting thin and becoming quite pale because the ogre was sucking her blood.

So then the two brothers asked her why she was getting so thin. She told them that the dog had put out the fire and that then she had gone to fetch some from the ogre. After that the ogre came to the door every day to suck her little finger.

The boys said, "The next time he comes back, tell him to

shove his head forward through the cat hole because you cannot stretch your hand to reach him."

So when the ogre came once more to suck their sister's little finger, she said just that, and then the two boys cut the ogre's head off.

After that, of course, the ogre's wife could no longer find her husband. The boys sold the ogre's head to her. So his wife made combs out of the bones from his head and then she sold them, but even then the combs were traps. Those who combed their hair with them fell sick and could never get well again.

•43• *Cinderella*

• ONCE THERE WAS a widower who remarried, and the stepmother did not like the husband's daughter by his first wife. This stepmother had a daughter of her own.

As for the husband's daughter, the stepmother called her *la Cendroulié* (Cinderella) because she was always to be found in the ashes in the hearth. Now the stepmother's daughter was called "Ram's balls" by everyone because she was so ugly.

The old woman and her daughter did not like the husband's daughter. The stepmother was always cross with Cinderella, and the other girl was no better to her.

One day the stepmother had said to her, "Go on off and look after the milking cow." Cinderella led the milking cow into the meadows to graze, but she had been given only dry bread to eat, so the Holy Virgin, who was this girl's godmother, gave her a hazel wand and said to her, "Give your milking cow a tap with this hazel wand, and she will give you something to eat." Then Cinderella took the hazel wand, tapped the cow's behind with it, and out fell bread and cheese.

From then on, Cinderella was well fed. The stepmother was very surprised. "How is it that Cinderella always has such a fresh complexion? All I give her is dry bread."

So then the stepmother's daughter watched to see what Cinderella did with the milking cow and then one day "Ram's balls" also took a wand to hit the milking cow, but the cow only presented her with a cowpat!

The Holy Virgin came along. So then what did the old hag and the girl do? They had the milking cow killed.

Poor Cinderella had no more bread and cheese. This time the Holy Virgin had an apple tree brought to Cinderella so that she could eat apples off it. The stepmother said once more, "How is it that Cinderella still has such a fresh complexion? She certainly hasn't any milking cow to give her food now."

So the stepmother's girl watched Cinderella once again. She saw her picking up apples. The apple tree would lower its branches to give her fruit, and then it would spring back up again. In this way the stepmother's girl could not get hold of these apples, and Cinderella went on having a lovely complexion. But the stepmother said, "You will not leave the house."

She gave her a mixture of millet seed and ash to sort out, but poor Cinderella had nothing to pull them out with. The old hag and her daughter went out for a walk, leaving her, by way of amusement, the ashes to sort out.

So the Holy Virgin brought her a hazel wand to sort out the ashes, and, quick as a flash, the millet seeds were separated from the ash. That evening the stepmother was more than surprised to see the ashes sorted out and the millet seed set aside.

Another time there was a ball in that part of the country. The old hag and her daughter went to it, but Cinderella looked after the house. She wished, however, that she could have gone, too.

So the Holy Virgin gave her a carriage drawn by two shining horses and a coachman to take her to the ball, and Cinderella had a beautiful dress and beautiful shoes. She climbed into the carriage and soon she went past the old hag and her daughter, who were on foot.

There was a Prince at this ball. When he saw this lovely girl, he wished to dance with her.

When the old hag and her daughter were still on their way home on foot, Cinderella had already reached the house in the carriage.

They told her, "If you only knew what a beautiful girl there was at the ball!"

"No fairer than Cinderella," said the girl.

Another time there was again a ball. Once more the Prince danced with the beautiful girl, but this time he wanted to know her name. So then Cinderella tried to run away, and one of her shoes slipped off her foot. The Prince was quick to pick it up while the beautiful girl was on her way home.

The next day the Prince said, "The girl who can slip this shoe on shall be my bride."

When the old hag and her daughter saw the Prince coming to their home, the woman said to her daughter, "Trim your foot, for heaven's sake! Then you will be able to slip the shoe on."

However, although "Ram's balls" tried hard to trim her foot, she could not slip on the shoe. Then the Prince noticed Cinderella, and he wanted to make her try it on. Well, the shoe was hers. She slipped it on at once.

When the stepmother saw that the Prince wished to marry Cinderella, she had her put in an attic, where she was locked up and no one could see her anymore.

Now there was a little dog who started yapping because Cinderella was shut up in this attic.

The Prince followed the dog and let Cinderella out of the attic.

Then the hag and her daughter were turned into stones. There was one on each side of the stairway in that house.

And so Cinderella married the Prince.

·44· *The She Donkey's Skin*

• THERE WAS a gentleman who had a very beautiful wife. His wife said to him before she died, "Do not marry again unless you find a woman as beautiful as I am."

When the gentleman became a widower, he looked everywhere for a wife as beautiful as his first but he could not find one.

This gentleman had a daughter. As she grew older, she looked much like her mother, so the father wanted to marry her. The girl would not listen to her father. She went to find her godmother, who was a *fado* (fairy) and who said to her, "Before you decide, ask your father for the most beautiful dresses in the whole world and wait and see what he does."

The father had people hunting everywhere for the dresses his daughter longed for, but the more she had, the more she asked for. In the end he said to her, "You'll bring me to ruin!" Still he pressed his suit.

The girl went to her godmother again, who said to her, "You are to run away from your father. I shall give you a chest, which goes underground, and a wand to make it do your bidding. You shall hide under a she donkey's skin (*peu d'anisso*), bringing the ears down over your face, and you'll leave your father's home."

The girl took the wand and the chest. When she said to the chest, "Open up!" the chest opened and she put her lovely dresses into it.

She dressed herself in rags and, hiding under the she donkey's skin, she fled during the night.

The next day she showed up at the King's farm. She was hired as turkey girl.

She looked so poor and dirty under her she donkey's skin that at first she was left to sleep outside with her turkeys. Poor Peu d'anisso! The turkeys came and rubbed against her, and this made her even more dirty. The Prince used to watch her going by and teased her because she looked so poor and so dirty.

When she was asked her name, she just replied, "I'm called 'Peu d'Anisso.'"

"'Peu d'Anisso'? What a gorgeous name for a turkey girl!"

The owner of the farm asked her, "What can you do while you look after your turkeys? Do you know how to sew or how to knit?"

Peu d'Anisso answered, "I know how to make lace." Now this was true. Peu d'Anisso made the most beautiful lace in the world. Seeing that she worked so well, the owner of the farm gave her a room to sleep in. Then Peu d'Anisso took her chest and touched it with her wand, saying, "Open up!"

The chest opened. All the lovely dresses were there, and every evening Peu d'Anisso would wash and comb her hair and try on one of her dresses.

One winter's day Peu d'Anisso was keeping warm in a corner of the hearth. The Prince went by there, and he picked up a poker and gave her a poke with it to keep her at arm's length.

The next day there was a big ball in that part of the country. The King's son went to it, like everybody else. When everyone had gone home, Peu d'Anisso came into her room and opened her chest and took out one of her loveliest dresses. Then she ordered her chest to lead her underground to where the ball was being given. As she came in, everyone stared at her. The King's son went over to fetch her to dance with him. When the dance was over, he asked her her name.

"I'm called 'Poker Poke.'"

"Ah-ha!" said the King's son. "'Poker Poke' is a good name. I'll remember that, all right!"

The next day the King's son called at the farm and talked of the ball and the lovely girl who had been there. He started to tell them, "I danced with the most beautiful girl I have ever seen . . ."

"No more beautiful than I! No more fair!" Peu d'Anisso began saying as she warmed her ragged clothing by the fire.

"Shut up, Peu d'Anisso!" said the King's son, teasing her, and he took the bellows and gave her a puff from them to shame her.

A little later on, another ball was being held. The same thing happened. The King's son begged the beautiful girl to come and dance with him. She had an even more gorgeous dress on and she looked so lovely.

"What is your name?"

"I am called 'Bellows' Puff.'"

"Ah! 'Bellows' Puff' is a good name. I'll remember that, all right!"

The next day he found himself once more with Peu d'Anisso and he talked of his meeting this beautiful girl again.

"No more beautiful than I, no more fair!" she said very softly as she stirred up the ashes in the hearth.

"Shut up, Peu d'Anisso!" said the King's son, who was irritated by all this. He picked up a *friquet* (stick) and stuck Peu d'Anisso with it.

Not long after, there was another ball given. The King's son met the lovely girl again. She was wearing yet another dress. He asked her her name.

"I'm called 'Blow from the Stick.' "

"Ah ha! 'Blow from the Stick' is a good name. I'll remember that, all right."

Without being any the wiser, the King's son went home while Peu d'Anisso, thanks to her chest, fled underground.

Some time later the King's son fell ill. He took to his bed because he was so sick with worry. By constantly thinking of the pretty girl's name, he had got to the stage of asking himself whether she had anything to do with Peu d'Anisso. Had she not said to him, "No more beautiful than I, no more fair . . ."? He was so sick with worry that he refused to eat any of the food brought to him. One fine day he said, "I don't want to eat anything but soup made by Peu d'Anisso."

"Oh, poor Peu d'Anisso! Surely you won't ask her to make you a soup?"

"I will eat only soup made by Peu d'Anisso."

The turkey girl was asked to make the soup for the King's son. She washed herself and combed her hair and put on one of her loveliest dresses so as to be clean to make this soup. The King's son got up without anyone knowing and looked through the keyhole. He saw the beautiful dresses spread all over the room. They shone like gold. As for the girl, she was surely the one he had seen at the ball.

"Open up! Open up, Peu d'Anisso!"

The girl opened the door, but she never again wore her *peu d'anisso* because the King's son did not want her to any more. I don't know whether he ate the soup made by Peu d'Anisso, but what is certain is that he married her and they both were very happy.

·45· The Two Brothers, or The Fox, the Wolf, and the Lion

• ONCE UPON A TIME there were two boys. They were off looking for a job. They were hoping for a few days' work, but they could not get themselves hired. So they said to themselves, "We have nothing left to eat. One of us must blind the other, and then he will lead him around begging for money from people who will take pity on him."

Then the two boys drew lots, each one hoping to draw the lot that would mean he would lead the other. The one who was led had the thin edge of the wedge; there was no doubt that the other ate much better and only gave him dry bread.

One day the one with good eyes said to the blind one, "Guess what? I'll go first in order to cross the ditch, but do keep an eye on it."

And then he left the blind youth at the foot of a tree and ran off after saying to him, "Get a good start and jump!" The blind man jumped and then he reached the foot of an oak tree. So what did he do? He climbed into the branches of the oak tree. When he reached the top, what did he see? A wolf arrived with a roast lamb, then a fox with a goose, and then came the lion with a barrel of wine. All three came under this oak tree to have supper. They ate, and after that they drank all the wine.

"So," said the wolf, "what's new? Over to you, little fox."

"There is a gentleman who has a girl friend. She is very ill. She could soon be well if they knew that by bleeding their old white mare and getting the girl to drink the blood they could cure her. She might even become a beautiful woman."

"Yes," said the wolf. "I know something else. You see this oak tree. Well, whoever, one-eyed or blind, tears off the third layer of bark and rubs his eyes very hard with it will see again."

How the youth listened to what the wolf said about the manner in which his sight could be restored!

In the end the lion said, "At this gentleman's home people go and fetch water from far away. If only they knew that by digging in their own fields they would find a spring which would yield enough water for the whole town!"

After this the fox, the wolf, and the lion left the place. The young man looked in his pocket. He said to himself, "Have I still got my knife?"

At last he found his knife at the bottom of his pocket. He dug into the oak, lifted the first layer of bark and took it off. Then he lifted the second layer of bark and took it off. Finally, he lifted the third layer of bark and used it to restore his eyesight. He took out the splinter of oak bark and rubbed it on his eyes. He saw a bit more clearly. He rubbed again, and then he could see perfectly. So he waited for daybreak to go and warm up in the sun. He walked right into town and asked a man for something to eat. Some people gave him bread. He asked for water to drink. "Oh, we'll give you gold aplenty, but no water. You have to go too far to fetch it."

So then he said, "If you will dig a hole in this gentleman's field, you will find a spring."

So great was their need that the people began looking for water by digging in the field, and they found it. What a miracle! A spring spurted up!

Then the young man went to this gentleman. He asked to go into this gentleman's house. Then he found himself at the door of an old oven. He found a servant and asked how the young lady was.

"Our young lady is very ill."

The young man said, "If they bled your old mare and gave its blood to the young lady to drink, she would soon recover."

The servant ran to tell his master, "A young man says that he could cure your daughter."

A fortnight later the young lady was convalescing. By the end of the year she was completely cured, and these people who had had to go so far to fetch water now had it in their homes.

This gentleman said to the young man, "You found a spring in my field to give us water, and you have also saved my daughter's life. Well, if you like her, I give you my daughter."

The other lad heard what had happened to the blind boy. He retraced his steps and went and found his friend to find out how he had recovered his sight.

"Ah, well, you must climb this oak where you left me all alone. You'll soon see what I found there."

A year went by. The fox, the wolf, and the lion came to see each other. Now the lion said: "One of us has given away the secret. It's you, little fox. You're nothing but a fool!"

"No," said the fox.

"Yes," said the lion, and he jumped on the fox, but the fox turned away with his foot up in the air. Then he saw a man in the tree and shouted, "Friend lion, take a look at this spy!"

So the lion cut the roots of the oak, and the oak crashed to the ground, and all three ate the man.

•46• Little Fourteen, or As Strong as Fourteen

• THERE ONCE WAS a very poor couple who lived in a shack close by the forest. They had a little boy, but they were so poor that no one wanted to be godfather or godmother to this child, and his parents just called him Petit.

The father died, and the mother was ill. There was so much missing in the shack, even wood for the fires. Petit was not at all strong, but he wanted to go to the forest to gather a small bundle of wood to make a fire and warm his mother. While he was gathering his twigs, a gentleman came toward him and said, "What are you doing there?"

"I am picking up a little kindling to start the fire and warm my mother, who is ill."

"What's your name?"

The boy answered, "As they could find neither godfather nor godmother, my parents call me Petit."

The gentleman said (this was God, by the way), "You will tell your mummy that from today on you shall be called Fourteen. I am your godfather, and the Holy Virgin is your godmother. From now on, you shall eat like fourteen. You shall work like fourteen, and you shall be as strong as fourteen!" Whereupon the gentleman disappeared.

Then as Little Fourteen wanted to lift his small bundle of

wood, he disappeared into the clouds. So he began again, making a huge pile of wood this time. There were oak trees and staddles, which he carried back to the shack on his shoulders. So in this way his mother had a good fire.

Little Fourteen wanted to learn a trade. He went to a smith, who took him on as apprentice, but he was so strong that he even broke the iron. The smith wanted to dismiss him. "Forge me a walking stick weighing five hundred pounds, and I'll go," said Little Fourteen.

He went far, far away with his iron walking stick. He had himself hired as a servant in a great house belonging to a timber merchant. He was sent to the forest with the other servants to gather wood. The others were used to eating a crust of bread before going to work. He swallowed half a loaf, and even then he had not had his fill. At last he went off tucking the other half of the loaf under his arm.

"He eats hearty," said the others. "Let's see if he works as well."

Each of them chose a team of oxen to saddle to a cart. For him they left two oxen who never walked in step. When he stung them with his goad, one would go this way and the other that way. He was very late in reaching the hedgerow. The two other servants were together loading a cartful of wood.

"It's my first time," said Little Fourteen, and, having watched how the other servants did it, he loaded his cartful of wood all by himself. Oh, he didn't take long loading it, but the oxen could not get the cart to budge.

"You'll never manage to take all that wood, will you?" shouted the other two.

"Yes, I will."

"Well, then, go on and try!"

There was no way of making his oxen work. So he unharnessed them. He led them up into the cart, and up onto his back went the whole load—cart, oxen, and all.

When they saw him arriving, one of the servants said to his master, "That's the Devil you've hired as a servant! If he's going to stay here, I'm off."

The second servant said the same thing. Then the master said to Strong as Fourteen, "You may leave."

Little Fourteen went on his way. A little farther on, he met
a man making up faggots in a clump of oak trees. He used a
whole oak to make the binding thongs.

"Hey, Oak Twister," said Little Fourteen, "come with me.
We will not be afraid of each other."

They walked on together. What did they find? A miller was
playing *palet*[1] with millstones.

"Hey, miller," shouted Strong as Fourteen, "come on with us.
We'll walk along together."

After a good walk, all three came to a castle. They went in.
There was no one there. They said to themselves, "We'd be all
right here if only we had something to eat!"

When they had really had a good search, they found enough
to make a supper. Then Little Fourteen said, "Let's stay here
for a few days."

The others were a little afraid of staying in this empty castle.
"Why not stay? No one interferes. If only we had a gun apiece,
we could go hunting."

They made a thorough search and found two guns.

"We are three," said Little Fourteen. "Two will go hunting
with the guns, and the third will make the soup here."

The first time no one wanted to stay alone in the castle.

"Who will stay?" said Little Fourteen.

"I don't want to!" shouted the miller.

"Oak Twister, you stay then and make the soup."

Willy nilly, Oak Twister ended by accepting. When the others had gone, he began to think. There was a big hole in the
square in front of the castle. Little Fourteen had said, "Be careful not to fall into the hole."

The two hunters were far away. Oak Twister saw coming
toward him an old man with a stick. He had come out of the
hole and seemed angry.

"What are you doing here?" he said to Oak Twister.

"Nothing."

"You wait and see what'll happen to you. How could you
allow yourself to come into my castle! I shall get you into the
hole."

The other did not trust him very far. He fought as hard as he

---

[1] Game resembling bowls played with flat stones.

could, but he was beaten by the old man and thrown into the hole.

And what about the soup? Oak Twister was to ring the bell to tell his friends that it was ready. The bell did not ring, however. The two hunters were quite surprised. The day was coming to a close, and still nothing rang.

"Let's go home and see whether he has made the soup!"

The table was laid. The plates were there, but there was nobody to sit down at the table.

"Where can he be?"

"Let's eat the soup. After that, we shall see."

As they ate the soup, they heard the other one sighing in the hole. He was crying out as if he had been hurt. Strong as Fourteen came to the edge of the hole and said, "What's the matter with you? I told you to be careful!"

"I went very close to the edge of the hole, and here I am in it."

Strong as Fourteen went into the hole to pull him out.

"Why did you fall so far in?"

The other would not say. A man capable of twisting an oak could not let himself be beaten by an old man!

That evening Little Fourteen said to the miller, "Miller, you will stay at home tomorrow to make the soup. Oak Twister and I will go hunting."

It was never Little Fourteen's turn to stay at home. Once the hunters were away, the old man came out of his hole. He caught the miller and beat him as he had beaten Oak Twister, and then he threw him into the hole.

However, the other one did not boast to Strong as Fourteen about what had happened to him the day before. Now they were waiting for the time when the bell would ring to tell them to go home and eat their soup, but it never rang. They decided to go back home. They saw the table laid but no one there.

Once again Little Fourteen had to go and pull the miller out of his hole, but he would not say a word about it. A man able to spin millstones could not allow himself to be beaten by an old man.

The two confederates, Oak Twister and the miller, said to

each other very quietly, "Tomorrow it will be Fourteen's turn."

The next day Little Fourteen said to them, "Go off hunting both of you! I won't fall into the hole." The others said to themselves, "You'll do the same as we did. The old man will come and find you."

Once the hunters were away, the old man came along. "What are you doing here? Do you want to be beaten and thrown into the hole like the other two?"

"Not I. You'll see."

Strong as Fourteen took his walking stick weighing five hundred pounds. It was the one the smith had forged for him. He beat the old man and threw him into the hole. "Well, now, don't you dare come out again."

After that he went home to put the bread in the soup, and then he rang the bell. The others arrived looking very surprised. It was then that Little Fourteen started teasing them. "Hey, you cowards! You wanted to see me caught like you two, but I did not let myself be beaten, I didn't. I even beat the old man and put him back in his hole. Now, let's eat."

When Little Fourteen dug his walking stick weighing five hundred pounds into the hole, the earth fell away under the surface. The chasm was so great there was no way of reaching the bottom. Then he said to the other two, "You must use a rope to reach the bottom of the hole." Neither the miller nor Oak Twister, however, wished to go down.

Fourteen said to them, "You shall stay up at the top to hold the rope, and I will go down."

When he reached the bottom, Fourteen left the rope and walked underground. He walked so far that he found three lovely girls whom the old man was holding captive, having kidnapped them from their parents. As the old man had been beaten by Little Fourteen, he hadn't enough strength left to hold onto the three girls, and he did not stop Fourteen from setting them free.

"You are going to go back up there," Fourteen said to them, and he shouted to his friends: "Hold onto the rope! I am sending a young girl up to you. She has been held captive by the old man."

When the two confederates saw the girl coming up, the first one said, "I want her for myself."

The other said, "No, she shall be for me!"

"Wait," said Fourteen, "I am sending another one up to you."

When they saw the second girl, who was prettier than the first, the two friends exclaimed, "She is for me!"

"No, I want this one!"

After that, Fourteen sent up the third girl, who was the prettiest of all. The two confederates, scorning the first two girls, both exclaimed, "That one is for me!"

"No," shouted Fourteen, "that one shall be mine." So then the other two cut the rope so that Fourteen would not get the prettiest girl, and they fled with the three girls.

Little Fourteen was underground. He could not get out of the hole. He said to the old man, "If you do not tell me how to reach the top, I shall kill you."

The old man said to him, "Listen. I have a creature who will take you up to the entrance of the hole. You will sit astride it, and each time the creature goes 'Coua', you will give it a lump of meat to eat."

The old man gave him some meat to take with him.

"That will not be enough," he said to Fourteen. "When you are nearly there, the creature will go 'Coua', and you will have no more meat. So you will cut off a piece of your leg and you will give it to her to eat. She will end by taking you up to the top. Take this little pot of fat to grease your leg where you will have cut the end off."

Little Fourteen did as the old man told him, and he recovered at once. The creature left him at the entrance to the hole. He was above ground again.

So then he went searching for his two companions, and he found them with the three girls. After that, I do not know what he did with the miller and Oak Twister, but it is certain that Little Fourteen married the prettiest of the girls for whom his friends had left him at the bottom of the hole.

The Master and the Tenant Farmer

· THERE WERE once a master and a tenant farmer who made a bet.

The master said to the tenant farmer, "We are going to make a bet on who will tell the biggest lie. The one who tells the biggest lie shall win part of the other's harvest."

"Oh, I don't want to," said the tenant farmer. "I need my share of the harvest to live on."

"Oh, well, it doesn't matter. Perhaps you will win."

In the end the farmer had to accept the bet. The master said to the farmer, "You speak first. Tell me your lie first."

So the farmer began like this, "Well, Master, one day I had a lot of work to do. I felt like being idle, so I began to count our bees. Well, Master, I found out how many bees we had, but I could not find a single one. I looked and looked for them. I went in the gorse bushes and then I found them. There were seven wolves busy eating them. Well, Master, I threw my ax at the wolves to send them packing. They had already swallowed half our bees. The other half gave me enough to feed the other bees for seven years. After that I tried to find my ax again. I looked for that ax without ever finding it. In the end I set fire to the gorse bushes. It burned them down and my ax too, but the fire left the handle intact for me. Well, Master, after that, so as not to waste the ashes from the fire, I looked in my pockets and found a bean, and I planted it in the ashes. Master, that bean grew so well. It was such a fine bean plant and so tall that I felt I must climb up it to see how far it went.

"Well, Master, I climbed and climbed from branch to branch and on and on from branch to branch again. In the end I went up and found God busy flaying oats. However, once having climbed up there, I couldn't come down again, so I had to make myself a stout rope. I asked God whether he would give me some oat husks to make into a rope. 'Ah,' said God, 'all right. If you wish it.' Well, Master, I knotted and reknotted oat husks. When I had made my rope of oat husks, I wanted to go down. When I reached the end of the rope, I saw that it was not long enough to touch the ground. Well, I let myself fall on a

rock and I sank into it up to my armpits. At that moment some
women were going to market with their eggs and their cheeses.
They broke the rock, and here I am. Well, Master, now you tell
your lie."

"Oh," said the master, "you've won my share of the harvest.
I can never match that!"

·48· *Fanfinette and the King's Son*

• A GENTLEMAN had three daughters. The youngest was called
Fanfinette. She was also the prettiest. The others were called
Catissou and Martissou, if you like it that way. Their real names
were Catherine and Marthe.

This old gentleman wished to go off on a journey, but next
door to them there also lived the King's son, who wanted to see
Fanfinette.

So the father went on his journey, but before leaving he said
to his three daughters, "Now you won't let anyone into the
house, will you?" Then he gave each of them a rose, saying:
"This goes without saying. Be very careful that they do not
wither."

The father left. It was a long journey. Now the King's
son always wanted to seduce Fanfinette. He said to himself, "Now,
how do I get into her house?"

The first time the three sisters sent him flying. So he dressed
as a beggar. He put on old rags. Now, maybe it was cold. Maybe
it was raining. At any event, he went to their door and he was
shivering—br, br, brr.

They gave him money, but now the King's son wanted to
come in and warm up by the fire. So the eldest of the three
sisters said, "We can let this old man in. He will do us no harm."
However, Fanfinette insisted, "Better let him go on his way."
(She felt he was up to something.)

So the King's son warmed himself for a while. He caught hold
of a piece of his suit and threw it into the fire, thus ridding himself of some of his rags.

"What are you doing, you poor old man?" asked the girls.

"Oh, it's only a bit of my suit that has got scorched!"

By repeating this performance, he ended up by throwing all his rags into the fire, and then he was revealed as the King's son in his proper clothes.

By evening he said, "This time I've got you. I'm going to sleep with Fanfinette."

But Fanfinette replied, "I should not have that honor. It should go to my eldest sister first."

Thus Catissou went to bed with the King's son that night.

Came the second night, and the King's son still wanted the prettiest of the girls. "It's going to be your turn, Fanfinette."

She answered, "Ah, no, the honor is due to my sister, Martissou."

During those nights when the King's son was with her sisters, Fanfinette lost no time. She broke up the floorboards under the bed. As for the King's son, he spent the night with Martissou, of course.

After the second night it was Fanfinette's turn. The King's son was looking forward to this so much, saying to himself, "This time I'll have you."

She said to him, "As you are so happy, I want you while in this happy state to leap into the air." The King's son leaped with such abandon that he went through the loose floorboards and fell into the cellar on top of some barrels, and so Fanfinette was rid of him.

So some time later the King's son, who was very put out, was still saying to himself, "I'll have you! I'll have you!" and now he wished to kill her.

With this goal in mind, he had lined a barrel with nails. Inside it was bristling with them, and he wanted to put Fanfinette in there to die. At the bottom there was one pointed nail which stood out above the others. So then she said to him, "I am quite ready to get into this barrel, but that point is so long it will prevent me from dying."

So then the King's son decided to get into the barrel to remove that nail. Fanfinette made the barrel roll right, left, and center, so that the points would prick the King's son all over.

He was bleeding from all his wounds. Then he wrenched himself out of the barrel as best he could.

Fanfinette went home. So then for a good long while the King's son stayed in bed, all swollen up. The servants wondered what was the matter with him, for he had told nobody about it.

Meanwhile, Fanfinette's two sisters each had a little boy. So then Fanfinette said to them, "You must feed your children well and keep them clean."

Then she made a bundle of the two babes. She dressed as a man and, disguised as a doctor, she arrived at the King's house. Then she said to the servants, "I have come to see your master. I heard that he was ill. I am a doctor. Even if you hear someone cry out, do not move. I will not need you."

Then she went into the room where the King's son lay in bed. She brought out a whip and she hit him good and hard. And did he yell! Fanfinette put the babies on each side of his bed. Then the servants came (she had finished her job). She went away. The two babies started bawling. The servants thought it was their master.

"It's not surprising that the King's son is so swollen. He has just given birth to two babies."

Then their master said to them, "Go and get nurses to suckle these babes and get them out of here!"

So they then did what they wanted with them.

As for Fanfinette, she went home. Soon after, her father came back from his travels. So then each of his three daughters had to show him her rose. Fanfinette's was the only one which had remained fresh. She handed it to her eldest sister, and then the eldest handed it to the second one, and then the second sister returned it to Fanfinette.

Then after this the father said, "This is all very well, but I would like to see all three of your roses at the same time."

Then their father saw that the eldest sisters' roses were faded, but he said nothing.

When the King's son was well again, he went and asked the old father for his daughter. By heaven, it was Fanfinette he wanted!

Yet she would have none of him. He wanted to marry her and kill her because she had made him suffer too much.

She did not want to accept. She took her time answering. Her father kept saying to her, "What have you got against him? He is rich. He is good-looking."

She ended up by saying, "Yes."

Now there was an old nurse who had brought up this son of the King's, and she had never left him. On the wedding night Fanfinette was not at all at ease. The nurse said to her, "My poor Fanfinette. You do not seem happy, and yet you are so pretty and so ready to please."

"Ah, yes! Tonight I shall die," replied Fanfinette. So the nurse answered, "Wait a bit now. I shall go and prepare the room."

She took an enormous marrow and filled it with honey. Then she dressed the marrow and put it in the bed as if it were a person with a nightcap on.

Then, when the King's son came into the room, he took his great sword to kill Fanfinette. He came forward. All at once— Pouf! Right in his face! He tasted a little of the honey which had fallen on his lips. He sucked it and said, "Unfortunate man that I am, I have killed Fanfinette, and she had such good blood." Then he cried and made an uproar in the room. The nurse came. He told her, "I am unfortunate. I have killed Fanfinette, and she had such good blood. Couldn't you bring her back to life?"

The real Fanfinette was hidden under the bed. She had gone, "Ha-ah . . ." when the King's son had pierced the marrow.

The nurse told the King's son to go away. "I'll do everything in my power to bring her back by breathing over her.

The King's son went out. The nurse said to Fanfinette, "Come on out, Fanfinette. I need your help."

So Fanfinette came out from under the bed. Together they took off the sheets full of honey, and they remade the bed.

The nurse said to her, "You will get into bed. If the King's son asks whether he hurt you, you will say, 'Yes.'"

The King's son came up to sleep next to his Fanfinette. Now he was happy to find her.

He said to her, "I hurt you so badly, Fanfinette."

"Oh, yes." She pretended to be suffering and spoke only in a whisper, as if she were in pain.

Then in time they made a good couple. The King's son did not wish to kill his Fanfinette any longer, as she had such good blood.

Part IX
Massif Central

·49· The Bear and the Beetle, or The War of the Animals

• I AM GOING to tell you the tale about the animals at the time when they made war on each other.

Once upon a time there were a bear and a beetle at the foot of a tree. The beetle climbed up the tree and fell off. Then the bear lifted his paw and put the beetle under it and held it there a good long time. Then he let him go. So then the beetle said to him, "You squashed me, and I declare war on you."

"Well," said the bear, "we'll make war by and by. Make up your army, and I'll gather mine." And they left each other.

The bear went and fetched the panther, the fox, and the wolf, but the beetle fetched the bees, the hornets, and the other insects. Then they all gathered at the bottom of a valley. When they arrived, the wolf was not yet there, and the bear said to the fox: "*Castafi!* Go and see if you can see them coming."

The fox galloped off and went and found the insects. When the creatures saw him coming, they jumped on top of his head and stung him all over. The fox had just time to throw himself in the water in order to get away from the insects, but later he was very careful not to let on that he had been stung by the bees.

When the other animals—the panther, the wolf, and the bear —saw him arrive soaked to the skin, they said to him, "Tell us, now. What did you get up to?"

"Oh, I am perspiring. I have walked so far my big toes are so exhausted I can stand up no longer."

"And did you find the insects?"

"Yes. They are up there and they are waiting for you."

"Up with you. Come with us, and we'll go and find them together."

"Yes, all right. I'll be ready to bite, but you go first and I'll follow."

When the other animals reached the insects, what did these creatures do? They did the same as they had done to the fox.

They stung them all over their bodies, and the great big animals lay beaten on the field.

· 50 · *Jean and Jeannette*

• ONCE UPON A TIME there were a man and a woman who had two pretty little children called Jean and Jeannette, but they were as poor as church mice.

One evening the children were in bed, and their father and mother were keeping warm by the fire. Suddenly the woman said, "My poor dear, there is nothing left in the cupboard. We can no longer feed our children. I have only a handful of flour left at the bottom of the basket. I'll make a little round bun, and tomorrow you'll take it with the children. You will go out and let them get lost. Someone is sure to take them in." Jean was not asleep. He heard his mother and saw that she was crying.

The next day their father put the bun in his pocket and, taking the children by the hand, he went off to the woods. On the way, Jean bent over and picked up some small stones, one here, one there, and put them in his pocket. No sooner was he in the forest than he began to drop his pebbles on the moss without his father noticing. When they were in the thick of the forest, their father climbed onto a height and then he said, "You see this bun. I'm going to let it roll down this slope, and it will be for the one who catches it." He did just that, and the bun rolled deep into the woods, and the children ran after it, laughing and shouting.

Jean got there first and picked up the bun. He brought out his knife and split it down the middle and gave half to his little sister, who had only just reached the foot of the slope. This was by a stream. There were lots of birds and butterflies, mulberries and raspberries to pick if they wished. They set to it and ate as many as they could. When they were satisfied, they looked for birds' nests and made whistles and picked flowers and had a lovely time.

After quite a while, the little girl said, "It will soon be noon.

We had better go back to our father." They hurriedly climbed up the slope again. When they reached the top, they began shouting, "Daddy! Daddy!" From all sides came the echo, "Daddy! Daddy!" but no one answered. They roamed around the woods all evening shouting, but search as they might, roam as they might, there was nobody anywhere. Then Jeannette started to cry.

"Don't cry, little sister," her brother said to her, "our father has lost us, but I'll find our way again." He did so by finding his white stones, and by going from one to the other, they came out of the woods. It was about time the sun was setting, and they saw their house far, far away at the end of the world.

When they reached the house, it had been dark quite some time, for the little girl's feet were cut and so she could only walk slowly. When they got there, they looked through the keyhole without anyone seeing them. The oil lamp on the table shone dimly. Their mother and father were eating their soup in silence. Drying her eyes, the woman suddenly spoke. "Who knows where my little children are now?"

"Perhaps they are hungry," said their father.

"Perhaps they are crying," said their mother.

"Perhaps the wolf has eaten them," said their father.

And they began to sob.

The children, who were hiding behind the door, could hold back no longer. They ran in and threw their arms round their parents. They were all crying and gobbling each other up with kisses.

All went well for three weeks, even a month—but the longer it lasted, the less they had to eat. Once more the wife said to her husband, "After all we have done we cannot let them starve to death. Go and lose them again. Perhaps some rich person will take them in." This is what they did.

The next day the father took the children out to pick up pine cones. This time, however, he cut straight through the fields. "Let's take the shortcut," he said.

When they had gone quite far, Jean thought that his father might lose them again, but what could he do? There wasn't a single stone on the grass, and they soon reached the edge of the woods. As Jean looked in his pockets, he found a piece of bread, and he began crumbling it little by little until it was finished. So they picked up pine cones from one side of the woods to the other, but after a while the little girl said, "I'm thirsty, Daddy."

"Me, too," said the boy.

"Don't worry," said the father. "I know a spring over there at the bottom of this gulley. There's fresh water there to slake your thirst." He pointed it out from afar, and while the children were running to it he slipped away. They did not delay long, however, and soon they were on their way back, but when they reached the spot where their father had been—no more father!

"He must have lost us again!" said Jean. "We must get home before nightfall. I'll find the way again." He set about looking for the bread crumbs, but he could not find them. The birds had pecked up the lot. Then Jeannette started to cry.

"Don't cry, little sister," said Jean. "I am going to climb this tree. Perhaps I shall see the house." In three leaps he was up in the middle of it.

"Can't you see anything, little brother?" said Jeannette.

"No, little sister."

"Climb up a little farther. Perhaps you'll see something. Can't you see anything, little brother?"

"No, little sister."

"Climb to the top of the tree. Can't you see anything now, little brother?"

"Yes, little sister. I can see a red house and a white house."

"Throw your knife at the red house and your hat at the white one."

Jean did this, but the wind carried his hat to the red house. "Then it's there we must go!" said the children.

Now the red house was the Devil's house, and the white one belonged to God. As they went into the red house, they saw a woman as ugly as sin sitting by the fire. She had a hooked nose and long teeth. Her hair was like a mare's mane. Her bonnet was all crushed with two little horns sticking out on each side.

"Good evening, woman," said Jean. "Would you let us sleep in your hayloft tonight?"

"I'll make a point of not letting you do any such thing," she said cantankerously, "for you'd set fire to it, no doubt. Hide under the bed, if you like, for my husband is the Devil, and if he finds you, he'll eat you." They quickly slithered under the bed. The Devil's wife threw them a crust. That was all they had for supper.

In the middle of the night, the Devil came home. They heard him dragging the chains through the house and grumbling like a tinker. Suddenly he began to scuffle around. "I smell . . . I smell . . . I smell . . . fresh flesh," he began saying. He picked up the oil lamp and looked under the table, in the cupboards, under the stairs, and in all the corners. At last he found them under the bed, and he pulled them out, one by the leg, and the other by the arm.

"Well, look at this! It couldn't be better. Here's a girl who can become my servant, for my wife's legs can barely hold her up, poor dear. And here's a boy who's a bit on the thin side, it's true (he was feeling his hips), but I'll shut him up in the pigsty, and I'll eat him when he's fat."

What he said came to be. Jean was shut up in the pigsty, and the Devil's wife kept the key in her pocket. Jeannette worked as the maid and was given a terrible time, as the Devil's wife was a fierce creature.

Every morning and evening she made the pig's meal and took it to her little brother and passed it to him through the cat hole. Sometimes she took him something a little better, like an apple, or a pear, or something else. From time to time, the Devil would slip his hand through the cat hole and touch Jean's little finger to see if he was fat enough. One day Jeannette found a rat's tail as she was sweeping the floor. She took it to her brother. "Take this rat's tail," she said to him. "When the Devil comes, you will get him to touch it. In this way he will never find you fat enough and he won't kill you."

All went well for a time, but one day the boy lost his rat's tail and he could not find it anywhere. He was obliged to let the Devil feel his little finger when he came. This time he found him fat enough. He sharpened an enormous ax and said to his wife, "Now that our meat to be preserved for winter is ready, I'm going to travel. You'll kill him, and when I come back I shall

eat him." The Devil's wife was very uneasy about this because
she had never done it before. She told Jeannette so.

"Is that all?" she said, trying to stop herself from crying. "I'll
show you. Put your head on the block."

The other one did this, and with one blow of the ax Jeannette
sent her head flying out in the middle of the house. She took
the key and went and opened the pigsty. Then they both hastened to wash away the blood. They carried the Devil's wife to
her bed and arranged the blankets to make it look as if she
were asleep. Then they went to the stable and harnessed the
white horses to the coach and the cart and galloped away.

When the Devil arrived, he was famished, and he saw his
wife in bed! He was as angry as a horsefly. "Well, well, well!
What do you know? You keep your old carcass in bed while I
split my gut going miles across the country!" He went over to
the bed to beat her. He took her by the hair, but the head came
off in his hands.

"*Fichtre!*" he said, "what is going on here?" He ran to the
stables. There were no horses there. In the shelter there was no
carriage, in the pigsty no boy. Then he understood, and he lost
no time at all! He took to the road like greased lightning. After
a little while, he met some haymakers, and he shouted to them,
"Have you by any chance seen my Jean and Jeannette with my
carriage and cart and my horses with shoes of gold and silver?"

"What are you saying? Is the hay ready?"

"I am not talking about that!" Off he ran like a man de-
mented.

He met a shepherd a little farther on. "Tell me, shepherd,"
he shouted, "have you by any chance seen my Jean and Jeannette with my carriage and my cart and my horses with shoes
of gold and silver?"

"What are you saying? Is my flock at rest?"

"I'm not talking to you about that!" He began running again.

He found three washerwomen by the side of a river. "Ladies,
have you by any chance seen my Jean and Jeannette with my
carriage and my cart and my horses with shoes of gold and
silver?" he asked them.

"Well, yes!" all three answered. "In fact they were galloping so fast that the cobbles were throwing off sparks. They went this side of the river. If you want to catch them, then cut off your legs and put them round your neck."

The Devil cut off his legs and put them round his neck. Then he fell into the river and was drowned.

The cock crowed, and the tale ended there.

· 51 · The Magic Napkin

· THERE WERE two children who had lost their mother and father. It was their stepfather and stepmother who brought them so much trouble. Because of them, they did not have enough to eat and they were crying in the middle of the woods. Suddenly a fairy appeared carrying a napkin.

She said to them, "What are you doing here, children?"

"Oh, we are crying because we haven't anything to eat and we have no money to go and buy food."

"Well," said the fairy, "here is a napkin. When you are hungry, you will spread it out on the ground and you will say to it, 'Napkin, do your stuff!' Then the napkin will bring out stew, bread and butter, and salt meat and fresh meat. When you have finished eating, you will say to the napkin, 'Napkin, do your stuff.' The napkin will then be empty. You will fold it up and take it with you."

The children took the napkin the fairy had given them, and that evening they went home and talked of the meeting they had had. Then the parents hurried the children off to bed and said to the napkin, "Napkin, do your stuff!"

Immediately the napkin brought out stew and salt meat and even fresh meat. After that the parents said to the napkin, "Napkin, do your stuff!" The napkin folded itself up again and looked all clean and neat.

The next day the children left, taking the napkin with them, but it wasn't the one given to them by the fairy. So they went once again to the woods and found the fairy. She asked them, "Well, doesn't the napkin give you anything to eat?"

The children said, "We are not the ones who have the napkin."

So then the fairy said to them, "Well, go to this donkey here, and when you need something, say to him, 'Donkey do what you know how to do!' The donkey, instead of shitting, will give you some five-franc pieces."

The children hastened to try the donkey that the fairy had given to them. The donkey shat five-franc pieces—you want some? Here they are! They quickly went back home to tell what had happened to them. So then the parents told them to go to bed in order that they could make the donkey do its work.

When the children were in bed, the parents said to the donkey, "Donkey do what you know how to do!" The donkey made as many five-franc pieces as they wanted. They kept them and went and found another rather weak-looking donkey to give to the children.

Then the children again went to the woods, but this donkey could not give them five-franc pieces. He could only pour out a few droppings. At that moment they once more saw the fairy who had already given them the napkin and the donkey. She asked them, "Well, are you pleased with the donkey, children?"

"Oh, no, this donkey doesn't give out five-franc pieces any more. He only gives droppings."

"Ah, well, children, here's a stick. When you reach home you will say to it, 'Stick, do what you know how to do!' and it will do this and that."

So when the children took the stick home, and once again they told their parents what had happened. The parents hurriedly took the stick and said to it, "Stick, do what you know how to do!"

However, the stick, instead of giving them five-franc pieces, gave them many a whack!

And now my tale is at an end.

Part X
Forez

• "Cric-crac, clog, kitchen spoon—walk today, walk tomorrow, by walking and walking we cover a lot of ground."

Once, on the day of Saint Sylvester, there was a little white goose who had quite a headache. She decided to go to Cervières in order to get better. To tell you the honest truth, I don't know why. Anyway, whichever way you take it, she was off up the stony paths and climbing, always climbing up toward the mountains. Now, it wasn't until some time later that a tiny cat, who was black as midnight, came out from under a bush and said to the little goose as he politely took off his hat, "A very good day to you, Friend Goose, and where are you going?"

"Good day, Tiny Black Cat. I am going toward Cervières to get rid of my dreadful headache."

"Would you like me to go with you? I'd like a change of air."

"All right. As you wish."

So up the stony path went our two little friends. A bit farther on, they met a smart, curly little lamb, who made a deep curtsy to them. "A very good day to you, little ones. Already up and on your way so early in the morning? And where are you going?"

Little Friend Goose answered, "Good day to you, Curly Lamb. We are going toward Cervières. I'm going to get rid of my dreadful headache, and Tiny Black Cat is going to get a change of air."

"Do you want me to come along with you?"

"Please yourself," purred Tiny Black Cat.

And there they went all three of them climbing up toward Cervières.

They went by a great meadow where a fine heifer was about to give birth to a calf. She put her snout over the hedge and said to them politely, "A very good day to you, you three beasties. It's a steep climb. Why don't you stop for a little while to get your breath back? And where are you going?"

"Good day, dear Heifer-Ready-to-Deliver. We are going off

in the direction of Cervières. I am going so as to get rid of my dreadful headache. Tiny Black Cat is going to get a change of air, and Curly Lamb is going along with us just for the walk."

"Would you like me to come along with you all? That would make four of us."

"Just as you like, dear Heifer-Ready-to-Deliver," said the cat, raising his tail.

"It's a great honor for us," bleated Curly Lamb.

By dusk they reached a shabby-looking house. They were rather keen to take shelter to avoid Mr. Wolf. They went to the little window where a light was shining. My dear friends, this was no castle. There was a tall bed with two puffed-out pillows and a neatly tucked red blanket. There were also a chair, a bench, and a big table. A chest in which to store clothes stood in the corner, and that was all. In the fireplace a lifeless little fire threw out a thin flicker which didn't look very hot. An old woman was sitting on the bench, and she was talking to herself out loud.

"Ah, my friends, what haven't I been through! To think that there are people who have bacon to eat and they complain. Ah, what a world! I don't even have a goat to give me milk, nor do I have a sheep to give me wool, so that I could spin and knit myself some nice warm woolens. I always have to drag about in rags. I don't even have a little hen to lay an egg for me. All by my lonesome self, all alone I live without even a cat to listen to me. Life is much too long for me."

Outside Friend Goose, Tiny Black Cat, Curly Lamb, and dear Heifer Ready-to-Deliver were all ears. All at once little Friend Goose said, "I haven't a headache any more. Let's go in."

She put up her foot and scratched gently at the old woman's door.

"Come on in," said the old woman, turning away slightly.

"Good day, old mother," said Tiny Black Cat, putting his hat under his arm.

Then he coughed, and while Friend Goose was putting her head on one side and tying her bonnet, and Curly Lamb was drying his eyes, and dear Heifer-Ready-to-Deliver stretched out her neck to see better—as she had stayed outside so as not to dirty the house—he spoke. "We are four friends, and we were on our way to Cervières. But we still have far to go, and the night is pitch black, so you shall put us up for the night. Friend Goose will go in the hen house. Dear Heifer-Ready-to-Deliver and Curly Lamb will go to the stable, and I'll stay by the kettle and keep an eye on the fire."

Did the old woman ever welcome all this! She kissed Curly Lamb and scratched dear Heifer-Ready-to-Deliver's forehead. She stroked Friend Goose and led them all to their beds. Then she picked up Tiny Black Cat in her apron and sang him a lovely song to send him to sleep.

They all lived together very happily. Never was the old woman hungry or thirsty again.

Little Friend Goose never had another headache, and never again did any of them want to climb to Cervières.

·53· *Half Chicken*

• ONCE THERE WAS a tiny little hen, so thin and so weak the mother hens called her Half Chicken. And what a life they led her! Those beaks were busy, believe me! Poor Half Chicken's head was quite bald because of it, and her wings were all plucked. Even at night the rooster and the hens gave her no peace. She had to go and crouch under the perch, and droppings would fall on her comb. The other hens were doing it on purpose.

So much so that one morning Half Chicken had enough. She took the little bit of grain the others had left. She put it in a small bag under her right wing and, as the door of the barnyard was open, she went away without saying goodbye to Tchouca or to Faverotte or to Rita or to White Jau.

The road was good and flat. The sun warmed Half Chicken's sticky feathers, and she felt so fit she began singing, "At Esser-tines at Chambest the hens crown the roosters!"

Well, then, as she was full of beans, she thought she would

go to the King. So off she went as fast as she could. The wee
hen's feet were steaming, she was going so fast. Every so often
she rearranged her small bag of grain under her wing and then
she was off again. As she went along by a pine wood she heard
someone calling her.

"Help, Half Chicken, help!"

The kind little hen left the path and began looking under
the junipers.

"Here, here on the right."

In the end she found the wolf lying on his side, and he
looked so tired it made Half Chicken sit up.

"Half Chicken, I am all in. Take me with you or else I shall
die."

"Come on, Sir Shaggy Wolf, come with me. Climb into my
neck, and I will carry you." Panting hard, Shaggy Wolf slipped
into the little hen's neck.

She went on her way just a little bit more slowly.

After going through another hamlet and another copse, Half
Chicken reached the bank of a river.

"Half Chicken! Half Chicken!" said the water, "I am quite
exhausted because I always have to flow in the same direction.
Take me with you."

Half Chicken took pity on Fair River, who was so bored.
"Draw in your claws a little," she said to the wolf. "The river
is coming in next to you. Come on, Fair River. Come along
with me. Climb into my neck, and I will carry you."

Fair River made haste and in a flash she went into Half
Chicken's neck, and Half Chicken started off again just a little
more slowly.

At four o'clock in the afternoon, they saw in the distance a
big city with golden tiled roofs and chimneys of finest silver.

"This must be His Majesty the King's city," thought Half
Chicken. She stood on the crown of the road to shake off the dust
on her wings. And then she made a face. "I smell something
jolly, like burning!"

In her neck Shaggy Wolf began to cough. A bonfire of couch
grass was smoking so much it was difficult to see through the
smoke.

"Half Chicken! Half Chicken! I am tired of burning and smoking. Take me with you and carry me."

Half Chicken flapped her wings a bit and said that before doing anything else she would put the wolf in the middle of her neck. Think of it—water and fire! What a life they would have led side by side! And also the river being on the right and Shaggy Wolf in the middle, the little hen turned to the fire and said, "Let's go, Burning Fire. Come along with us. Climb into my neck, and I will carry you."

Burning Fire was soon ready. He crouched in the hen's neck and, as he had good manners, he made himself very small so as not to heat Half Chicken or roast Shaggy Wolf or make Fair River have the vapors. So Half Chicken, who by now was heavily loaded, moved off very slowly.

Just as the sun was setting, Half Chicken reached the King's house. She scratched at the great door. A footman dressed in greenish silk opened it, and without further ado the little hen headed for the King's room. My dear children, you should have seen it. My, it was something! On the wall hung masses of huge embroidered cloths. Sheepskins and hides of all sorts of strange animals lay scattered on the floor. A table was loaded with ham, roast rump of veal, little suckling pigs with mustard under their tails. The King, seated on a glittering throne, wore a great red cloak, and he had a nice new hat on his head.

Half Chicken came in carefully lifting each foot so as not to get tangled up in all the skins lying there as carpets. She made three curtsies before His Majesty the King, and, stretching out both her wings, she said, "A very good day to you, Your Majesty. I have come on foot from near Poncins to see you. I was so weak the other hens tore my feathers out. I come to ask you for a new coop and a handful of grain and some clear water. In return I shall lay one egg for you every morning."

The King started to laugh. He did not reply at all, but he beckoned to a long tall weed of a servant, who was looking his way, and Half Chicken found herself in a hen house with mother hens ten times larger than Tchonca and a golden rooster like one I saw as a weather vane some time ago. Think of it! The King's hens!

Yes, only these hens were as mean as they were large. As soon as Half Chicken had settled on her perch and was getting out her little bag of grain to eat, they began to shove her about with their wings and with their claws and made her take that on the head and take that on the rump. Filthy words showered down on Half Chicken. Suddenly she said, "Shaggy Wolf! Shaggy Wolf! Shaggy Wolf! Come out of my neck now, or I am a poor lost chick!"

The wolf came out, and in a minute all the hens fled.

The next morning when the footman came in he found all the hens with white combs and stiff legs, and Half Chicken was all alone on the perch.

"You spiteful fool of a hen! Look at your handiwork. Don't you budge, my little friend. You'll see how you get roasted!"

The screams from Half Chicken's throat were enough to deafen one. It wasn't long before the poor little hen was thrown before a roaring fire with her feet tied. This was a fire worse than the one used to boil the Devil's cauldrons.

The little hen thought the end had come, and in a tiny voice, which was all choked up, she said, "Fair River, Fair River! Come out of my neck, or else I am a poor lost chick!"

And here came my Fair River, murmuring softly as she flowed on and on. She put out the fire and upset the kettles and threw down the servants in the kitchen. She rose and rose, drowning everything except the King, who had climbed on top of a cupboard with his wife, and Half Chicken, who was stuck atop a dresser. Only the water was still rising and was going to spoil everything, so, with all the power she could muster, the little hen said, "Burning Fire! Burning Fire! Come out of my neck, or else I am a poor lost chick!"

Burning Fire came roaring down worse than the wind in the great pure forest. Things soon dried up, believe me! Half Chicken flew down to the ground and shook herself. She put up a small ladder and made the King come down. He put out his hand for his wife, so that she, too, could get out. They were all there on the ground. The King said, "My little Half Chicken, you have caused me a lot of trouble, but you were no coward and you saved both of us, my wife and me. I shall give you a fine house. I shall give your wolf a forest, and your river shall have a country, and your fire shall have all the chimneys."

The King did as he said, and they lived to such a ripe old age that no one in their lifetime could tell my great-grandmother about the end of their lives.

Part XI
Franche-Comté

·54· *The Wolf and the Fox*

• THERE WERE once a fox and a wolf who got together. They bargained for a field of grain, which was to be harvested. As they cut it down, the fox had an awful backache—so much so that he stood up and yelled, "Excuse me, please!"

The wolf said to him, "So, what's the matter with you?"

"Oh, I think I'm being called upon to be godfather."

"Oh, well," said the wolf, "you'd better go. One can't refuse a christening."

By golly, that fox picked up three sheep's droppings, rolled them in flour, and then he dipped into the butter in the pot, and after that, believe it or not, he went back to the wolf and said to him, "Look, here are three *dragées* [1]. We haven't bought any. You see, we are not well off. Well, what d'you think of them?"

"Well, they're not so bad. What kind of name did you give him?"

"Gobbled."

"Oh," said he, "that'll do."

Anyway, they went back to work. The fox's backache came back. He started to yell, "Excuse me, please!"

The wolf said, "Well, now, what's the matter?"

"Well, I'm needed to be godfather once again." Then the fox went on to say to the wolf, "You ought to go."

"Oh, indeed no. It's better if you go. You walk better than I do."

So the fox went off. He picked up two or three more sheep's droppings and then he ate half of what was in the butter pot. Back he came to the wolf and he gave him the sweets. "I just can't buy any as I am godfather so often."

"What sort of name did you give him?"

"Half."

Back to work they went, and they scythed more of the harvest.

---

[1] Sugared almonds, a traditional sweetmeat offered at christenings.

Then about an hour later the fox began to yell again, "Excuse me, please!" The wolf did not listen. He was making haste. Then the fox yelled again, "Excuse me, please!" and said to the wolf, "They want me to be godfather again. Go on, Wolf. You go, Wolf. You ought to go. Run along and give yourself a bit of a rest."

"No, indeed not. I don't want to go. I can't read or write. What should I go for? Go there, Fox. You go once more."

So, by my faith, off he went, that fox. When he got there, he licked the butter pot clean and he didn't bring back any sweets.

Then the wolf said to him, "What name did you give him?"

"Well-Licked."

Well, when evening was coming, the wolf was dead tired. The fox said to him, "Wolf, you don't know it, but you've got to go and make the soup, and you're dead tired."

The fox worked on till night and then he came home. The wolf was in bed. The fox said again, "What you doing in bed? You haven't made the soup, then?"

"What would I have put in the soup, I'd like to know, seeing as how you've eaten everything. Three times you went off to be godfather—some godfather! You came after the butter pot. You gave it a name all right—Gobbled, Half, and Well-Licked. Fox, I've got to eat you."

Fox said to him, "No. The one who feels like going to bed will be the one who's eaten the pot of butter."

"Fine!" said he. "I don't want to go to bed. I haven't eaten anything. I haven't had any supper. This time I've got to eat you."

"Wolf, I know you like meat. A butcher comes by there on the road every Tuesday. You ought to go out there and pretend to be dead. Then, when the butcher goes by, he'll say, 'Oh, I won't skin him just now. I'll throw him into my cart like that.' You'll grab the pieces of meat and run off."

Well, now, the wolf went away and pretended to be dead. The butcher came along and stopped his cart. Then he said, "Here's a dead wolf. What shall I do with him? Well, I'll take my knife and I'll skin him." When the wolf felt that the knife was pricking him a bit, he ran away. He came back to the fox, and this one said to him, "Then you didn't do as I said?"

"Oh, yes, I did, but, instead of just chucking me in his cart, the butcher wanted to skin me, so I ran away," said he. "So I've got to eat you this time."

"Well, no, Wolf. There's going to be a wedding in the village nearby. Now that means we'll both go there while they're all at the Mass. We'll have a good tuck in, and then we'll run away."

So off they went. They got to the wedding. The windows were open. They slipped through the bars. They got through those for sure. Then the wolf dived into one dish and made a pig of himself—that's for sure! The fox would grab something and eat it and then jump out again. That wolf really set to it and stuffed himself.

Then after a long stretch the fox came out and yelled at the wolf, "Get out of there, Wolf. Here come the wedding guests."

The wolf tried to get out, but he'd eaten so much he couldn't slip through the bars this time. When the guests came in and saw all the dishes knocked over, they grabbed some clubs and they hit the wolf. The wolf came out quite exhausted, and the fox said to him, "Well, Wolf, did you dine well this time? Did you really have a good feed?"

"Yes, I had a good feed but I've had quite a bash."

"Should have done the same as me, Wolf. You should have come through the bars. I kept taking a piece, and then I would come out to see if I could still get through."

"But, Fox, you ought to have told me. This time, Fox, I must eat you."

"No, Wolf, no. I know you like fish. We'll go on a night when there are lots of fish. You put your tail in the water, Wolf, and when you feel them biting, we'll pull it out and then you'll have a fish."

So there he was putting his tail in the water, and it froze solid. When it was good and frozen, he pulled out his tail, but it was all skinned.

"This time, no fooling, I must eat you."

"Well," says he, "no. Look here, Wolf. Tonight I know where there's a lovely bit of cream cheese. I know you like it."

So then he was off that night. It was a lovely moonlit night. The moon was full. He led him to a well and said, "Wolf, you take a look and see if there isn't a fine cheese? Now you need to go down in a bucket. I'll let you down, and then when you reach the cheese you jump onto it."

When the fox heard the wolf jump onto the cheese, the fox brought up the bucket and the wolf drowned. So be it.

·55·   The Wolf and the Fox in the Well

• THE WOLF FOUND the fox and said to him, "Ah, here you are. Well, you'll make two nice mouthfuls for me."

"Oh, I do beg your pardon! I do beg your pardon!"

"Well, find something for me."

"I'll find something."

"Now, what are you going to find for me? I want you to find me a whole cheese."

"Oh, I'll find that for you."

"Agreed."

They crossed three orchards and went round Benjamin's place (the Faivret used to live there), and then they crossed the garden belonging to the Chalandre (between Benjamin and Fortunat). Then they were in Fortunat's yard. There was a well there with coping stones around the edge. It was a well with two buckets and a chain and pulley.

"I can't see anything there."

"Yes, wait a bit. It's here at the bottom. There is something. There's cheese there, I promise you."

Now the moon was shining down directly into the well, so the fox said to him, "Look!"

"Well, then, go on down."

"Oh, what a millstone of a cheese! Look how big it is! Look at that millstone of a cheese!" he shouted from the bottom. Then he said to the wolf, "Climb into the other bucket."

As the wolf was heavier than the fox, he was soon down at the bottom, and the fox was overhead.

"Well, you wanted to eat me. This time you come up. I'm safe!"

The wolf kept saying, "Draw me up. When I reach you, I'll gobble you up."

But he didn't reach him. He drowned instead.

· 56 · *The Black One, the White One, and the Plucked One*

• ONCE UPON A TIME there were three ewes. There were a black one, and a white one, and the plucked one. They had been together in the same pen for a long time. They went to the fair—the Gendrey fair—and when they reached the corner of the wood, there was the wolf waiting for them.

"Oh!" said he to the black one, "Black ewe, you black one, I must eat you!"

"Oh, poor wolf, help yourself to the white one who is behind me, for I am too thin!"

"White ewe, you white one, I must eat you!"

"Oh, do eat my sister who is behind me!" (This was the plucked one.)

"Oh, plucked one, plucked one, I must eat you!"

"Oh, poor wolf, eat me if you like! I am nothing but skin and bone."

"Oh, really? Well, I'll wait for you to come back."

So they went off and reached the fair at Gendrey. There they began browsing in a field of clover. Oh, they really ate well for eight long days! They were much more plump than when they had set off.

Now they were on their way back. They were no longer thinking of the wolf, but he still had his mind on them.

"Hey, black ewe, I must eat you!"

"Oh, wolf, let me by! Eat my sister who is behind me!"

(The narrator stops at this point, and the audience asks, "And what about the plucked one?")

"Kiss her on the backside so her feathers will grow back again!"

Part XII
Dauphiné

· 57 · *The Girl and the Thief*

• A FATHER and mother with a daughter had gone to the fair. They had asked a neighbor to come and sleep with her. As she bent down, this neighbor saw a man lying under the bed. She said to the girl, "I must go and get my bonnet and I'll be back."

As she did not seem to be coming back, the girl said her prayers and went to bed. Now the man came out from under the bed and said to her, "You must give me everything you own in the house."

After that they made bags out of the linen. When he was ready to tie up the bags, he asked her for some string.

She answered, "Oh, I haven't any string. When my father wants to tie up a bag, he climbs up the tree outside and cuts off little twiglets that bend easily."

He said, "All right. Come and give me some light." The girl lit the lamp and went out to give him some light. When he was at the top of the tree, she put out the lamp and went in. She locked herself in and barricaded the door. He came down from the tree and began scrabbling under the door. He said to himself, "I'm getting my hand through. I'll manage the rest."

As he put his hand under the door, the girl cut it off. When her parents came home she was so scared that she did not want to open the door to them. But they made themselves known, and as soon as they were in, she explained to them what had happened.

A few years later a boy showed up and asked to marry her, but the girl recognized him. He had one gloved hand and the other was bare. She said to her parents, "Next time he comes, ask him to take off his glove."

So when he came back, the father said to him, "I wish you would take off your glove."

The other answered, "It isn't the fashion in my part of the world. When you ask a girl to marry you, you keep your gloves on."

In spite of this, the father wished his daughter to marry this man at any price.

When they were alone together, he took off his glove and said to her, "You see this one is sister to that one—you cut it off but you'll be sorry."

As soon as they were back in his home, he tied her to the foot of the bed and he said to his mother, "Keep an eye on her and see that she does not get away. In the meantime I shall get the knives ready to bleed her."

Then the girl started begging her mother-in-law to let her go.

"Here are some pins. Scratch your face with them and say that it is I who scratched it and that you could not hold me back any longer."

Well, after that, she went away and reached home, saying, "I told you he was the one. He wanted to kill me."

Her parents kept her in their house. Then one Sunday she was with her mother and father at Mass. The girl turned round and saw the thief at the foot of the church. She told her father. The father went out to warn the police, who then arrested the thief. The girl then went on living with her parents. That is the end.

· 58 ·   *The Devil's Boot*

• A LANDOWNER's SON had used up every penny of what his father had left him. When he discovered he was bankrupt, he made the acquaintance of a young lady who owned a castle and was of his class. So he went to her father to get permission to marry her. Her father said to him, "How can I give you my daughter—you who got through a fortune in such a short time! But as you love each other, I'll give you my daughter if you manage to remake your fortune within the next year."

So the landowner tried to get a loan to show he had done something, but as his credit was bad, he found no one who was ready to lend him anything.

One day as bankruptcy approached, he was standing on top

of his castle pulling his hair out, when he shouted, "Only the Devil can get me out of this one!"

That very minute he smelled sulphur, and a man dressed in red appeared before him. He had horse's feet. He said to him, "You called for me? What do you want me for?"

So the landowner explained his situation. He said that it was gold he wished for. Only gold would save him. The Devil answered, "You wretch! We make all the gold where I come from. I'll give you as much as you like and more!"

"Yes, but what will I have to give you in exchange?" he retorted.

The Devil said, "Not much. There is nothing you need give me during your lifetime. Only, after your death, you shall give me your soul."

So then he thought and said to himself, "I would like his gold but I would not like to give him my soul forever." He said to the Devil, "Come back at the same time tomorrow and I shall give you the right answer."

So then he thought again. He took a boot and punctured the bottom of it and he placed it at the top of his castle, having first pierced the floorboards and emptied the rooms. When the Devil appeared, he said to him, "If you fill my boot in one hour you shall have my soul, but if at the end of one hour the boot is not full I shall keep your gold and my soul."

The Devil answered, "That's a deal. Tomorrow at the same time I shall be here with the gold."

The next day the Devil arrived with several of his minions, each of whom carried a bag of gold on his shoulders, and he made them empty them into the boot. However, at the end of an hour, the boot was still far from full, as it was punctured. My grandfather used to say that it was a riding boot.

So after that the Devil went away swearing stormily, and the landowner kept his soul, and with the help of the Devil's gold, he was able to marry the girl.

Well, now, that really is the end.

·59· He Who Speaks First

• A YOUNG married couple, who were not very rich, had, during the first few months of their wedded life, to borrow a small kettle for boiling their soup. Then later when they had to return it to its owners, neither husband nor wife could make up his mind to go. The wife would say, "Well, then, you go and give it back!"

Then he said to her, "Look, we'll do this. The first one to speak shall take back the kettle. You can sing as much as you like, and I can whistle."

This man was a shoemaker, and his wife was a weaver. They spent their days singing and whistling. She sang as he wove, and he whistled as he drew the awl.

Now it so happened that the King and his following came out hunting in the vicinity. Night came upon them in the wood. Suddenly their lantern went out. Then they saw light coming from this house, and the King sent his servant there to get a light for the lantern. The servant went into the house and spoke to the woman, saying, "Would you allow me to light my candle from your lamp, Madam?"

The woman showed him her lamp, singing. The servant said to himself, "Either that woman is crazy or she is mute." And he turned toward the man and asked him, "Would you allow me to light my candle from your lamp, sir?"

The man pointed at the lamp with his awl, whistling. The servant went to the King and said ot him, "Those poor people must be out of their minds. I can't understand it. They don't speak!"

So then the King came to see to satisfy himself. He asked the woman, "Would you allow me to light my candle from your lamp, Madam?"

The woman began to sing as she pointed at the lamp with her finger. Then the King said to the shoemaker, "Allow me, Sir, to light my candle from your lamp!"

Now the man pointed at the lamp with his awl, whistling. The

King said, "Poor wretches! We must have them taken away
from here!"

He started by taking the woman on his back, but when the
shoemaker saw his wife going off, he wept and said, "Oh,
Sir, please, Sir, give me back my wife, and I'll return the kettle!"

·60· *The Fearless Shoemaker*

• IN THE OLD DAYS people were very much afraid of having to
keep watch over the dead.

There was a shoemaker who was not afraid, though. So a
man said, "I am going to scare that shoemaker, I am."

He pretended to be a dead man, and the shoemaker went and
watched over him, having brought some of his work with him.
Now, during the night the other man sat up and said, "When
one watches over the dead, one does not work!"

However, the shoemaker replied, "When one is dead, one does
not speak!"

He gave him a blow on the head with his hammer and really
did him in.

It was the other man who got caught!

Part XIII
Savoy

• THERE WAS an old woodcutter who lived with his wife at La Fraissette. Now his wife was called Jeannette. They were the only ones to live there all the year round. They would spend the winter there.

One night they were going to have their soup. The woodcutter was making up a basket. As it was hot, they had opened the door. Coming back to the table to put down her pot, Jeannette let out an "Ah!" of surprise as she stared through the half-open door. Her husband turned round, and what did he see? There stood a wolf, a huge one. This wolf was a big as a donkey. Jeannette was standing there with her tureen in her hand. Her husband shouted at her, "Pour away, Jeannette!" So then his wife tipped the pot over the wolf. The animal gave one howl and fled into the depths of the forest. He was steaming all over. They quickly closed the door, and that night they went without soup, but they were only too happy to have rid themselves of the wolf.

Some time later, when it was fine, our woodcutter went off to the forest. He went to the Replat to make a few faggots. His wife had packed his game bag. He began making a faggot, and he did not notice the time going by. Dusk came and he found he had strayed a bit in the forest. It took him quite a while to find his game bag. Well, by the time he had finished roaming around looking everywhere, night had fallen and he could hear the howling of the wolves. He set off for home as fast as he could, but the howling began again and he climbed up a fir tree. Now what did he see coming out from a corner of the clearing? There was a huge wolf. It was their wolf, the scalded one! The woodcutter recognized him. His coat had not yet grown back. The wolf stopped at the foot of the tree. He sniffed the air and he, too, recognized the woodcutter, and with his wolf's brain he worked out: "This is it. This time I have him." He let out a terrifying howl and called his brothers. A few seconds later the whole pack arrived. There were ten, fifteen, twenty. There was a whole pack! They formed a circle round

the tree. Then at a given moment the wolves stood aside and
held a meeting. After a minute or two they came back to the
foot of the tree. The scalded one placed himself at the foot of
the tree, and the wolves made themselves into a ladder. One
climbed up, then another, then a third, and a fourth. The woodcutter, who could see them coming, climbed higher, too. In
this way they reached the top of the fir tree. Our poor woodcutter felt that he was caught, and he saw the wolf climbing
and climbing and knew that he could be reached. Then the
woodcutter shouted, "Pour away, Jeannette!" The scalded one,
remembering the words referring to the tureen of boiling soup,
took off at once, but it was he who was holding up the column
of wolves, and so down they all came. They fell at the foot of
the fir tree and, limping as they went, they ran back to the
depths of the forest. The woodcutter went home.

Soon it was Christmas, and there was a little snow. One day
Jeannette said to her husband, "Next week it will be Christmas.
We must go down to Chambéry to buy some food. You'll take
the small sledge to cross the Col des Prés, and you'll put a small
barrel on the sledge."

She gave him a snack and a little wine, and the woodcutter
left, drawing his barrel along on the little sled. He went by
the Col des Prés and went down the other side. When he
reached the Croix de Fornet, he met half a dozen brigands,
who asked for his money. Afterward they said, "What are we
going to do with this man?"

The leader said, "We've only to bring him down and throw
him into the ravine." But one of the younger brigands said,
"After all he is an old man. We are thieves, not murderers. We
must let him live."

Then the leader said, "We've only got to put him in his
barrel and then we'll run away."

They took out the bottom of the barrel and put the woodcutter
into it. They put back the bottom and the bands, and then they
left it. The leader sent the barrel rolling down into the ravine.

The barrel came to a halt against a bush, and our woodcutter
came to. He wondered how he was going to get out of the
barrel. He tried calling through the bunghole, but no one

answered. Night fell. He felt cold, but luckily he had his little bottle of wine to keep him going. The night was followed by another day spent in the same manner. A second night fell. Our woodcutter felt all was lost. He said to himself, "This time this is the end."

There was a moon, and the cold was even more intense. Now, in the middle of the night he heard a noise. He glanced through the hole, and what did he see? The scalded one!

The scalded one came up to the barrel and sniffed at it, and then he began to scratch around it a little, growling. In the end he went right round it. Now at one point the wolf stopped, and the woodcutter saw the wolf's tail swinging in front of the hole. He put his hand through the hole and grabbed the end of the tail and pulled it in. Then he shouted, "Pour away, Jeannette! Pour away!" Our wolf at once imagined the kettle of boiling soup hanging overhead. He set off as fast as he could, dragging the barrel and the woodcutter after him. He climbed up the ravine in this fashion, and helter-skelter they went over the Col des Prés again. Then he reached the chalets of La Fraissette.

When the woodcutter saw the smoke from the chimney of his house, he let go of the wolf's tail and came to a halt in front of his home. He called his wife, "Jeannette!" Jeannette!" Jeannette came up to the barrel. She saw that it was her husband shut up in there and she set him free.

The scalded one was never seen again.

.62. *Princess Elisa*

• THERE WAS once a beautiful Princess called Elisa. She wished to marry a man who could stay hidden either in the heavens or on earth or in the sea, and she gave him only three days in which to hide.

Now there was a man who had found an eagle fallen from its nest. He put it back in its nest, and then he went and found the Princess. She said to him, "I am quite willing to marry you, but do try and hide well."

So then he went away to hide. He met the eagle whom he had helped. The eagle said to him, "Well, now. You are going to climb onto my back and hang onto one of my feathers. I shall fly so high up into the sky that the Princess will not find you."

So then off went Princess Elisa to look for him, and she began shouting, "Earth, give him back to me! Heavens, give him back to me!" Right then the man came down on his eagle and appeared before the Princess.

Now another man found a fish dying out of water as he was coming to see the Princess. He took it and put it back in the water. After that he went to see the Princess. She said the same thing to him, "You will have to hide so that I can find you neither in the sky nor on the earth nor in the sea."

So he left to hide. He went by the seashore and said to himself, "Where could I hide really well so that the Princess cannot find me?"

The fish leaped out of the water and said to him, "You will come down with me, and I shall take you so deep down in the sea that the Princess shall not find you."

After three days Princess Elisa began saying, "Heavens, give him back to me!" But nothing came. "Sea, give him back to me!" And he came up to the surface and he had to appear before the Princess. She was stronger than he was.

So, then, a third man came forward. On the way he had helped a drowning ant. He said, "Oh, poor little thing!" Now he took the ant and put it back in the ant-hill. Then he appeared before the beautiful Princess, saying he wished to marry her. She said to him, "I shall marry you on condition that I find you neither in the heavens nor on earth nor in the sea."

He left. He too had only three days in which to hide. He said to himself, "So, where can I hide then?"

Now he met an ant, who said to him, "You helped me. You will take me in your hand and you will turn into a little ant like me. You shall climb into the Princess's garter and she will not find you."

The Princess went away. She began saying, "Heavens, give him back to me!" Nothing came. She turned toward the sea. "Sea, give him back to me!" Still nothing happened. Then she

shouted, "Earth, give him back to me!" Ah! Always nothing.
She said to herself, "That one really does know how to hide."

Well, when the three days were up, the man came down from
the Princess's garter, and she said to him, "As you know exactly how to hide, I shall marry you." And they were duly
married.

·63· The Little Devil of the Forest

• THERE WAS a mother once who had a dinner to prepare, and
she had wanted to make some cakes. She had made five cakes
and she had placed them in the room next door.

She said to her little girl, "Go and see if the cakes are cool."

As they smelled so delicious, the little girl ate one. She came
back and said, "No, Mother. They are not yet cool."

A little later the mother again said, "Daughter, go and see
if the cakes are cool yet."

The little girl ate them all, and came back and said, "No, they
aren't cool yet."

Then her mother lost her temper and said: "It's impossible.
They must be cool by now."

Then the girl said, "No, Mummy, they aren't cool."

Her mother, who could tell that she was lying, went to see
and found no cakes left, which made her furious. She went out
onto the balcony and shouted, "I am going to tell everybody
about you, you greedy girl!"

She sang in her anger:

My daughter has eaten five cakes today!

Then a handsome young man went by on the road. Her mother changed her tune. "My daughter has spun five spindles of wool today!" He asked her what she was saying, and she repeated:

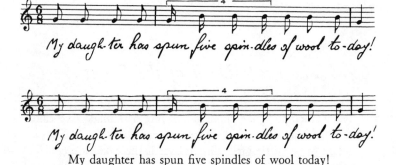

My daughter has spun five spindles of wool today!

"Oh, she must spin well, your daughter, to have spun all that. And my mother, who has so much wool to spin!" (You see in those days there weren't the machines we have now.)

"Well, come on up. She'll go with you." Now the girl whispered to her mother, "You know well that I can't spin!"

Her mother answered, "That will teach you to be greedy."

It was time to go. Without further ado, she left with the young man. They reached a lovely castle standing at the edge of the forest. He said to his mother, "Here you are, Mother. I have brought you a girl to spin your wool. Apparently, she can spin five skeins a day."

His mother said, "Ah, well, my girl, I'm thrilled. We shall put you in the room behind the castle so as not to disturb you."

They got the spindle ready and the five lumps of wool to spin. They gave her her tea, and her supper, and her bed, and they left her there.

Now once she was alone, she began to cry, as she did not know how to spin. She tried to place the spindle correctly for spinning, but she could not manage it. Then she heard someone scratching at the window pane. She went up to the window and saw a little devil. Now it didn't say what this little devil looked like. It was one of those little devils of those times!

The little devil said to her, "I'll spin for you, I will." Then she said, "You know how to spin!" He could not talk very well. He said to her, "You'll have to guess my name, and then I'll weave the lot. When I bring you the wool in the evening, you will have to guess my name, or else if you have not guessed my name on the last night, I'll take you off to the woods."

She had eight days in which to spin that wool, and every evening the little devil would appear with his five spindles all spun, and well spun at that. Then he would say, "What's my name?" The girl had nothing else to do all day but find a name for him. She would say, "Tonight I'm going to say François." When he handed her the wool through the window he would say, "What's my name?"

"François."

"No, no, no. I am going to catch you and carry you off to the woods."

The week went by like this. For five days, every evening she would say a name like that—"Auguste"—Now on the sixth evening the young man came up to bring food to the girl. He said to her, "I went for a walk in the woods. Guess what I saw there."

"I don't know."

"I saw a little devil spinning there. He spun and spun saying:

> You'll never know my name.
> I'm called Mimi Pinson, Mimi Pinson.

Then the girl, who was very surprised, said to him, "What did you say, Sir?"

"Yes, yes. I saw a little devil spinning and singing:

> You'll never know my name.
> I'm called Mimi Pinson, Mimi Pinson.

And so she began trying out "Mimi Pinson" so that she would remember it clearly when the little devil came and asked her for it.

There was another evening, when she was going to use another name, Robert. So there you are. At last the final evening

was at hand, and the little devil entered the house through a
window instead of scratching on the window pane. He gave her
the remaining wool, saying, "What's my name?"

"Mimi Pinson."

He gave an awful groan and fled into the forest. Well, since
then the mother was thrilled with the gorgeous wool in the
end, the son married the daughter, and as for me, they left me
here.

Part XIV
Pyrenees

• THERE ONCE WAS a charcoal burner up in the mountains. One day during the winter, when snow was falling and it was very cold, he had made a good fire. During the night he heard someone knocking at the door—bang, bang, bang. The charcoal burner did not want to open the door. He asked, "Who's knocking? I am not opening for anyone." It was a bear knocking.

"Open the door for me, I beg you. I'm cold and shivering. I want to warm my paw."

"Who are you?" asked the charcoal burner.

"The bear."

"But, my poor friend, if I let you in, you would eat me up."

"No, I wouldn't eat you. Please let me in." He let him in. The bear lay down near the fire. He was cold and he dozed off. After a while someone knocked at the door with a stick— Bang, bang.

"Who is there?" said the charcoal burner.

"It's me, the wolf. I see you've made a fire. If you want me to get warm, please let me in."

"No, I won't let you in. You would eat me."

"No, I won't eat you. Let me in, I beg you, for I am shivering with cold," said the wolf.

In the end he let him in. When he was inside, he lay down next to the bear by the fire and there he lay dozing in the warmth.

After a while there was a knock at the door.

"Who is there?" said the charcoal burner.

"Me," answered the fox. "I am the fox, and I would like to get warm."

The charcoal burner answered, "No, you would eat me up."

"Of course not. I wouldn't eat you up." So then the charcoal burner let her in. She settled by the fire and she dozed off next to the wolf and the bear. There were all very happy. A few minutes later someone was knocking at the door again—Bang, bang. It was the hare. "Open the door! I'm so cold!"

The charcoal burner asked, "Who's there?"

"It's the hare."

"You would eat me up," said the charcoal burner jokingly.

"No, I wouldn't eat you up. Let me in." So the hare came in and settled by the fire to get warm. Then the charcoal burner saw that they were all sleeping there because the fire was giving a good blaze. After a while they all woke up and said to him, "As you let us get warm, let's all have a good meal together."

"I know where there is a young calf on a farm. I'll go and fetch it," said the bear.

The wolf said, "I know of a fine, fat little lamb. We'll go and get it."

"And I," said the fox, "I know of a lovely pair of fowl. They are plump and juicy. I'll go and get them."

"And I know of a fine cabbage with a big heart," said the hare. "I'll go and get it." So they all went off at the same time. Very soon the bear was back carrying the calf. He had killed it, and now he put it down there on the floor of the shack and warmed himself.

Soon after, the wolf arrived carrying a fine lamb. He put it down and warmed himself.

Shortly after this the fox arrived. He was carrying a pair of chickens. He put them down and did as the bear and the wolf had done. He warmed himself.

Very soon the hare arrived. He carried a gorgeous cabbage with a big round heart. He put it on the ground and he, the hare, warmed himself, too.

When the charcoal burner saw that all these animals were falling asleep because they were tired out and cold, he thought to himself, "If I killed the bear, the wolf, the fox, and the hare, I could have a feast. I would have the calf, the lamb, the chickens, and the cabbage." So in a flash he took a great club—really a big hammer—and he put it in the fire to make it red hot. When the tip was red hot, he gave the bear a blow on the head with it, and the bear fell to the floor half dead. He gave another fast blow to the wolf. He was in a hurry. The wolf fell to the ground like the bear. He could not stand up. Then he put the tip of the hammer up the fox's arse and he gave the hare a blow on the head which killed him. When the hare was dead, he opened the door, and the bear, the wolf, and the fox went out. They could not walk very well, but nevertheless they made their way out, and as he fled the bear was groaning. "Aï, aï, aï! Help! He gave me a blow on the head which is making me go dingdong."

The wolf was saying, "Help me, too! He gave me a blow on the back and the head which is making me go dingdong."

"And I," said the fox. "He put the tip of the red hot iron up my arse. It will never be the same again."

Would you believe it? The charcoal burner had the calf, the fine lamb, a couple of chickens, the hare, and the cabbage, and so he had enough to eat the whole year long.

And so, tric-trac, my tale is at an end. [*Et tric-trac, Moun counte es acabat.*]

.65. *The Three Deserters*

• ONCE UPON A TIME in a village there was a family who got their living from the soil. They were father and mother and three small boys.

After some time, the father decided to leave, as he could not even support his family by his hard work. One fine day they all left together in the direction of Paris. After a long journey they reached Paris, where they had a great deal of trouble finding shelter. At last, after having looked for work just about everywhere, they ended up by tagging onto a family of rag-and-bone men. Two years later the wife died, and he remained a widower with his three boys, who were now much older.

The eldest, François, was eighteen years old. The other, Jean, was sixteen, and the youngest, Paul, was fourteen. The job of rag-and-bone man did not appeal to them very much. So the eldest said, "Father, I would like to join up." His father ended up by consenting, and he enrolled with the Twenty-fourth Colonial Regiment, which was at Perpignan. At the end of six months, he was made a corporal. At the end of a year, he became a sergeant. With his sergeant's pay he was able to send some money to his father. At the end of two years, Jean was eighteen, and he asked his father whether he, too, could join up. By golly! The father didn't really want it, but in the end he agreed to his going. So then he enrolled in his brother's regiment. He left to join the Twenty-fourth Colonials. He was made a corporal. Meanwhile, the eldest had been made quartermaster sergeant.

After another two years Paul, the youngest, wished to join up. His father would have liked to keep him. He saw himself growing old alone. He did not want to give his consent, but in the end he let him go. Paul chose his brothers' regiment, the Twenty-fourth Colonials, and after six months he was made a corporal. Meanwhile, his elder brother was made sergeant major. His brother Jean became a sergeant, and he, by golly, became a corporal! When they received their pay they sent some money to their father every month. Thinking himself wealthy, he gave up the job of rag-and-bone man and made the most of being a small stockholder.

By the time two years were up, the eldest began gambling and having a wild time. He got himself into bad company, and it brought out the bad side of his nature. He started to gamble, and one evening he gambled away all the money he was supposed to pay his whole company. When he got home, he found he was in trouble. He tried to borrow money from his friends. No one was ready to lend him any. He wanted to kill himself, but he thought, "What are your brothers going to say?"

So he went and found his brothers, and he told them what had happened to him. His brothers saw that it would be wrong of him to commit suicide. They said that it would be much better to become a deserter. So at dusk on the following night they left the barracks and set off dressed as soldiers. They walked all night, and at daybreak they hid in a wood.

The next morning the captain of their company wondered what had happened to them. He did not yet report them as deserters. This allowed them to make good their escape. Only on the third day did the captain report them as deserters. Meanwhile, the three brothers had gone quite a long way, keeping hidden as much as possible. The eldest was surviving well, but the second one was hungry, and the shoes of the third one were hurting him so much that he could hardly walk. At last, by nightfall, they reached a huge castle, and they said, "Let's knock."

They knocked on the door, but no one answered. There was no light, nothing at all. They skirted the castle grounds and went a little farther on, when they saw a small cottage, where there was a light. They knocked there, and a nice old woman came and opened the door to them. When she saw that three soldiers had come her way, she was not afraid, and she asked them what they wanted. The eldest said: "Dear lady, we are three soldiers from the French army. We went astray during maneuvers, and we would like to ask you whether we could spend the night here tonight."

The good woman answered, "Come in, you fine soldiers."

And the good woman made them come in and said to them, "My husband will be here soon. He is gamekeeper for the castle."

After a while the gamekeeper came in, and when he saw the three soldiers, he asked them to join him at table and share their meal. As they were eating, the sergeant major said to them, "We knocked on the door of the castle, but no one answered us." Then he said to them, "You see! One is received far better by the poor than by the rich!"

But the gamekeeper answered, "Let me put you right, men. The reason why no one answered at the castle is that it is haunted and nobody can live there."

Then the sergeant major said to him, "But hasn't anyone been in to see what's going on?"

"There have been some who have tried, but they were so frightened that no one could get anything out of them."

"Well," said the sergeant major after having talked to his brothers, "if you will accept our help, we shall keep guard at the castle."

His two brothers answered, "Yes," and the old people, too. They decided to begin their watch on the castle that very night. A cold meal was prepared for them with a few bottles of good wine, and they were given a long key to the front door of the castle. With this and a packet of candles, the three of them left after having wished the old folk good night.

They left for the castle. They opened it and locked it again.

They lit a candle and had a look at some of the inside and, after having started a good fire in the kitchen hearth, they sat down again at the table to eat their cold meal. After a couple of drinks, they began to talk. The eldest said, "You think this castle is haunted! I don't believe it."

"Oh, well, perhaps," said the others, "perhaps."

"Never mind."

"Ah, well," said the eldest, "it is not worth all three of us staying up. I shall be the first to keep watch. Each of you two can go into a room and go to bed."

The two brothers went to bed comfortably. Meanwhile, the sergeant major filled his pipe, and while he waited he took the odd swig from the bottle. At about midnight a great storm gathered. The wind blew and someone knocked at the window. He asked, "Who is there?"

The answer came, "You are bragging, you poor deserter from the French army. You want to stop me coming in. You are a poor good-for-nothing without a penny to your name. If you let me in, I'll make you rich. I shall give you a purse in which you will always find one hundred francs wherever you are and whenever you like."

He said, "Come on. Give me the purse so that I can try it."

"No. Let me in."

"No, no, no. Give me the purse, then we shall see."

So the Devil slipped the purse through the window. It was the Devil himself! The sergeant major climbed onto the table. He opened the purse and spilled out the contents. A hundred francs, another, and another came pouring out. There was a pile of hundred-franc notes, and more one hundred franc notes. He was rich! He said to the Devil, "I accept." And he opened the window. The Devil came into the castle. After a while he again heard a loud noise and then nothing more. He fell asleep on the table until the following morning.

At daybreak his two brothers came and found him in the kitchen. After having said good morning to each other, they asked him, "Well what happened? Did you see anything? Did you hear anything?"

"No, nothing. I went to sleep. They're just tall stories. There is nothing."

They closed up the castle. All three went off again to the little cottage, where the old people were waiting for them wreathed in smiles. They gave them coffee and asked them what had happened. They said that they had gone to bed and that the eldest had seen nothing. The old folk said to them, "Would you mind keeping watch one more night?"

They accepted, and that evening they left for the castle again. That evening it was the second one's turn. The sergeant, Jean, was to keep watch. The other two brothers went to bed. Like the other one, he had a swig or two as he waited by the table keeping watch. At midnight torrential rain hit the window panes of the castle, and he heard a tapping on the pane. He was a little afraid. He asked: "Who is it? Be careful. Don't move, otherwise I shall shoot through the pane and do you in."

The answer came, "Poor deserter from the French army, you are dying of hunger and you make believe you are strong. I want to reward you. If you let me in, I'll give you a magic napkin which has the power to lay the table. You've only got to say 'Napkin lay the table!' and the table is laid. The best wines and the most delicious dishes appear on the table."

"Let's see. Give me the napkin."

"No. First let me come in."

"No, no. Give it to me. Then I'll think about it."

So the Devil passed the napkin to him through the window. He said, "Napkin, lay one hundred places at this table!" In a flash the table was laid for a hundred.

The sergeant said, "All right. I'll let you in. I'm keeping the napkin."

The Devil came in. He went all round the castle and disappeared with a bang. After having kept watch all night, the sergeant fell asleep. The next morning his two brothers came to find him, and after wishing each other good morning they asked him what had happened.

"Oh, nothing at all. I saw nothing. I heard nothing. Those were just stories. It is quite possible to live in the castle."

They went back to the little cottage, and the old folk asked them to keep watch a third night. They accepted once again. On the third night they settled once more in the castle, and it was the youngest, Paul, the corporal, who took the watch. His brothers went to bed after a hearty meal, and he began his watch. At midnight a hurricane blew up and snowflakes fell on the window panes of the castle.

"Well, well! So you are the unlucky one!"

Paul said, "Who is it?"

"You also make out that you are strong, you poor deserter from the French army. You can no longer walk, but still you want to confront me."

"Go back, or I shall bust your gut with my bayonet."

So then the Devil said to him, "You are a strong man. Calm down. Look, as a reward for letting me in, I will give you a magic coat which has the power to carry you wherever you like."

"Let me see. Hand it to me."

The Devil handed him the coat through the window. He put it over the shoulders and said. "Coat, make me go round the room!" He began whirling around, and in the twinkling of an eye he had been round the room over a hundred times.

"Well, well," said he, "that's not bad."

"So, will you let me in?"

He said to him, "No."

"And why not?"

"I wish to know what you are up to in the castle. I have the coat and I'm going to keep it."

"And suppose I don't tell you?"

"You shall not come in. I'll bust your gut!"

"Well, I'll tell you. In the castle cellar where it says number nine there is a treasure hidden inside. It is my job to look after it. That is why every night I come and make sure nothing has been tampered with. This money does not belong to me. It will not become the castle owner's property until the treasure has been blessed, and once it is blessed, then they will be able to make good use of it. I shall not came back any more then, and the castle will be a pleasant place to live in."

"Is that all?"

He said, "That's all."

"All right then. Come in."

The Devil did his work and went away. The next morning the

brothers met once more, and they wished each other good morning and the youngest was asked whether he had seen anything. He said to them, "No. I neither saw nor heard anything at all. The castle can be lived in."

So they went back to the old folk. They told them, "The castle can be lived in. We have seen nothing there."

The old fellow said to them, "I can no longer keep you here. I thank you."

And so they left. As they reached a crossroads, the sergeant major said, "As we are three deserters and they are looking for us, it would be better if we separated. Each one must find his own way to Paris, where we shall meet at our father's house."

They said, "Yes," and they separated. After a day's walking, the youngest came back to the castle. He had put his coat over his shoulders and said to it, "Coat, take me back to the castle which I have left." Sure enough he landed like a tornado in the courtyard of the castle. He folded his coat and went to the cottage where the old folk lived. He knocked on the door, and the old folk opened it. They had thought the lad knew something, but had seen that no one would let on. Then Paul told them what had happened between them and the Devil. He explained the whole thing to them.

At once they sent for the owner of the castle, who arrived by coach and went to find the treasure and bless it. Then the owner shared it with everybody. He gave it as a gift to the poor. He wanted Paul to stay in the castle, but Paul would have none of it and he went away. When he was at some distance from the castle, he put his coat back over his shoulders and said to it, "Coat, take me to Paris!"

That very evening he was in Paris. He came back to the place where his father lived. The latter, as he had no longer received any money from his sons, had been forced to become a rag-and-bone man again. He had left the place, and Paul did not find him. Paul went looking for a job, and he stayed in Paris. His brothers, by golly, also came to town.

This was at the time of Louis Philippe, and the King announced publicly that he wished his daughter to marry the richest man in the world. Well then, by golly, plenty of suitors showed up. François, too, came forward with his magic purse as the richest man in the world. He was asked for his credentials and he said, "My credentials are this purse."

"What do you mean, this purse?" They teased him.

"Well, have you a big room?" he said. "Now, I'll fill it with hundred-franc notes." He took his purse and opened it. He began emptying it out. One hundred francs and more and more and more. Still they came, those hundred-franc notes. When he saw this, the King said, "Well, yes. He is the richest man in the world. He always has one hundred francs in his purse."

So he dismissed everybody, as he had now found the richest man in the world. He introduced him to his daughter. "Here you are, Daughter. He is the rightest man in the world."

When she saw him, she made a face and whispered in her father's ear, "I don't like him."

Then the King answered, "Well, you know what you have to do."

"All right."

She summoned him and said: "Ah, how d'you do, Sir, how d'you do. It seems that you are the richest man in the world because of the magic powers of your purse. Well, while we wait to get married, you shall stay at the castle. You shall take a room, and, as proof of your friendship, you can in the meantime leave me your purse." By golly, the unsuspecting François handed it over to her. She called a servant and said: "Take this gentleman to room number twelve. See that he has everything he requires." He was led to his bachelor's room, and, after having spent a whole day in the castle, he went to bed. At one o'clock in the morning a spring was released, and he found himself flung into a drainage ditch. Having run along a sewer for most of the night, he then found himself at the opening, where there was an old fellow who pulled him by the shirt tail. It was his father. He said to him, "Well, what sort of place are you working in now!" He took the lad back to his apartment, and he went back to working as a rag-and-bone man for his father.

Well, some time after all this had happened, the King proclaimed once more that he wished to marry his daughter to the man who was the best cook. Having the magic napkin, Jean

came forward as the man who was the best cook. He was
tested by being asked for his credentials.

"My credentials," he said, "here they are—this napkin."

"What do you mean, this napkin?"

"With the help of this napkin I can be responsible for laying
the table for two hundred or one thousand people, as you wish."

"Well," said the King. "Here is a dining room where one
thousand places may be laid. Get to work."

Jean took his napkin and said to it, "Lay the table for a thousand people. Do not forget a thing." To the King's great aston-
ishment, all this was done like magic. The King said, "All right,
young man. You are the finest cook in the world." He said to
the others, "You may go. Here is the finest cook in the world."
He said to his daughter, "There you are. Let me present you with
the finest cook in the world." She made a face and whispered
in his ear, "I don't like him." Her father said to her, "You know
what you have to do now."

She played the same trick on this man as she had played on
the other one. She asked him for the napkin, and at one o'clock
in the morning he found himself in the sewer. Once again his
father fished him out of the opening of the sewer. He said to
him, "But you all work in the same place!" He again worked for
his father as a rag-and-bone man.

After some time the King proclaimed that he wished to marry
his daughter to the best horseman in the world. Then the youngest Paul came forward as the best horseman in the world. And,
by golly, he bought a horse which was an old nag. The other
competitors started laughing when they saw him. He kept mum,
by golly! When they gave the starting signal, he put the cloak on
his shoulders and said to it, "Cloak take us on this horse to the
end of the field and back as fast as possible—flat out!"

As quick as a flash, the horse set off and he came back at a
terrific speed. The others could not get over it. In fact, by
golly, he became the best horseman in the world. So much so
that an Englishman wanted to buy the horse from him, and he
sold it to him at a fantastic price.

"I am going to win all the races in England!"

"Yes, you will win them."

When he witnessed this, the King said to his daughter, "That is the best horseman in the world." The King suspected something. "As you are to marry him, here he is."

She whispered to him, "I don't like him."

"Well, then, come to some arrangement with him." So she took him to the castle. In her room she said to him, "Why did you sell your horse?"

He said, "My horse had nothing to do with it. It wasn't the horse who won the race!"

"I should have liked to keep an animal like that."

"Oh, no! That had nothing to do with it. What won the race was the cloak."

"How?"

"You'll see. Open your window." Then he said, "Come here next to me."

They stood at the sill like this. He put his cloak over his shoulders, and then he placed a fold of his cloak over the shoulders of the Princess. At the same time he said to the cloak, "Cloak, take us to the most secluded island in the world!"

Well, the cloak actually took them to such an island. They stayed there. Night fell and they lay down one next to the other. He put the cloak under his head so that she could not steal it from him. The next morning they went all over the island. They found some apple trees and they picked apples from them and bit into them. As soon as they had eaten some apple, their noses grew longer, and in the end they could reach anywhere with their noses. They reached into all the streams all over the place.

When night fell, they again lay down and he put the cloak under his head. Only the Princess stayed awake and for so long that he fell asleep, and she stole the cloak from him. Then she put it on and said to it, "Take me once again to my father's castle in Paris."

The next morning she was back in the royal castle. Her father recognized her as soon as he saw her, but she had a nose which reached all over the place. She told him what had happened.

The next day, when Paul woke up, he found himself alone and with an elongated nose. Well, by golly, he went over the island, and as he was doing this, he found a pear tree. His hunger made him taste the pears. As he began eating one, his nose shrank, and finally fell off. So then he said to himself, "This is a cure. The apples make one's nose grow, and the pears make it drop off. So be it!"

He brought in a store of apples and pears. He went along the shore and was rescued as a castaway by a ship. He landed in France again with the apples and pears and came back to Paris.

The King called for the most famous doctors in the world to come and cure his daughter. Then Paul showed up as an American doctor. He made some apple ointment and pear ointment smartly presented in labeled pots. He arrived at the castle disguised as a doctor. He said to the King, "I wish to cure your daughter."

"Good! But where are your medicines?"

"I have them here."

"You must be just another quack!" But he brought him to his daughter, who did not recognize him. He said to her, "Now I can see that what ails you is serious. You must have done a few wicked deeds during your life. If you don't tell me about them, I don't know whether I shall be able to cure you."

The girl said to him, "Yes. My father wished me to marry the richest man in the world. He had a purse, and I stole it from him."

"Is that all?"

"Yes. That's all."

"Right! Well you must give it back to me." She gave it back to him. He said to her, "Try this ointment." It was the apple one, and her nose grew longer still. So then he said to her, "You see you must have done something else which was bad."

"Well, yes. In the same way my father wished me to marry the best cook in the world. He had a magic napkin. I stole it from him."

"You must give it back to me. We shall try." He took the purse and the napkin and put them in his pocket. Again he tried the apple ointment. Her nose grew even longer. So then he said to her, "You must have done some other wicked deed."

She said to him, "Yes. Some time ago my father wished me to marry the best horseman in the world. He had a cloak, and after the adventure which earned for me this long nose, I stole it from him."

"You must give it back to me." She gave it back to him. Then he said to her, "Is that all?"

"Yes."

"Well, we'll try the experiment again."

He rubbed her nose with pear ointment, and her nose grew smaller again. He gave her a little more to eat, and it grew still smaller. Then he made her eat some of the apple paste and rubbed her with it. Again her nose grew so long that she could not turn round in the room any more. She began to cry. He left her just like that, promising her he would come back.

The King, who was waiting to hear whether he had cured her, received this answer, "I'll come back and see her, but I am not certain that I can cure her."

He was able to leave the castle, and the King's daughter kept her long nose. He never went back there. Finally, after a long search, he found his father and two brothers again. He gave back to them what was theirs, and the two brothers were very surprised. However, he explained everything that had happened. As for him, he came back to the magic castle. The owner greeted him with open arms. He had a young daughter, and Paul married her. They had a magnificent wedding celebration, which his father and his brothers attended. They lived happily for a long time and had many children, who brought him much happiness.

As for the King's daughter, she died, having kept her long nose all her life.

Cric-crac. My tale is at an end.

.66. *The Laurel Flower*

• THERE WAS ONCE a father who had three sons. He said to the eldest, "If you bring me the laurel flower, you shall be my heir." His mother did not want to let him go. "You will not find it! You will not find it!" She was very sad to have to let him go. Her son wanted to leave in spite of her. So his mother packed a game bag for him and gave him bread, wine, and an omelet. He picked up his walking stick and left. He went far, far away from home right into a large forest to go and look for the laurel flower.

When he was in the forest, he was walking along a little path when he felt very tired and he had a rest there. While he was eating, a lady came along and this lady asked him for a little bread, for she was hungry.

He said to her, "No, no, I don't want to give you any. I have just enough for myself."

The Holy Virgin did not reveal herself. She said to him, "What are you doing there, my lad?"

The lad answered, "My father has told me that if I bring him the laurel flower he will make me his heir, and I cannot find it anywhere."

He had looked for it all over the forest. She thought to herself: "You shall not find the laurel flower. You are a bad boy."

He started to go home, as he had looked everywhere without finding it. There his father said to him, "Did you find the laurel flower?"

"No, I have not found it."

The younger brother said, "Father, I want to go. I believe I shall find it!"

He left. He found the lady, just as the first had done, and he would not give her any bread, either, and he, too, did not find the laurel flower. He went home and said to his father, "I looked all over the forest for it, and I have not found it!"

So then the third and youngest brother said to his father and mother, "I want to go and find the laurel flower."

His mother said to him, "Don't go, child. You see your brothers have not found it, and you won't either."

However, the youngest insisted. "Mother, do let me go. I want to go and find it. Let me go."

So she packed a game bag for him, as she had done for his brothers. She put in bread, wine, and sausage. When he found himself in the forest he came across a fountain, and he sat down next to the fountain to eat his snack, as he was tired out. He ate the lunch he had brought with him. Then a lady appeared before him, and she came and stood next to him. This lady asked him, "What are you doing there, child?"

He said to her, "I have come to get the laurel flower because my father has told me that if I brought it back, I would become his heir."

She said to him, "Won't you give me a piece of bread, child, as I am so hungry?"

The youngest answered, "Yes, Madam. If there is enough for one, there is enough for two."

The youngster gave her some bread and sausage.

"Here you are, Madam."

She answered, "Thank you, my child. I can see that you are very polite and good and you think well of the poor. Thank you, my child."

She did not take any.

"I am the Holy Virgin. You are kinder than your brothers. I asked them for bread, and they did not give me anything. As you are so kind, I shall show you the laurel flower. Look at that flower at the foot of that rock next to the fountain. Take a sprig of that."

The boy went and cut a sprig of it, and he went home singing this song:

> Tran la la,
> Tran la la.
> I've found the laurel flower,
> I shall be the heir.

As he came nearer to his home, he was going down hill. His brothers heard him singing:

> Tran la la,
> Tran la la.
> I've found the laurel flower,
> I shall be the heir.

They said to themselves, "He's carrying the laurel flower. He will be the heir, and we will have to leave home!" The two brothers then said, "We must go and kill him!" They met him later in a meadow. They went up to him, and they killed him and they buried him under a heap of stones. Then they came home with the laurel flower.

Later, one fine day, there was a shepherd looking after the sheep. He went up to the pile of stones and noticed an instrument like a trumpet or something like a bone. They said that the Holy Virgin had had something to do with this. He took this flute or this trumpet and put it to his lips, and the trumpet began saying:

> Oh, shepherd,
> Oh, dear shepherd,
> It is not you who killed me
> To get the laurel flower.

Then this shepherd came down to the village, and he made the trumpet sing out wherever he went. Good Lord, everyone was anxious to hear this man! There was a merchant in the village who said to him, "Do you want to sell the trumpet, Sir?"

He answered, "No, I don't want to sell it. I want to keep it for myself."

The other insisted. "Do sell it to me. Sell it to me!"

He wanted it, so he said to the shepherd, "I'll give you six hundred francs for it." Six hundred francs was worth a fortune in those days, so the shepherd sold it to him. The merchant put the trumpet to his lips and the trumpet said to him:

> Oh, merchant,
> Good merchant,
> It is not you who killed me
> To get the laurel flower.

The merchant went from village to village, always playing the trumpet. It always said the same thing, "Oh, merchant . . ."

So imagine what happened. This merchant went to the youngster's village. He began playing the trumpet, and it was still saying, "Oh, merchant . . ." So then this boy's father and mother and sister heard this and said to themselves, "What is the meaning of this?" They said to the merchant, "Would you by any chance like to sell us that trumpet?"

"Oh, no, Sir."

The father and mother said to him: "You must sell it to us! You must sell it to us!" They went on, "How much do you want for it?"

He said to them, "I want two thousand francs." He gave them the trumpet. Once the sale was over, the father put the instrument to his lips, and the trumpet began to sing:

> Oh, father,
> Good father,
> It is not you who killed me
> To get the laurel flower.

Good Lord! When the mother heard this, she said to him, "Lend me the trumpet." She put it to her lips, and the trumpet began to sing:

> Oh, mother,
> Good mother,
> It is not you who killed me
> To get the laurel flower.

Well, you should have seen the father and mother when they heard this.

"What is the meaning of this? What does it mean?"

Then the sister said, "Mother, hand the trumpet to me."

She put it to her lips and the trumpet began to sing:

> Oh, sister,
> Good sister,
> It is not you who killed me
> To get the laurel flower.

That trumpet said the same thing over and over again. So then the brothers who had killed him said to their sister, "Lend us the trumpet."

("This is it. Now we have it," warned the teller of this tale.)

One of the brothers put the trumpet to his lips, and it began to sing with a dark and angry voice:

> Oh, brother,
> Wicked brother,
> Yes, it was you who killed me
> To get the laurel flower.

The same thing. Always the same thing. Then the other brother said to him, "Let's see what happens if you lend it to me."

It sang again even more angrily:

> Oh, brother,
> Wicked brother,
> Yes, it was you who killed me
> To get the laurel flower.

Imagine the father and mother's reaction when they heard that! They said to them, "It is you who killed your brother! It is you who killed him! Scoundrels!"

The father said to them: "So that's the way you thought you would become the heir?" He got hold of one of them and beat him up. He hit him in the face and threw him down the stairs, and he died. He did the same to the other one. And now it's over.

Part XV
Corsica

·67· The Legend of the Oxen's Pass

• At the foot of the Rinuccia at the edge of Lake Nino is the Oxen's Pass, which is also called Forge Pass. Now this is why it bears that name.

One day the Devil was plowing near the pass with a wooden plow drawn by a pair of oxen like the ones still seen around here sometimes. At one point the Devil wanted to adjust the blade of the plow with a hammer, and he gave his fingers a blow with it. Enraged, he flung the hammer through the mountain we now call Cabu Tafonatu; that is to say, Pierced Peak. After having gone through the mountain, the hammer fell on the sands of Calvi beach.

Since then, too, they show you the furrows drawn by the Devil. In the direction of Rinuccia you can see them engraved in the stone. As for the oxen, two enormous stones of their shape can be seen silhouetted in the distance. From afar it looks like a mountain plowed with long lines.

As for the Devil, if he was turned into stone like the oxen, he was not to remain visible! On the other hand, one can still see the floor of the forge where he mended his tools. There are pieces that look like lumps of coal in that place. So they sometimes call that Forge Pass, and sometimes the Oxen's Pass.

·68· The Fox and The Blackbird

• One fine morning a blackbird sang cheerily from her perch on the branch of a tree. A fox happened to go by and, speaking to the blackbird, he asked her why she felt so happy.

"What makes you so happy, friend blackbird?"

This one answered, "I am so happy, friend fox, because I had three young last night."

"May I see them?" added friend fox.

"Oh, no," said the bird, "you are quite capable of eating them."

"I swear to you I will not touch them."

Trusting the fox's oath, the blackbird showed him her nestful.

Friend fox looked at the little birds and said to himself, "That could make a good mouthful."

The first time the blackbird flew away, he made the most of it. He ate them up. When the blackbird came back to its nest with a bit of food it had gone to get, it found the nest empty. A few days later a dog went by and, seeing the blackbird crying, asked her what had happened, and the blackbird told him of her misfortunes. Friend dog promised to avenge her. "To accomplish this," he said, "this is what you must do. You have noticed that every morning the shepherds go along this path carrying cheeses. They take them to the caves for them to dry out there. Among these shepherds there is a boy you can entertain somewhat. Place yourself in his path and pretend to limp. Then he will put down his cheese-draining board and try and catch you. Meanwhile, I'll eat his cheese, and then I shall pretend to be dead in the bushes. When friend fox goes by once more, you will sing like last time. When he asks you why you are singing, you will say to him, " 'The dog who has eaten my young has been killed by a shepherd because he had eaten his cheese.' "

And the fox actually did go by once again, and, seeing the blackbird singing, he said to her, "Friend blackbird, have you had more young to be as happy as that?"

"No, friend fox, but the dog who ate my young has been killed by a shepherd whose cheese he had eaten."

"Serves him right!" said the fox. "If that is true, I knew the varment. He was a greedy one. I wonder where he is now. I would go and spit in his face."

"He is lying in the bushes," the blackbird said, and she showed him the path.

The dog was there with his four feet sticking up. The fox stood over him to carry out his threat, but he did not have time to spit in the dog's face. The latter grabbed him by the throat and killed him.

So in this way the blackbird found herself avenged.

·69· *The Shepherd and the Snake*

• ONCE THERE WAS a shepherd who took his sheep to graze in the meadows. On his way there he came across a fire. A little farther on, he suddenly heard a whistle, and he tried to find out where it came from. He saw a snake. It was a large one, and it was burning. So what did the shepherd do then? He pulled the snake out of the fire.

When the snake was out of the fire, he said to the shepherd, "I am a magician's son. Come and see my father. My father will be pleased that you have saved my life, and he will reward you generously."

"But I must look after my sheep."

"Don't worry about your sheep. Let's go to my father's. He will offer you a pile of gold, and a pile of silver, and a little box of notes. Don't take them; they would all turn into coal. Then be careful and answer him in this way, 'If you want to reward me, I wish to get to know the language of the animals.'"

The two took to the road. They reached the magician, and his son explained to him, "There was a fire, and this shepherd pulled me out of it. You must reward him, for he saved my life."

"What's that? This shepherd saved my son's life?" The magician showed him a room where there was a heap of gold, a heap of silver, and a heap of small change.

"Oh, no," said the shepherd, "I don't want that."

"What do I do now? Don't you want a reward?"

"If you want to give me a reward, then teach me the language of the animals."

The magician said to him, "All right, I'll teach it to you, but if you give away the secret, you are as good as dead."

"Right! I'll not talk about it."

And so he went off. The shepherd left. Goodbye! Goodbye! He went to join his sheep and ran far, far away. At last he lay down under a tree. A crow happened by who said as he turned to the shepherd, "You sleep now, but if you knew what treasure lies buried here under this chestnut tree you wouldn't sleep."

No sooner had he said this than the shepherd rose. He left his ewes to rest with their lambs and went home. Then he left home once again taking a pickax with him. He went back to the chestnut tree pointed out by the crow.

He started using the pickax there, and little by little he picked up the gold. Out of caution, he took the gold home only a little at a time. In this way he became rich, leading all the while his shepherd's life and looking after his ewes every day. He sold his animals and he set himself up as "the Frenchman." In the end, his wife grew astonished by all this wealth and asked him, "How is it that you have all this money?"

"Well, I earn it by keeping my ewes!"

"They couldn't bring you in all that money. Come on, you've got a secret."

"Well, I've worked hard, so I have sold my ewes."

"That isn't true. If you don't tell me where you got this gold, I shan't give you a moment's peace."

His wife never let him be after that. She grew more and more anxious as the days wore on, and she showered him with questions. Finally, the shepherd said to her, "If you want to know the secret, get my coffin ready, for if I tell you, I'm as good as dead."

Right then the shepherd heard the cock in the barnyard scuttling about among the hens saying, "Cock-a-doodle-do! Cock-a-doodle-do!" So then the dog said to the cock, "Our master, the shepherd, is about to die and you sing, rooster?"

"Our master need only do as I do. Look how many wives I have, and they have given themselves up to me."

So the man understood the lesson. He said to himself, "This rooster has given me an example. I've only to do the same thing."

And to his wife he said, "So you want to know. Well, go and fetch my whip."

The shepherd suddenly took his whip made of bull's tendons and began beating his wife. The blows showered down. He hit her as hard as he could. "Well, now do you want to know?"

"No. Now I have had enough."

They walked together up to the fork and nothing more was said.

> *Fola foletta*   Fable, little fable,
> *Dide la vostra*   You tell yours;
> *A mea è detta.*   Mine is told.

·70· *The Child Promised to the Devil*

• ONCE UPON A TIME there were a husband and a wife. They had already been married ten years, but they had no children. The husband was upset because his wife gave him no family. Every day when he went home everything was set on the table, but there was no child at the table.

So, weary of seeing her husband's unhappiness, the wife would go off alone and, despairing, prayed to the Lord, saying, "Send me a son to satisfy my husband."

One fine day the Devil appeared. He was smartly dressed in a suit and a bowler hat, with a cane in his hand. He said to the wife, "What are you requesting?"

The wife answered, "Send me a son to satisfy my husband."

"If you want a son to satisfy your husband, promise to give me your son's soul when he is eighteen years old. You will be expecting a child, and in nine months' time you shall give birth to him."

The woman began her pregnancy. She said to her husband, "Oh, if only you knew, husband! You would be so happy!"

He said, "Well, what is all this about?"

"I've something to tell you. I am pregnant, and in nine months' time I shall give birth to a boy."

Nine months later a son was born. He was a fine boy. Every day the father would come home all happy because his son was there, and his wife was happy, too. They laughed to have him there with them. When the child was four or five, he began to go to school. When he was ten, he was already very learned, and everybody was pleased with him. When he was seventeen, the boy noticed that his mother's eyes would fill with tears as she looked at him, and then she would start crying. He asked her, "Until now you have shown me that you are proud of me, and I am proud of you. Now you are crying. Why?"

"It is because I am so happy to see you so handsome and learned," said his mother.

The next day, however, his mother began crying again, and the following day there were more tears. So, then, the boy could stand it no longer. As he could get no other answer from her, he ended up by saying to himself, "They are hiding something from me."

He went and found the schoolmaster to explain his parents' attitude.

The schoolmaster said to him, "You are sad. You are not as you were before."

"I've something to tell you. There is something wrong at home. My parents are in tears every day, and I cannot find out why."

The master said, "Well, buy yourself a dagger. Point it at your heart and say to your parents, 'If you do not tell me the reason why you are crying, if you have deceived me, I shall kill myself!' You'll see. Your parents will not deceive you."

The young man took his advice. He went and bought himself a dagger and held it to his chest. Once he was at home and everybody was sitting at table, he began eating, and his parents started to weep because it was nearly the end of the year and he was going to be eighteen years old. The young man said to them, "Why do you deceive me? Let me tell you. I have a dagger and I am going to plunge it into my heart. Yes, if you go on deceiving me, I shall kill myself."

Then the mother said to him, "Don't kill yourself. We shall tell you everything. As you wish to know, this is what happened. Your father complained every day because he had no son. So one day I went out begging God to give me a child, and the Devil appeared before me. Then he said he would send me a son but that he would come and fetch you when you were eighteen years old."

Now when the youth heard that his soul was to be the Devil's, he was not at all pleased. He went back to see his master.

"I took your advice and I have succeeded. I found out some amazing things. Mother and Father told me they had promised the Devil my soul when I reached eighteen years of age."

The master said to him, "You are freed from this agreement, as your parents accepted these conditions as far as your soul is concerned, but not your body, and so you shall go and fight the Devil." Then he added, "Take a large sword and a horse and go before the Devil as soon as you are eighteen years old."

The young man bought himself a large sword and put on his great cape. He mounted his horse and left when he was eighteen. On the morning of the day he reached his eighteenth year he met the Devil. The Devil said to him, "You belong to me."

The young man answered, "No. My mother agreed with you to certain conditions regarding my soul, but you had better know that I am going to fight you."

"How?"

"Let's fight a duel. The one who wins shall have my soul."

So, baring their chests, they flung themselves into the duel one against the other to find out who was to have the youth's soul. The Devil struck, and lost.

Then he said to the youth, "You are free."

The Devil went away in a terrible rage, and the young man went home. There his father and mother were already in mourning. They fell into each others' arms. Then they had a splendid meal, to which the schoolmaster was invited, and henceforth the young man went on with his studies and remained free.

Notes
to the Tales

PART I

LOWER BRITTANY

·1· Yann the Fearless

Type 326, *The Youth Who Wanted to Learn What Fear Is.*

Recorded in 1953 in the course of my research in the Trégor area in Prat (Côtes du Nord) from a sixty-seven-year-old peasant, Veuve L'Héréec.

The name of the hero—*Yann* (John) *heb aon* (without fear)—which has no connection with King John the Fearless, serves also as the title of the folktale type chosen by Paul Delarue for his *Catalogue des Contes Français* (Paris, 1957, p. 293), in which he uses a version found in Nivernais. Very popular among French storytellers, this theme seems to have spread throughout several provinces: Delarue cites sixty-three versions. It also occurs frequently among the French of North America, notably in Canada, in Michigan, and in Missouri. To this list could be added variants recently recorded in Corsica (*Le Neveu du Curé:* cf. my *Contes Corses*, No. 48, p. 116) and in the Lower Marche region (*Richard Sans Peur*).

Even though the first European version of this theme was given by Grimm at the beginning of the nineteenth century, Delarue calls attention to the fact that a direct allusion to it is found in France in the seventeenth century in the *Mémoires* of Roger de Rabutin, which appeared in 1640 (I, 76–77), and in which he writes: "I remember those tales that are told to children, of meals served by strangers, and then of arms, heads, legs, and the other parts of the body falling out of the chimney and forming people who disappeared after having taken a drink." In this passage can be recognized Motif H1411.1 of of Stith Thompson's *Motif-Index*, which is well represented in our version from Lower Brittany. The first two episodes of *Yann Heb Aon*, which end with the release of a soul in torment, relates this version of Type 326A. The final episode of the blackbird enclosed in a loaf of bread—a last attempt to frighten the hero—is also found in the Corsican variant mentioned above.

·2· Old Fench

Type 516, *Faithful John.*

Recorded in the village of Prat (Côtes du Nord) in 1954, from the same informant as the previous tale.

As in many of the tales of Lower Brittany, the hero, *Fench* [Francis], is a Breton (and, in this case, an old servant) who has entered the service of the King of France. When questioned about the nature of the three mysterious figures who gathered at the foot of a tree at night in order to trade secrets, the informant stated that she believed them to be *korrans,* or dwarfs, or *korrigans,* as they are more often called, supernatural beings who enjoy playing tricks on men and who especially enjoy luring them around the fire at night.

The theme is rather widespread in France, where it is associated with several separate motifs, so that there is a great deal of variety among the different versions. It is equally popular in the folklore of the American French, and I have also recorded a version of it in Corsica (*Contes Corses,* p. 277). German and Chilean versions can be found in *Folktales of Germany* and *Folktales of Chile,* other volumes in this series.

The final motif of the child sacrificed by his father in order to bring a faithful friend back to life (cf. Stith Thompson, *Motif-Index,* S268) appeared in the Middle Ages in the epic poem *Amis et Amiles.* Amiles slits the throats of his two sons and uses their blood to heal Amis, who has become a leper (cf. Gédéon Huet, *Le Conte Populaire,* p. 148). In his tale of the *Corbeau,* Basile (*Pentamerone,* Fourth Day, story No. 9) has Millucio kill his twin sons in order to smear their blood over the body of his petrified brother.

·3· Ugly Yann

Type 675, *The Lazy Boy.*

Recorded in 1953 from the same informant as the two previous tales. This old peasant woman—a rival of Marguerite Philippe, from Plouaret, the famous informant of F. M. Luzel for his *Contes Populaires de Basse Bretagne*—knew by heart countless stories handed down to her orally; she told me a good thirty of them during my 1953 and 1954 vacations. Most of the stories in her repertory belong in the category of tales of magic, but they still include fiercely critical or sarcastic touches in the morals of the treated themes.

In this version, the initial motif of the hero doing a superior being a service is missing. In a variant recorded in Upper Brittany, the superior being is a fairy transformed into a snake by a jealous rival; the hero takes pity on her, and is rewarded by having his wishes granted. The motif of the bundle of firewood which becomes a means of transportation because the young man is tired of carrying it on his shoulders, is found in Corsica, associated with Type 851 (cf. my *Contes Corses,* No. 66, *Pedi Untu,* p. 145, discussed p. 320); it can be compared to Motif D441.3.1, "faggots transformed to chargers," which Thompson and Balys discovered in India (cf. Stith Thompson, *Motif-Index*).

This theme does not seem to be widespread in French folklore, since the last edition of Aarne's and Thompson's *The Types of the Folktale* lists only thirteen versions in France and eight among the American French.

·4· *The Tailor*

Type 1640, *The Brave Tailor*.

Recorded in 1953 from an old man in the forest of Loc-Envel (Côtes du Nord), François Thomas, who made wooden shoes and spoons.

This theme first became famous when the Grimm brothers published a version which went back to an old German book published in 1557 by Martinus Montanus of Strasburg. Motifs from Type 1045 (where the hero's mere threat intimidates the ogre) and Type 1060 (characterized by the episode of the "crushed" rock) are also included in the story.

This folktale type, categorized in the series of "Lucky Accidents," is rather popular in French folklore, in France as well as among the francophiles of North America, even though the last edition of the Aarne-Thompson type index does not indicate it. In 1961 I recorded several variants of it among the French of Nova Scotia in which the battle against the unicorn (Aarne-Thompson, Type 1640—III b) plays a prominent role. In our version from Lower Brittany, however, the plot is centered in the series of tricks used by the tailor, whose bluffs get the better of his adversaries, the giants. On the other hand, the episode of the tailor's marriage to the King's daughter is missing here.

Cosquin, in his *Contes Populaires de Lorraine* (II, 95–102), has studied this tale-type in great depth in relation to a variant recorded at Montiers-sur-Saulx, *Le Tailleur et le Géant*.

·5· *The Priest's Pig*

Type 1792, *The Stingy Parson and the Slaughtered Pig*.

Recorded from the same informant as the previous tale, the old shoemaker of Loc-Envel.

The 1961 edition of the Aarne-Thompson classification indicates that this theme is relatively little known in folklore, except in Germany. In France, eight versions have been recorded. Aarne-Thompson classify this Type 1792 among the jokes about "Parson and Sexton" (Types 1775–1799). In this variant from Lower Brittany, the initial motif which reveals the parson's stinginess is missing, and there is no sexton in the story; instead, the theft is motivated by the extreme poverty of a large family.

The little verse with which the thief's son mocks the victimized parson, and which he repeats in the pulpit, altered only so as to be slanderous, reflects an attitude commonly found among the people of Lower Brittany, for whom a deep attachment to traditional religion does not exclude a critical mockery of the members of the clergy when they are found to be at fault. This exchange of rhymed sentences can be compared to Type 1831, *The Parson and the Sexton at Mass,* in which the theft of a lamb is discussed in antiphony.

PART II

UPPER BRITTANY

·6· *The Devil and His Three Daughters*

Type 313, *The Girl as Helper in the Hero's Flight.*

Recorded in 1958 from a farmer, Jean Belliot, who had learned it from his father, Jean Belliot, known as Guineau, a basket maker who lived in La Chapelle des Marais, in Brière.

In the past the story must have been part of the vast repertory of the "basket makers' tales," described in a masterful way by my colleague Ariane de Félice in her *Contes de Haute Bretagne* (Paris, 1954, pp. i–xiv). As she points out (p. v), over a hundred years ago Gérard de Nerval, in his *Chansons et Légendes du Valois* (Paris, 1854), made this comment about a part of a tale: "Here is a folktale that I remember hearing the basket makers tell of an evening." Recently one of my colleagues from the National Center of Scientific Research, who is studying the old crafts of Limousin, shared with me his observations on the culture of the basket makers of this area, who have also inherited a rich folklore tradition.

The theme is a favorite among French storytellers, as my teacher Paul Delarue has pointed out, because it is one of those tales of magic that lend themselves the best to a stirring and vivid exposition and that at the same time combine motifs of magic inherited from the ancient past. In the first volume of the *Catalogue des Contes Français* (I, 199–241), Delarue lists 118 versions in French, to which must be added the Canadian collections—Luc Lacourcière lists eighty-one Canadian and Nova Scotian variants in *Mémoires du IVe Congrès des Investigateurs des Contes Populaires* (Kiel-Copenhagen, 1959, p. 148)—and those versions recently recorded in France. (I recorded five versions in Corsica and a sixth unpublished version has been given to me.) A version from Norway is contained in *Folktales of Norway,* another volume in this series.

Our version from Upper Brittany, which preserves fairly well the series of tasks, attaches to the episode of the flight that of the forgotten fiancée, which can also stand alone as a story in itself (according to the wife of the informant).

·7· *The Boy Whose Mother Wanted to Throw Him in Boiling Water*

Type 314, *The Youth Transformed to a Horse.*

Recorded in 1954 from a sixty-year-old housewife, Jean Broussard, in La Chapelle des Marais, Brière.

Like the previous tale, this story was part of the repertory of the basket makers, of whom the informant's husband was one of the last to know how to "spin a yarn." It includes a few motifs which do not properly belong to it. The coach carved from a turnip by a fairy and drawn by four white rats brings to mind the pumpkin transformed into a coach in Perrault's *Cinderella* (Type 510A). Delarue, in his commentary on the *Contes du Nivernais et du Morvan* (p. 279), points out that this motif of the transformation of animals and objects into a coach is frequently found in French folklore. And the three beautiful suits, the colors of the sun, of the moon, and of the stars, which the hero received from the fairy are reminiscent of the marvelous dresses in Perrault's *Peau d'Ane* (Type 510B).

In French folklore, the hero usually has golden hair, which he covers up under the pretense of having ringworm until the moment when its beauty is publicly revealed. The Brière version omits the magical episodes I, II, and III, and opens with episode IV, in which the hero is hired by the king to care for his animals. This theme has already been recorded in Upper Brittany by Paul Sébillot, the great folklorist of the nineteenth century (the versions numbered 26 to 31 by Paul Delarue, *Catalogue des Contes Français,* pp. 255–56) and by Ariane de Félice (*Contes de Haute Bretagne,* No. 2, p. 24); in one of the versions recorded by Sébillot, the reason behind the hero's departure is the cruelty of his parents, as in this story.

Other versions of this tale may be found in *Folktales of Japan* and *Folktales of Chile,* companion volumes in this series.

·8· The Seven-Headed Monster

Type 317, *The Stretching Tree,* Type 300, *The Dragon-Slayer,* Type 303, *The Twins or Blood-Brothers,* and Type 314, *The Youth Transformed to a Horse.*

Recorded in 1954 from an old farmer from Missillac (Loire-Atlantique), Jean Tobie, who had heard the story from his mother, a well-known storyteller; he told me thirteen of her tales.

This tale combines in an interesting way elements from the narrative defined by Delarue (*Catalogue des Contes Français,* p. 275) as Type 317, with a battle against the seven-headed monster—an episode belonging to Types 300 and 303—and with episodes reminiscent of Type 314. The hero goes back to his menial job in the service of the King, and reveals his identity only after having pranced about on three magnificent steeds, in contempt of the fences raised by the King in order to stop him.

Type 317 has only a narrow distribution in France as a whole, but it is well represented in the folklore of Upper and Lower Brittany and in that of French Canada. Kurt Ranke has pointed out in his monograph *Die Zwei Brüder* (FFC 114, p. 197) the frequent association of this theme with that of the seven-headed monster (just as in this case). Delarue (p. 279) notes that in France this theme serves rather often as an introduction for Type 300 (seven times), more rarely for Type 314 (once, in a tale recorded by Luzel, *Robardic le pâtre*) or for Type 530 (once, in a tale published by Cosquin, *Lorraine,* II, 89, *Le Petit Berger*). In his commentary on this latter story, Cosquin compares it to several versions from other parts of Europe (Tyrol, Hungary, Moravia, Italy) and points out the frequency of the motif of the "triple appearance of the hero in a tournament, on three horses of different colors" (II, 97).

·9· The Beast

Type 425, *The Search for the Lost Husband.*

Recorded from the same informant as the previous tale.

This theme, which was made famous by Leprince de Beaumont's adaptation, is also widespread in the oral tradition of French folklore, in France—where there are sixty-six versions according to the Aarne-Thompson type index, of which a few show traces of the eighteenth-century literary version, which was widely circulated by peddlers —as in North America, where forty-three variants have been collected. Additional versions may be found in *Folktales of Ireland, Folk tales of Israel,* and *Folktales of Japan,* other volumes in this series

Maurice de Meyer has brought to light the characteristics of French folklore in *Amor et Psyche, Etude Comparée de Variantes Recueillies en France, en Belgique et an Allemagne (Folk-liv,* II, 1938, 197–210). In our version from Upper Brittany, the motif of the three drops of blood that the wife lets fall from her finger onto the shirt of her husband when he is forced to leave her stands in opposition to the motif of the harmful drops of water which the jealous sisters-in-law pour on his pelt. In contrast to those spots of blood that Lady Macbeth thinks she sees on her hand, these indelible spots are the symbol of the wife's faithful love, and will enable her to later make herself known to her husband.

The expression *l'eau d'endormie,* which designates the sleeping potion used by the second bride to put the prince to sleep, is a vestige of Old French. Godefroy (*Dictionnaire de l'Ancien Langue Française,* III, 132) cites these medieval verses: *"Avez-vous beu de l'endormye / Que dormez si grant matinée?"*

· 10 · John of Calais

Type 506A, *The Princess Rescued from Slavery.*

Recorded from the same old basket maker of Brière as No. 6, *The Devil and His Three Daughters.*

This story was sometimes known as *John of Pontchâteau,* from the name of a small town close to the village where the basket makers lived, to which they went to sell their baskets at the fair. Type 506A, to which it belongs, was made famous in France by the version circulated by the peddlers under the name *John of Calais.* Our version from Upper Brittany reflects both the peddlers' booklets (the names of the hero and the heroine's cousin, Don Juan and Isabella, suggest the literary version) and traditional folklore traits: the seven-year sojourn of the hero on a desert island, the little scene in which he becomes a woodcutter and is referred to as *"barbu peillu guenillu,"* his recognition by means of a handkerchief embroidered by his wife, and so on. The reproach to the woodcutter cited above reflects the local speech, in which the term *peille* means "rag" and *peillu* means "ragged." Furthermore, the informant seems to want to suggest from the very beginning that the area around Saint-Nazaire, at the mouth of the Loire, a site close to Brière, is the setting for the story, when he says, "He sailed away on the river."

Marie-Louise Tenèze has devoted a praiseworthy study to "Jean de Calais (Type 506A) en France: Tradition Ecrite, Tradition Orale, Imagerie," in *Mélanges Archer Taylor* (pp. 286–308). Few French folktales have been so widely circulated by means of peddlers' booklets; of the 32 versions recorded from the oral tradition (and half of them are Breton), only six versions seem untouched by any literary influence. However, the majority have still preserved the episode of the buried corpse, a typical episode of the universal theme, which is missing in the French literary version written by Angélique Poisson Gomez, born in Paris in 1684.

· *11* · Gold Feather

Type 531, *Ferdinand the True and Ferdinand the False.*

Recorded from the farmer from Missillac (Loire-Atlantique) who provided me with the story about *The Beast* (No. 9 of this collection).

As often happens, the initial episode of this variant—in which a poor child's eyes are put out to make him a beggar, and who is then purposely lost—is not peculiar to this type; it is also found in association with Type 613 (see No. 45 of this collection). The same thing is true of the next episode: three figures with supernatural and even magical powers—in this case, they are three giants —gather beneath the tree in which the child has taken refuge, and they interpret even the blunders he makes while perched in the tree in a quaint way, and always in his favor (see also my *Contes de l'Ouest,* Paris, 1954, No. 21).

The story of *Gold Feather* has also appeared in the repertory of the basket makers of Brière: the oldest of my informants in this region, Pierre Thureau, who was eighty-eight years old in 1950, told me its beginning that year. It is interesting that my informant from Missillac, who owed his stories to his mother, had learned from her a "literary" version belonging to the same Type 531, *Avenant*. In this version the features characteristic of Mrs. d'Aulnoy's story are clearly repeated; but for this peasant storyteller, who was ignorant of the international classification of types, these stories—incorporated into the local folklore from different sources—were entirely distinct.

· *12* · The Orange Tree

Type 313, *The Girl as Helper in the Hero's Flight.*

Recorded from the same informant as the previous story.

This story belongs to the same type as No. 6, *The Devil and His Three Daughters,* but its moral is completely different, even though Missillac (the informant's home) is geographically close to Brière, the home of the basket makers. The initial episode of the golden fruit—oranges in this case—stolen from a lord is not peculiar to this theme, and is frequently found in France as the beginning of Type 301A. But in this story, the bird-magician who stole the oranges does not lead the pursuing hero underground; instead, he forces him to rejoin him in an ivory castle. The motif, which is unclassified, of the castle all in bone or ivory is also found in Lower Brittany: the tale of *Luduenn* which I published in *Rencontre des Peuples dans le Conte* (Munich: France-Allemagne, 1961, ed. G. Hüllen and M. L. Tenèze, I, 92–94) has as its hero a "Cinderella," the youngest of three brothers, who successfully performs the task of constructing a "castle all in bone"; in that story, a dragon surrounds the bone castle "with its tail curved around it like a golden ring."

This story, *The Orange Tree,* includes the episode of the bird's daughters bathing in the pond, which is missing in the version from Brière. On the other hand, even though after the performance of the series of tasks, and the transformations of the flight, there is indeed a kiss which makes the hero forget his fiancée, she immediately makes herself known to him; therefore the episode of the forgotten fiancée is not included in this story, as it is in the Brière version.

· *13* · *March and April*

Type 1000, *Bargain Not to Become Angry.*

Recorded from the same farmer of Missillac as the previous tale.

This theme is known in neighboring Brière by the title of *Premier Lassé* (cf. my *Contes de l'Ouest,* p. 98), and even of *Cendrillon* (cf. *Contes de Haute Bretagne* by Ariane de Félice, pp. 66 and 255). In this version the names of the heroes—who are two brothers, the eldest and the youngest—bring to mind two successive months at the beginning of the year, as in a variant that I recorded in Lower Brittany, *Janvier et Février;* this feature also recurs in other provinces of France.

This folktale type is usually associated with other themes of the series "Tales of the Stupid Ogre," as is noted in the latest edition of *The Types of the Folktale* (p. 340); however, in this version it is found in its pure form. The punishment reserved for the first one to become angry—a strip of skin will be removed from his back

—is the one that appears the most frequently in the versions from different parts of France; I also encountered it in a Corsican version, *Les Trois Tranches de Peau* (cf. my *Contes Corses,* Gap, 1963, No. 23, p. 53). But this annoying punishment can just as well be the loss of the loser's ear or nose, or even death, as Delarue has pointed out in his commentary on the work by Ariane de Félice mentioned above.

For a Chilean version of this tale type, see *Folktales of Chile,* a volume in this series.

PART III

PAYS DE RETZ

·14· *The Tale of La Ramée*

Type 559, *Dungbeetle.*

Recorded in 1958 from a seventy-one-year-old farm woman, Clémentine Lezin, in Sainte-Pazanne, in the Retz region. Lying to the south of the mouth of the Loire, this region forms a transition between the area around Nantes (which belongs to the ancient duchy of Brittany) and Lower Poitou, to which it is related by its dialect.

My informant had learned this story as a young child from an old basket maker. There are only a few versions in French folklore of Type 559, which is not widespread in the rest of Europe either, except in Ireland. However, Aarne-Thompson lists sixteen French versions in America. The motif of the suitor who must make the Princess laugh in order to marry her, which here is related to the series "Animals as Helpers" (Type 530–Type 559) within the category of "Tales of Magic," also belongs to Types 571–574, and is often enjoyed as a humorous tale by the storytellers and their audiences.

G. d'Aronco has devoted a paragraph in his *Fiabe di Magia in Italia* (Udine, 1957, pp. 78–79) to the theme of *La Principessa che non Ride.* A version of Type 559 appears in the *Pentamerone* (Third Day, Story 5, *La Sorece e lo Grillo*) in which the hero, instructed by his father to purchase some goods, buys for a hundred ducats each of the three helpful animals—a mouse, a dungbeetle, and a cricket. Our variant from the Retz region features as its hero an old man, or perhaps an old soldier (for the name "La Ramée" was a common nickname for a soldier under the *ancien régime*), who simply meets a mouse, a beetle, and a cricket on the road, and who welcomes them as companions, somewhat in the manner of

Demi-Coq (Type 715), a tale which is widespread in this part of western France.

PART IV

LOWER POITOU

·15· *The Goat Who Lied*

Type 212, *The Lying Goat,* and Type 123, *The Wolf and the Kids.*

Recorded in 1960 from Mme Pierre Péau, aged sixty-seven, in Saint-Hilaire de Riez, where the salt marsh borders on the freshwater marsh, close to the mouth of the Vie River.

Lying to the south of the Retz region, the Vendean Marsh (sometimes incorrectly called the Breton Marsh) is an area which is still strongly steeped in its old traditions, even now in the middle of the twentieth century. *The Maraîchins* (as the inhabitants of the Marsh are called) are especially well known as singers and dancers, and their gay spirit, sometimes touched with melancholy, lends itself more to these two popular media than to the folktale.

Type 212 and Type 123 are both found throughout western France (especially the latter), as well as in Upper and Lower Poitou, in Aunis, in Saintonge, and in Angoumois. They are frequently combined in the folklore of the rural areas: Ellenberger noted their association in Upper Poitou (cf. *Arts et Traditions Populaires,* 1960, No. 3, p. 139) and Maugard in the Pyrenees (cf. his *Contes des Pyrénées,* 1955, No. 26, p. 211).

In French folklore, the development of these two tales is marked out by means of set phrases, which are generally in either rhyme or assonance, and which are modified as the plot progresses. A great Walloon folklorist, Elisée Legros, has emphasized the importance of these formulas in her work, *Trois Récits de Lutins et de Fées dans le Folklore Wallon et le Folklore Comparé* (Liège, 1952), and especially in *Quelques Formules de Contes d'Animaux en Wallonie et en France* (Brussels: *Les Dialectes Belgo-Romans,* 1953, pp. 149–68). These formulas have generally been adapted to the dialect of each region in which they have taken root, and therefore sometimes contain archaic terms and symbolic allusions.

The Vendean folklore tradition is rich in stories studded with this type of short verse; some are simply rhymed (as in this case), while others are sung (see my *Contes de l'Ouest,* No. 12, *Les Brigands,* and my *Poésie Traditionnelle Enfantine* [Poitiers: *Bulletin de la Société des Antiquaires de l'Ouest,* 1958, pp. 540–43]); almost all can be beautifully adapted to stories suited for children.

A version of Type 212 from Germany may be found in *Folktales of Germany,* another volume in this series.

· 16 · *Boudin-Boudine*

Type 333, *The Glutton.*

Recorded in 1958 from Mme. Panetier, aged eighty-five, in Gué-de-Velluire.

The marsh of the Sèvre River, also known as the *Marais Feuillu,* is on the border of the present departments of Vendée and of Deux-Sèvres. Its inhabitants, who used to be called *huttiers,* lived in huts (*huttes*) on the islets of the Sèvre River, surrounded by its many channels, and conducted their agricultural affairs with boats as their sole means of transportation. Their speech, very different from the *maraîchin* used in the Vendean Marsh to the north, has preserved until the present some peculiarities which make its set expressions and short verses almost impossible to translate. I have therefore incorporated them in this story as they are.

This story is a local variant of the well-known *Little Red Riding Hood* (Type 333), which, like another version recorded in La Taillée in this same Marsh, features a little boy rather than a little girl. Furthermore, this little boy does not take his grandmother a cake and a small pot of butter as in Perrault's version, but instead, after the Vendean fashion, some black puddings from a freshly killed sow on his parents' farm. He also takes her some *friture,* a local dish made with pork rinds boiled in a pot, for one local custom requires that when a pig is killed and butchered, the best pieces be shared with neighbors. The name Courtine for the sow indicates that she was *écourtée*—that is, that her tail had been bobbed. The informant sets the story in the marsh of the Sèvre River (just as her grandfather did when he told her the story, she said), which is alluded to in several place names: the Grand Veurdé, the Bas Galioux.

The motif of the wolf who dips his black paw in the semolina in order to whiten it belongs to another type, Type 123, *The Wolf and the Kids,* which was also discussed in relation to the previous tale. As to the term *bouillie bordelaise,* it seems to have been the name the informant's mother used for a white semolina probably made from wheat. The happy ending of this story is not unusual, for Paul Delarue (Paris: *Bulletin Folklorique d'Ile de France,* 1953, pp.

513–14) notes that this ending is found "in certain versions from France, Italy, and Tyrol, and in a tale related to the Far East, *Le Tigre et les Enfants.*"

A variant of this tale can be found in *Folktales of Japan,* in this series.

·17· *The Iron Pot*

Type 400, *The Man on a Quest for His Lost Wife,* and Type 401, *The Princess Transformed into Deer.*

Recorded in 1958 from an old peasant woman from the center of the island of Yeu, Eugénie Lacroix, aged seventy-five, who had heard it from her great-grandfather.

The island of Yeu, which is farther from the shore than Noirmoutier and which has also been more influenced by maritime life, has well preserved its traditional customs and its oral literature.

This story is an altered version of Types 400 and 401 (deliverance of the lost wife). Interestingly enough, another tale known by this same title, which I heard that same year in the unique village of the island of Yeu, is related by one motif to Type 401A (with the three nights of torture endured in silence) even though it belongs as a whole to Type 425, *The Search for the Lost Husband.*

In this version, the informant has emphasized the role of the eagle, which as the hero's guide helps him to identify and to deliver his future wife, who is enclosed not only underground but also in an iron pot. To this role has been added the motif of the hero pulled from the underground world up to the light by the eagle, which he must feed with the game he kills and then with a piece of his own flesh. This feature, which frequently serves as a conclusion to Type 301A in France, has in this case been altered in an ingenuous way: the hero's wound is simply due to his fall, and it is in another underground hunt that he kills the game which will give the eagle the strength to carry him back up to the surface. Here his delivered wife-to-be and his dog wait for him, for they had been carried up first.

·18· *The Little Lad Who Became a Bishop*

Type 671, *The Three Languages.*

Recorded in 1958 from Delphine Soupault, aged seventy, who worked in a sardine-packing house on the island of Noirmoutier.

In the universal theme, three successive episodes correspond to the

three categories of animals—dogs, birds, and frogs—whose languages the boy learns. This folktale type is fairly widespread throughout the different provinces of France; a more complete version of it
has been published in my *Contes de l'Ouest* (No. 4, p. 36, *Le Pape;*
commentary by Paul Delarue, p. 249), and another one in F. Cadic's
Contes de Basse Bretagne (No. 12, p. 133, *Le Pape Innocent*). The
theme of animal languages appears also in my *Contes Corses* (No. 2,
p. 4), but this variant clearly belongs to the related Type 670, as does
another Corsican variant mentioned in my *Commentaires* (p. 268).

We know that the understanding of animal languages by a man
is a motif that goes back to antiquity. Melampus, a Greek magician,
raised some young snakes he had rescued. One day his snakes cleaned
out his ears so well that when he woke up he was astonished to discover that he understood the languages of mammals, birds, and
reptiles. Later, this motif appears in *Gesta Romanorum* and in the
Roman des Sept Sages; the theme of Type 670 was itself treated by
Morlini around 1520 in one of his *Novelle* (No. 71).

19 · *Tom Thumb*

Type 700, *Tom Thumb.*
Recorded in 1960 from Mme Bellion, aged sixty-five, from Brétig-
nolles (Deux-Sèvres).

The name *Petit Poucet,* which Perrault gave the hero of his famous
tale (derived from Type 327, *The Children and the Ogre*), actually
belongs to a different theme, Type 700, which is that of *Tom Thumb,*
the French *L'Enfant Gros comme un Pouce,* or the German *Daumes-
dick.* In order to avoid confusion, Paul Delarue has proposed the
name Pouçot, which appears frequently in Nivernais, for the folklore
versions of Type 700 (see his commentary on my *Contes de l'Ouest,*
p. 269).

This tale is an example of this theme, which is widespread in
western France, where the adventures of Pouçot are well known
and are often interspersed with brief rhymed verses, smatterings of
which quickly come to the minds of the old peasant women, even
when they think they have forgotten the main content of the story.

A version of this tale may be found in *Folktales of Japan,* a
volume in this series.

20 · *The Tale of Jean-le-Sot*

Type 1696, *What Should I Have Said (Done)?*
Recorded in 1958 from Mme Chevalier, aged eighty-three, a farm
woman in Chaillé-les-Marais (Vendee).

This story is studded with chanted phrases in deliberate imitation of religious chants. Paul Delarue realized that his country's many versions fell into two categories according to the interpretations of the foolish young man: Type 1696A, "What should I have said?"; and Type 1696B, "What should I have done?"

Our Vendean version has the originality of taking place in this marsh of the Sèvre River, which extends into the departments of both Vendée and of Deux-Sèvres. The local setting is reflected in the episodes of the cracked ground, which the hero treats with butter, and of the frogs croaking in the ditches, which he bombards with eggs. This quick-moving story is also characteristic of the rebellious spirit and in particular of the sarcastic attitude toward the clergy which are typical of this small region.

PART V

UPPER POITOU

· 21 · The Wolf and the Soldier

Type 157, *Learning to Fear Men.*

Recorded in 1960 from Olivier Sennegon, a seventy-three-year-old farmer, in Martaizé (Vienne).

This type is widespread in the Nordic areas of Europe, and is also well represented in France. The informant, who had learned this variant from his grandmother, faithfully retained the old woman's local references, identifying the setting by referring to places allegedly in his own village: the Fontaine blanche, the Croix cassée, and La Chausse en l'air. This is a technique old people frequently use when addressing children, in order to bring an extraordinary story close to home.

An interesting aspect of this tale is the fact that the wolf, eager to fight "a creature called man," does not ask a fox for directions but, instead, an old woman, who sends him out against a soldier armed from head to toe. And after his unfortunate fight, the wolf relates his defeat not to a fox but to another wolf.

Sixteen variants of Type 157 collected by Richard M. Dorson from Negroes of the Southern United States are given in his article, "King Beast of the Forest Meets Man," *Southern Folklore Quarterly,* XVIII (1954), 118–28.

· 22 · *The Little Elves of La Chausse-en-l'Air*

Recorded in 1960 from Mme Brissaud, aged seventy-nine, in Martaizé (Vienne).

This legend is a "news item" about those evenings of long ago which is widespread in all of France. The original term used in this story, *fadet,* designates in the west of France those small elves who came down chimneys, as distinct from the *lutin,* those elves (who were no less mysterious) who used to haunt stables. Cosquin includes in his famous *Contes populaires de Lorraine* (II, 288–89) an analogous legend, *La Fileuse,* recorded in Montiers-sur-Saulx, and notes that a Basque tale and an Angevine are similar to it, except that the mysterious figure has become a fairy. The general meaning of the little verse, which is rhymed in the local speech and which provokes the anger of the man disguised as a spinner, is "Last night's spinner spun a lot better."

· 23 · *The Piece of Cloth*

Type 402, *The Mouse (Cat, Frog, etc.) as Bride.*

Recorded from the same informant as No. 21.

This type owes its fame in France to a literary version by Madame d'Aulnoy, *La Chatte Blanche (Contes Nouveaux ou les Fées à la Mode,* Paris, 1698, II, 89), but it is also well represented in French folklore, where it has been little influenced by the literary version. In our variant from Upper Poitou, the motif of the father promising his niece in marriage to his three sons also suggests Type 653, interesting versions of which have been found in Lower Brittany (cf. F. Cadic, *Contes de Basse Bretagne,* Paris, 1955, No. 13, p. 142, *La Fille du Sabotier*) in the Pyrenees (cf. Maugard, *Contes des Pyrénées,* Paris, 1955, No. 2, p. 7, *Le Rusé Voleur*) and in Corsica (cf. my *Contes Corses,* p. 139, No. 61). As I have noted in the commentary on the Corsican version, *La Fleur, le Miroir et le Cheval* (p. 315), this motif is found in *A Thousand and One Nights* in the first part of a tale entitled *The Story of the Prince Ahmed and of the Fairy Pari-Banou,* where the King's three sons are in love with his niece, Nourounnihar. But in Type 653 the three rare objects that the suitors must bring back later help to save the life of their fiancée, whereas in Type 402 the items found by the youngest of the three brothers enable the animal that helped him through his trials to return to human form; in the end the hero marries, not the original object of his desire, but the Princess (or the fairy) to whose deliverance he contributed.

For a Chilean version of Type 402, see *Folktales of Chile,* a companion volume in this series.

·24· *The Three Gold Hairs from the Devil*

Type 461, *Three Hairs from the Devil's Beard.*

Recorded in 1960 in Martaizé (Vienne) from a ten-year-old girl, Marie-Renée Baudouin, who had heard it from an elderly neighbor woman.

This variant contains the essential elements of the theme, but it does not include the series of questions the hero must answer, except for the last one, the ferryman's. However, the informant greatly elaborated the amusing dialogues between the hero, the old housekeeper, and the Devil over the pulling of the three golden hairs.

The initial motif—the King's jealousy of a poor newborn baby who, according to prophecy, would become king (cf. Motif M312— "Prophecy of future greatness for youth") is not peculiar to Type 461; it also appears at the beginning of the Corsican tale of *Tignusellu,* the rest of which belongs to Type 516. (Cf. my *Contes Corses,* No. 14, p. 31, commentary pp. 277–78; by mistake I wrote Type 314 instead of Type 461, Motif 321 instead of Motif M312, and Motif 461 instead of Motif M314.) Types 930 and 1525R also begin with a similar motif.

The basket in which the newborn child is placed is probably the Poitou *bourgne,* a basket formerly used by peasant women in the fields to lay their babies in.

Other versions of this tale may be found in *Folktales of China* and *Folktales of Germany,* additional volumes in this series.

·25· *Puss in Boots*

Type 545, *The Cat as Helper.*

Recorded from the same young informant as the previous tale.

This variant of Perrault's famous *Chat Botté* reflects in a fanciful way the story which is probably derived through many intermediate forms from the original literary version. The cat's first thefts for his master's sake and the sharing of the spoils (the cat gets the black puddings and a draught of wine) are touches added by the common people which are told with great zest. The transformation of the cat into a young man after his short-lived marriage to a rat is inserted into a scene which probably originated with one of the people in the line of those who handed down this story. On the other hand, the dialogue which characteristically enhances the Marquis of Carabas is lacking in our Poitou version. We know that oral versions of Type 545 are rare in France.

· 26 · The Pea

Type 555, *The Fisher and His Wife.*

Recorded in the spring of 1960 from an old farm woman from Marçay, in Vienne, Mme Fraigneau, who as a small child heard it in dialect form from an old woman who was a cowherd.

This theme was illustrated in Old French literature by the *fabliau Merlin-Merlot,* which corresponds to Type 555. The hero's benefactor (the hero is the head of a poor household) is often a fish, as in *La Petite Sardine,* in my *Contes de l'Ouest* (No. 18, p. 164); but the pea or bean which, when planted, climbs to the sky is an initial motif common to this folktale and to Type 563.

Paul Delarue, having published a charming Nivernais version entitled *Pourquoi les Chats Huants Sont des Personnes* (*Contes du Nivernais et du Morvan,* No. 10, p. 96), considered comparing it to a story of the *Pantachantra* (*Les Souhaits,* trans. Lancereau, p. 333; see his commentary on *Contes de Gascogne* collected by Perbosc, No. 7, p. 253). He had already counted thirty-three French versions of this theme and was thinking about commenting on it at greater length in relation to a variant recorded in Lower Brittany by F. Cadic (No. 8, p. 92), *Pourquoi le Hibou Fait-Il Hou! Hou! et la Chouette Ha! Ha!*

PART VI

LOWER MARCHE

· 27 · The Black Hen

Motif N555.1, "Between midnight and cockcrow best time for unearthing treasure."

Recorded in 1960 from Mme Bourot, aged twenty-three, who had learned it as a child from her grandmother.

The informant used landmarks allegedly in her native village of Bouresse (Vienne)—*La Crêpe-au-lait,* the *Logis des Barres*—as the background for this legend, which also strongly suggests the former

Poitou mentality. It contains some well-known motifs: the search for a mysterious treasure which appears only as midnight approaches, and the interruption of the search by the cackling of a hen at midnight; the lord's greed, which is greater than the beggar's; the punishment of the greedy lord; the diabolical nature of the apparition (the black hen). The expiatory pilgrimage to the Holy Land suggests the faith of the Middle Ages, which remained evident in the rural areas of Poitou up to the beginning of the twentieth century.

·28· *Jean of Bordeaux*

Type 307, *The Princess in the Shroud*.

Recorded in the fall of 1960 from M. Boutin, a farmer in his sixties, in the village of Asnières-sur-Blour (Vienne), on the northeastern border of the department of Charente. This village had preserved its folklore exceptionally well.

The story of *John of Bordeaux* is a variant of Type 307; Delarue has listed thirteen versions in France (cf. his *Catalogue des Contes Français,* Paris, 1957, p. 172). In French folklore, the Princess is not a diabolical creature but instead is simply enchanted, and the hero disenchants her at the end of three nights spent not in prayer but in undergoing trials. The version from Lower Marche does not feature a soldier, like most of the French versions, but a poor swineherd in wooden shoes who finds himself pursued by the Devil himself. (Uusually the hero is pursued by the enchanted person.)

The final episode is the hero's return to his parents, his loss of everything to an innkeeper after a card game, his successful search for his wife, and the final recognition scene. This episode is not included in the description of the theme in the international classification and in the *Catalogue des Contes Français* mentioned above. However, it is found in a less detailed variant recorded in Ariège by Charles Joisten in 1953, also known as *John of Bordeaux.*

A German version of this tale may be found in *Folktales of Germany,* in this series.

·29· *Golden Hair, or The Little Frog*

Type 310, *The Maiden in the Tower,* and Type 402, *The Mouse (Cat, Frog, etc.) As Bride.*

Recorded in the fall of 1960 from Mme Rouyer, a farm woman in her sixties, in Bouresse (Vienne). She had learned it from her mother, Mme Grelier, born in 1865, who had heard it as a child from an old woman who was a cowherd.

Like many French versions of this type, this story is contaminated at the end by another tale, in this case Type 402. Delarue (*Catalogue des Contes Français*, p. 181) notes that this merger and this ending are brought about by the transformation of the heroine into a frog, a motif common to these two types. He then points out an original feature peculiar to French folklore—the parrot who spies on the lovers. Our variant from Lower Marche also contains an adaptation which is peculiar to it alone—the young girl's godmother, generally a jealous fairy, is here the Virgin Mary, who, far from punishing her goddaughter, comes to her aid by assisting her fiancé.

The theme of Type 310 was already known by Basile (*Pentamerone*, Second Day, Story 1) and by Mlle de la Force (the story of "Persinette" *Le Conte des Contes*, 1698).

· *30* · The Comte de Mes Comtes

Type 621, *The Louse-Skin,* and Type 900, *King Thrushbeard.*

Recorded in 1960 from Mme Barbier, aged ninety, a farm woman originally from Queaux now living in Luchapt (Vienne).

This strange title designates the hero of a popular theme of French folklore, known notably in Vendée by the name of Monsieur de Montanville (cf. *Arts et Traditions Populaires*, 1953, p. 111), a member of the nobility who disguises himself as a poor man in order to better test his beloved, and who reveals his true identity to her after a series of trials. This combination of Type 621 and Type 900 is not unusual in France.

The suitor who correctly solves the riddle is sometimes disguised as a beggar (cf. Vendée) and sometimes as a pilgrim (Charente); here he is a coal merchant. In its Vendean form, this quick-moving story is studded with disappointed remarks by the young lady as she is led by the poor man through her beloved's property: "Oh, how I loved Monsieur de Montanville!" Ariane de Félice has studied these characteristic recurring remarks in a suggestive article (*Internationaler Kongress der Volkserzählungsforscher in Kiel und Kopenhagen*, 1959, pp. 93–97).

It is interesting that in my Limousin version the lord's name is Marquis de Keraba. It has evidently been influenced by Perrault's *Chat Botté* (Puss in Boots), in which an analogous stylistic motif is developed in relation to the Marquis de Carabas. In our version from Lower Marche, the peasant humor is given free rein in the little scenes of local color where the disguised count enjoys making his wife steal napkins on the day of the *bugée* (the large annual washday), and then black puddings on the day of the *boucherie* (the slaughtering of the hogs), and all this takes place on the estate of his own castle.

·31· *The Woman with Her Hands Cut Off*

Type 706, *The Maiden without Hands.*

Recorded from the same informant as No. 29.

The medieval antecedents of this tale have been thoroughly studied, notably by Suchier and Puymaigre. This theme, which was included in Basile's *Pentamerone* (Third Day, Story 3) and in Straparola's *Facétieuses Nuits,* seems still to be greatly enjoyed by audiences of folktales throughout the different provinces of France. I recently recorded four versions of it in Corsica (cf. my *Contes Corses,* Nos. 59, 75, 81, and 104; commentary, p. 312) one in Lower Marche, one in Upper Brittany, and one in Lower Brittany, and also I found many variants in the course of my research among the French of Nova Scotia.

This story reflects the influence of Christianity, as do many stories recorded in this area, which was influenced by the Langue d'Oc civilization. The kindly figures who help the heroine during the delivery of her twins are the Virgin Mary, Saint John, and Saint Paul, who then serve as godmother and godfathers to the twins. The motif of the splinter driven into the leg of the executioner, which only the heroine can remove, is typical of French folklore. In Brittany, it is generally a thorn which takes root and grows in the foot of the guilty person.

Other versions of this tale may be found in *Folktales of Japan* and *Folktales of Germany,* volumes in this series.

·32· *Souillon*

Recorded in 1960 in Moussac from Mme Loiseau, aged seventy, born not far away in Luchapt (Vienne).

Paul Delarue noticed in the folklore of southwestern and midwestern France a theme not classified in the first edition of Aarne-Thompson, dealing with *La Soeur Propre et la Soeur Sale* (The Clean Sister and the Dirty Sister), for which he suggested the number 915B (see his commentary on Perbosc's *Contes de Gascogne,* p. 248). In the 1961 edition of Aarne-Thompson's *The Types of the Folktale,* the outline of Type 915, *All Depends on How You Take It,* is described, but in only one of the forms observed in France: the two different ways in which two daughters interpret their mother's precepts when they marry.

The variants that I recorded in France—one in Corsica, two in Lower Marche, three in Upper Poitou—correspond to Delarue's indexing of Type 915B rather than to the Aarne-Thompson form. However, this latter type is represented in Upper Poitou by an interesting version recorded by Ellenberger, mentioned by Delarue in *Contes de Gascogne* and published in *Arts et Traditions Populaires* (1960, No. 1, p. 115; commentary by Marie-Louise Tenèze, p. 138). Type 915B of Delarue's catalogue, like this story of *Souillon*, features a mother and her two daughters. The favorite daughter, who is lazy and spoiled, is not compelled to do any work, whereas her slighted sister is given the most tiresome jobs. The clean, hardworking sister manages her home very successfully, for she had the better training, whereas the dirty, lazy sister becomes poor.

· 33 · The Devil and the Good Lord

Type 1030, *The Crop Division,* and Type 1097, *The Ice Mill.*

Recorded in 1960 from Mme Faideau, a seventy-five-year-old farm woman who had heard it from her husband in Bouresse (Vienne).

This story joins the Devil and the Lord. It reflects both Type 1030, which is often associated with other themes, such as Type 9B (cf. my *Contes Corses,* No. 5, p. 10; commentary, p. 270), and Type 1097, which is well known in France as a separate story (there are nine versions). It is interesting that the Devil here plays the role of the stupid ogre, and God that of man, "weak," according to the informant, but intelligent (by implication). We have already seen in relation to tale No. 31, *The Woman with Her Hands Cut Off,* that the Christianization of the characters was a trait characteristic of the areas of midwestern France which were originally part of the Langue d'Oc country.

· 34 · The Rat and the She Rat

Type 2022, *The Death of the Little Hen.*

Recorded in 1962 in Pressac (Vienne) from Mme Boutant, aged fifty-two, who had learned it at the age of five from her grandmother, who was originally from Availles-Limouzine.

This *randonnée* is very popular among children. The story is developed through a series of enumerations, but is not summarized by beginning with the last verse and working backward, as in the

Chanson de Bricou, the song *Biquette A Tout Mangé Nos Choux,* and the following *randonnée* about the little hen.

Our version from Pressa is one of the most complete of its type. After telling of the drowning of the rat's mate and the rat's tears, it sets in motion the bench, the table, the door, the cart, the magpie, the fountain, the woman carrying pitchers, the man at his oven, the man leading a horse; then the water spreads over the body of the disemboweled horse, marking the end of the *randonnée,* and drowning out the "news story" originated by the tears of the unfortunate rat. The brief dialogue terminating this story introduces the usual set expression given in answer to children's requests for the sequel of a story.

·35· *The Little Hen*

Type 2032, *The Cock's Whiskers.*

Recorded in 1960 from Mme Benaîton, an eighty-two-year-old farm woman, in Adriers (Vienne).

The *randonnée* about the little hen and the little *jau* (rooster) is one of the favorite tales of children, who enjoy both its content and its form. These enumerations and then the summary, which are generally in rhyme or assonance form, enable the child to follow the evolution of a story, and even then to retrace it himself. When I watched in person the method used by a mother to transmit the story orally to her ten-year- old daughter, I noticed that she tirelessly had the girl repeat each fixed formula in order to have her memorize the progressive stages of a rather long *randonnée,* which she then had her recapitulate.

PART VII

ANGOUMOIS AND RUFFECOIS

·36· *The Goat, the Kids, and the Wolf*

Type 123, *The Wolf and the Kids.*

Recorded in 1959 from an old peasant woman, Mme Lavaud, aged seventy-nine, in Montjean (Charente), at the northern edge of Ruffecois.

This variant of Type 123 represents the form this theme most frequently takes. It is still very much alive in the folklore of western France, and is perhaps the animal tale country children enjoy most, with its rhymed verses, its rich dialectal resonant tones, and its mysterious rhythm, set by the grandmother's cane or her wooden shoes.

The heroine of the story is usually a nanny goat, but she is sometimes also a sow (in a variant from the island of Yeu) or a hen (in a variant from the Pays de Retz). The local customs are reflected in the description of the dishes enjoyed by the wolf: the *froumajhé* or *tourteau froumajhé* is a cake stuffed with fresh cheese, popular in a small area running through the southern ends of the departments of Deux-Sevres and of Vienne and the northern end of the department of Charente.

In the twelfth century Marie de France (in her Fable 90, *De la Chèvre et ses Chevreaus*) and later, in the seventeenth century, de la Fontaine (in his Book IV, Fable 15, *Le Loup, la Chèvre et les Chevreaux*) already put this traditional folklore theme in verse form in French.

· 37 · *The Sleeping Beauty*

Type 410, *Sleeping Beauty*.

Recorded in 1959 in Ambérac (Angoumois) from a farmer, M. Ganachaud, aged seventy-four, who learned it as a child from an old Vendean immigrant (a common case in Charente, where the immigrants of Vendean origin now constitute an important proportion of the rural population).

The beginning which properly belongs to Type 410 is missing here. The story begins instead with episode IV; owing to the initiative of a fairy, the beauty's godmother, a Prince arrives a hundred years after the young girl was put to sleep. Several traits characteristic of our story from Angoumois are not included in the "international" theme: the monster with seven heads and seven paws with claws (cf. Types 300 and 303), a magic sword which increases in length by two meters to strike the monster, the cawing of the crow to announce the breaking of the spell, the transformation of the monster's seven heads into seven golden balls which announce the birth of the seven children to the couple.

The strange motif of the sword which increases in length is found in the folklore of Armenia among the attributes of a *dève* (a seven-headed dragon), and the hero or heroine must seize it in order to kill the *dève* (cf. Lalayantz, *Revue des Traditions Populaires,* 1895, X, 193).

A version of this tale from Chile may be found in *Folktales of Chile,* in this series.

·38· The Three Innocents

Type 1450, *Clever Elsie.*

Recorded in 1959 in the Ruffecois area from Mme Latinois, aged seventy-six, in Villiers (Charente).

This story is widespread in Ireland and Sweden as well as in France, where it is frequently associated with Type 1384, *The Husband Hunts Three Persons as Stupid as His Wife.* In his commentary on a version of the *Three Innocents* recorded by Ariane de Félice (*Contes de Haute-Bretagne*, No. 21, p. 277), Paul Delarue expressed the opinion that the two associated themes (a combination represented in France by thirty versions) should be considered a distinct type (see also F. Cadic, *Contes de Basse Bretagne*, No. XV, p. 160, *Les Surprises de Jean le Rigodon*). It is interesting to note that in Charente, however, a version of Type 1450 has circulated in its independent form. We have already seen in relation to No. 30, *The Comte de Mes Comtes,* the frequency in French folklore with which two types are associated (in this latter case, Types 621 and 900 were combined).

Another version of this tale may be found in *Folktales of Germany,* in this series.

·39· Coué or Couette

Type 2015, *The Goat Who Would Not Go Home.*

Recorded in Montjean from the informant who told me No. 36.

This little *randonnée* is characterized by the final recapitulation of all the set phrases, only now inverted, beginning with the last one. Here, the initial motif—the attitude of the ram which refuses to return to the sheepfold—is explained by a trait suggestive of Type 212, *The Lying Goat* (cf. our No. 15): "My mistress has done nothing but make me run all day long." The local names Coué or Couette are probably related to the dialectal word *coué*, meaning "tail"; thus a sheep or goat with a long tail (a rather rare phenomenon).

PART VIII

LIMOUSIN

·40· The Gold Ball

Type 425, *The Search for the Lost Husband.*

Recorded in the spring of 1961 in the Limousin dialect in Chassenon (Charente) from an octogenarian, Mme Rougier, who had learned it as a child from her father, who was originally from the neighboring village of Saint-Quentin.

On the borders of the departments of Charente and Upper Vienne, a small region, centered in the two towns of Confolens and La Rochefoucauld, stretches along both banks of the Vienne River. Here they still speak the old Limousin dialect made famous in the Middle Ages by the first troubadour, Bernard de Ventadour.

This story does not begin with the usual initial motif for this type—an animal-husband—but instead with the indiscreet behavior of some old neighbor women, who surprise a newlywed couple in bed. The golden ball which the Virgin Mary gives the young wife, and which leads her to the spot where her husband has taken refuge, brings to mind a variant of Type 451, *La Boule Rouge* (The Red Ball; cf. my *Contes de l'Ouest,* No. 20, p. 175). It would seem that the golden ball became confused with the first of the three magic objects the maiden received to use in exchange for her brothers, the two others being a golden hen and her chicks and a golden bobbin. In French folklore the magic objects are usually a spindle, a spinning wheel, and a bobbin.

·41· *The Brother Who Was a Lamb*

Type 450, *Little Brother and Little Sister.*

Recorded in the spring of 1961 from Mme François Audonnet, a farm woman, aged fifty-nine, in Esse (Charente).

This type is represented by several versions in Lower Marche and in Limousin. The motif of the three fountains, the first two of which transform into an animal anyone who ventures to drink from them, while the third one transforms the young girl into a pretty, well-dressed lady, is particularly widespread in this area, where it is sometimes added on as an episode of Type 327. In this story, another woman is not substituted for the wife (cf. Type 450, episode IV), but instead the mother-in-law pretends to be ill in order to persuade her son to kill the lamb. It is at this point in the story that the rhymed verses are placed, exchanged at the edge of the well by the sister, a Queen, and the brother, a lamb. This final episode is frequently found in the versions of Type 451 which come from the western and midwestern parts of France.

A German version of this tale may be found in *Folktales of Germany,* in this series.

·42· *The Ogre* (*Malbrou*)

Type 451, *The Maiden Who Seeks Her Brothers.*

Recorded in the fall of 1961, in Alloue (Charente) from a spry eighty-three-year-old shepherdess, Mme Delage, who had learned it as a child from an elderly neighbor.

The local name for the evil figure—*malbrou*—suggests the Poitou term *lebrou* or *brou,* the ogre's name in certain versions of *Tom Thumb* (Type 700), and the Nivernais term *loup-brou* (cf. Paul Delarue and Achille Millien, *Contes du Nivernais et du Morvan,* p. 148).

Other local terms are the *ponne* (a large washtub) and the *gabiote* (a forester's cabin). The final episode of the brothers' transformation into animals because they ate vegetables growing on the ogre's grave is missing in our variant; but even so, the *malbrou* remains harmful after his death, since the combs made from his bones cause an incurable illness.

Another version of this tale can be found in *Folktales of Germany,* in this series.

·43· *Cinderella*

Type 510A, *Cinderella.*

Recorded in the spring of 1961 from a seventy-three-year-old peasant woman, Mme Joly, at Saint-Maurice des Lions (Charente).

This variant of Type 510A, which is generally known in France by the name of *Cendrillon,* is of this area.

The motifs of the food-providing animal—in this case, the milking cow which the little girl strikes with a hazel wand as the Virgin Mary, her godmother, told her to—and of the magic tree that bends down to feed the disinherited girl, are considered by Delarue characteristic of a related type which he calls Type 511A, while he reserves the classification Type 511B for another type, *Le Petit Taureau Rouge* (cf. his commentaries on *Contes du Nivernais et du Morvan,* p. 268). On the other hand, the ugly sister who trims down her foot in order to be able to slip on the shoe, and the animal which reveals the place where the pretty sister is hidden, are both typical of Type 510A. The transformation of the two jealous women into stones flanking the staircase or into doorjambs is found in other folklore themes as the punishment for jealousy: in our tale No. 9, *The Beast,* the two sisters who drenched the animal-husband's pelt are changed into *coulombres* (doorjambs).

Other versions of this tale can be found in *Folktales of Japan* and *Folktales of Chile,* companion volumes in this series.

·44· *The She Donkey's Skin*

Type 510B, *The Dress of Gold, of Silver, and of Stars.*

Recorded in 1960 from a seventy-eight-year-old peasant woman, Veuve Delage, a native of Le Lindois, who lived not far from there, in Vitrac-Saint-Vincent (Charente). She had heard this story from her deceased husband.

This theme, which is closely related to the preceding tale in the international classification, is characterized in French folklore, according to Delarue, by the motif of the Prince's three encounters with the heroine dressed as a servant. The Prince strikes the servant successively with three household objects; in this case, a poker, a bellows, and a *friquet*—the local name for the stick used to stir the meat to make *grillons* or potted minced pork. Interestingly enough, in spite of the local setting for this variant in which the heroine is a turkey girl, the story has assimilated a feature of literary origin—the chest which goes underground—probably a reminiscence of Perrault's famous tale *Peau d'Ane.* This story, which is still popular in the countryside, is one of the earliest recorded in French folklore. Noel du Fail mentions the tale *Cuir d'Asnette* (The She Donkey's Hide) in his *Propos Rustiques* (1547), and Bonaventure des Periers alludes to the story *D'une Jeune Fille Surnommée Peau d'Asne* (A Young Girl Nicknamed "Donkey Skin") in his *Contes ou Nouvelles Récréations et Joyeux Devis* (1557).

Another version of this tale may be found in *Folktales of Chile,* in this series.

·45· *The Two Brothers, or The Fox, the Wolf, and the Lion*

Type 613, *The Two Travelers.*

Recorded in 1961 from an eighty-eight-year-old peasant woman, Mme Dumaine, who told it to me in the Limousin dialect, in Esse (Charente). Another elderly person from the same village told me the same story, but with a different setting.

Thirty French versions of this theme have been recorded. Cosquin has pointed out how extremely old it is by comparing it to an ancient Egyptian tale (*Les Deux Frères,* fourteenth century B. C.; cf. *Contes Populaires de Lorraine,* I, Appendix B, LVI–LXVII), and yet it is interesting to see how alive this type still is in French folklore now in the twentieth century. I myself have recorded four variants in Corsica, all of them rather different from each other (cf. my *Contes Corses*, Nos. 43, 51, 82 and 88; discussed, pp. 299–300), and one in Upper Brittany which is contaminated by Type 300; Ariane de Félice has found in this same area a version which has merged with Type 531, *La Belle Kévale* (cf. *Contes de Haute-Bretagne*, No. 8, p. 87).

In the universal tradition, the heroes generally have symbolic names: Bien-Faire et Mal-Faire (Good-Doer and Evil-Doer; as in the case of our Corsican variant No. 43), Bonne-Foi et Mauvaise-Foi (Sincerity and Insincerity; *ibid.*, No. 82), Loyal et Déloyal (Loyal and Disloyal; the title of a Norwegian tale mentioned by Cosquin, *Contes Populaires de Lorraine*, I, 88). Delarue writes about a third-century Chinese version, the story of Fait-Bien et Fait-Mal (Does-Good and Does-Evil) in his commentary on the story *Secret des Bêtes* (cf. Perbosc, *Contes de Gascogne*, p. 254). In this concise story recorded in Esse, it is simply a matter of drawing lots: the one who loses has his eyes put out in order to solicit alms, which the other one gathers but does not divide evenly. We have already encountered this initial motif in the story of *Gold Feather* (No. 11 of this collection).

Other versions of this tale may be found in *Folktales of Israel* and *Folktales of China*, in this series.

·46· *Little Fourteen or As Strong as Fourteen*

Type 650A, *Strong John,* and Type 301B, *The Strong Man and His Companions* followed by *Quest for a Vanished Princess* (Type 301A).

Recorded in 1960 from a farmer from Saint-Christophe (Charente), Jean Chansigaud, aged sixty-seven, who had heard it from his mother, and who remembered the final episode during my second visit in 1961.

These two themes are frequently associated in French folklore, as Delarue has noted. The symbol of strength multiplied fourteen times is not peculiar to our version from Saint-Christophe. Sébillot recorded in Upper Brittany a story of *Quatorze* (Fourteen), which is more distinctly related to Type 301B (cf. Delarue, *Catalogue des Contes Français*, p. 125, No. 56).

The initial motif of this variant tells of a child so poor that no one is willing to be his godfather, but who in the end becomes the godson of eminent people (generally a king or queen, and in this case, the Lord and the Virgin Mary). This is a beginning common to several themes, notably to Type 531 (cf. *Motif-Index*, N811). Once again the characters have been Christianized, a trait characteristic of the Marche and Limousin areas.

·47· *The Master and the Tenant Farmer*

Type 852, *The Hero Forces the Princess to Say, "That Is a Lie."*

Recorded in the spring of 1961 in Esse (Charente) from an old farmer, François Audonnet, whose father was still famous as a story-teller at evening get-togethers.

This story belongs to the special category of "fibs," for Type 852 is usually about a Princess to whom her suitors must tell a story so preposterous that she says, "That is a lie." The central motif (Type 852, episode IIb) of a tree growing up to the sky overnight, which the hero climbs and then descends on a rope made from bales of oat husks, is preceded and followed in our variant by a series of original "fibs." In addition, and most importantly, it has a highly character-istic local setting. The story is not about a princess and a suitor, but a master and a tenant farmer who in a way is driven to tell these "fibs" in order to preserve his share of the harvest, which is at stake because of a bet imposed on him at his master's whim.

·48· *Fanfinette and the King's Son*

Type 883B, *The Punished Seducer.*

Recorded in the fall of 1961 from a seventy-seven-year-old peasant woman with a remarkable repertory, Mme Bertrand, in Saint-Claud (Charente).

The last edition of the Aarne-Thompson type index lists only one version of this theme in France, which became famous as Miss Lhéritier's story of *Finette ou l'Adroite Princesse* (published in 1696: *Revue des Traditions Populaires*, 1888, III, 275, and St. Prato, *Giornale della Società Asiatica d'Italia*, IX, 229).

The motif of the flower which fades (*Motif-Index*, E761.3), symbolizing the young girl's seduction, is replaced in a variant that I recorded in Upper Poitou by a distaff which breaks. Léon Pineau found in the same area a combination of the two traits: the father gives a rose to the two older sisters and a stick to the youngest (cf. *Revue des Traditions Populaires*, the tale of *Finon-Finette*). Pineau also ran across the motif of the cask lined with nails in which a person is rolled in this Poitou variant. However, I recorded this same motif in Vendee in association with a version of *The Giant Killer and His Dog* (*Bluebeard*) (Type 312: cf. my *Contes de l'Ouest,* commentary p. 259, No. 19, version C).

The giant gourd placed in the bed to look like a person and take the sword's blows is a trait found in another theme, where a poor young girl's guile is also set against a prince's seductions. This is *La Jeune Fille au Pot de Basilic,* not classified in the Aarne-Thompson index. Delarue has analyzed a version in *Incarnat, Blanc et Or* (Paris, 1954, p. 67; see also my *Contes Corses,* p. 37, No. 18; commentary, p. 280).

PART IX

MASSIF CENTRAL

·49· The Bear and the Beetle, or The War of the Animals

Type 222, *War of Birds and Quadrupeds.*

Recorded in 1951 in Crandelles, to the west of Aurillac, from an octegenarian, Mme. Fournier, and her forty-eight-year-old daughter, who had heard it from her mother as a child. It was recorded during the research done by the *Atlas Linguistique et Ethnographique du Massif Central,* and comes from the collection of its director, Pierre Nauton, made in the department of Cantal.

This story belongs to the category of animal tales, which are always enjoyed in the rural areas. The conflict is actually between the insects, offended in the person of the beetle which the bear held under his paw, and the quadrupeds, the bear's colleagues. The role given to the fox—that of a messenger who is careful not to admit that he was stung in order to let the others run the same risk—is consistent with his character as presented in oral French folklore. In his commentary on a Gascon variant of this theme (cf. Perbosc, *Contes du Gascogne,* No. 26, p. 271, *Le Loup et le Grillon*), Delarue notes that this theme was already well known in the Middle Ages, and that from it "Marie de France took her fable *D'un Loz è d'un Escarboz* (fable LVI, p. 241 of the Roquefort edition)." He lists thirteen versions of this type in France, almost all in the Langue d'Oc country.

·50· Jean and Jeannette

Type 327, *The Children and the Ogre.*

Recorded in 1941 from two elderly peasant women in Saugues (Haute-Loire), to the north of the Margeride mountain, by Pierre Nauton, the author of a remarkable monograph on *Le Patois de Saugues* (Clermont-Ferrand, 1948), and the director of the *Atlas Linguistique et Ethnographique du Massif Central.* Nauton heard this tale himself in Saugues around 1920, when he was a child.

He has specified that this is one of those evening stories which children were formerly told while their mother or grandmother was sewing or knitting. With his background as a linguist and dialectologist, Nauton is primarily interested in these dialectal tales because their content has not been suggested to the informants, and their style and syntax present original forms often missed in direct questioning. Folklorists consider the story of *Jean and Jeannette* to be a version of Type 327, in the form which is characteristic of the center of France, but at the same time a little different from those already published by Paul Sébillot in his *Littérature Orale de l'Auvergne* (p. 33, *Les Enfants Égarés* from Cantal; see *Revue des Traditions Populaires,* 1887, II, 146), *L'Almanach de la Lozère de 1928* (p. 42, le diable et la diablesse), and by Léon Pineau in *Les Contes de Grand-Père* (Paris, 1938, No. 6, p. 47; a variant from the Loire region).

We have already discussed the Christianization of themes in the Langue d'Oc country; in this case, the evil character is not the ogre but the Devil, in his "red house," and his pursuit of the fugitives gives rise to dialogues in verse form between the Devil and the haymakers, a shepherd, and the washerwomen who finally cause the Devil's drowning. The motif of the child considered too thin and placed in a pigsty to fatten up, as well as the pretense to help the Devil's wife, who must kill the child, are found in association with Type 327 as well as with Type 328.

The episode of the rat's tail which the child substitutes for his own finger when the Devil comes to feel it is an intrinsic part of Type 327 (cf. Delarue, *Catalogue des Contes Français,* p. 311, Episode III, Motif F3), but it also suggests Type 451, in which the ogre comes and sucks through the cat hole the finger of the little girl, who is wasting away (cf. No. 42 in this collection).

·51· The Magic Napkin

Type 563, *The Table, the Ass, and the Stick.*

Recorded, in June, 1952 in Lozère, in a hamlet close to Mende,

from a seventy-year-old woman who had learned it at fifteen, by
Pierre Nauton in the course of his research for the *Atlas Linguistique
et Ethnographique du Massif Central*. Like the two preceding tales,
this one was recorded in dialect form; though the informant knew
French, she was used to telling stories in her local dialect. The
following text, like the preceding ones, is a translation by Nauton.

The theme is here prefaced by a brief introduction describing two
hungry children abandoned by bad parents (cf. Type 327). A fairy
brings objects to the children that will relieve their misery, somewhat
in the same way she helps the orphan who, in the folklore of the
central France, is the heroine of local forms related to Type 510A
(*Cinderella*) and Type 511 (defined by Delarue according to the
motif of the food-providing animal). In this version a particularly
cruel trait should be noted: the first two magic objects are not stolen
by an innkeeper but by the two children's foster parents.

Other versions of this tale may be found in *Folktales of Israel* and
Folktales of Germany, companion volumes in this series.

PART X

FOREZ

· 52 · *The Four Friends*

Type 130, *The Animals in Night Quarters*.

Recorded in Poncins, in Forez, from an old miller's wife, by
Marguerite Gonon, who collaborated on the *Atlas Linguistique et
Ethnographique du Lyonnais*.

This story is preceded by the peasant storytellers' favorite introductory rhyme.

The departure of the four animals on a trip the night of Saint
Sylvester is generally motivated in French versions by their master's
or mistress's plan, overheard by one of them, to kill them for the
New Year's banquet (usually Christmas, and they leave on Christmas
Eve). Friend Goose, Tiny Black Cat, Curly Lamb and Heifer Ready-
to-Deliver are the four companions of Type 130, forty-five versions
of which have been recorded in France, according to the latest edition
of the Aarne-Thompson type index; the rest of the story seems to
have been altered, perhaps in order to arrive at a more peaceful ending. In this version the four friends do not encounter thieves in the
house in which they take shelter but a poor old woman who is very
happy to receive them and to keep them with her.

·53· Half Chicken

Type 715, *Demi-Coq*.

Recorded by Marguerite Gonon shortly before 1939 in Poncins (Forez).

Aarne-Thompson list seventy-two versions of this theme in France, where it is one of the most popular among the peasants, plus five among French-speaking Canadians and one in the French West Indies. In his discussion of this story's fame in France, Delarue quotes from Destouches' *La Fausse Agnès* (1759), in which a young girl, when asked what she knows about fables, answers: "I know the tale of *Peau d'Ane* of *Moitié-de-Coq* (Half a Rooster) and of Marie Cendron." In addition, he points out that Restif de la Bretonne gives a Burgundian version of it in *Le Nouvel Abailard* (1779).

The initial motif of this folklore theme is missing in our Forez version. Usually an egg is divided in two and from one of the two parts Half a Rooster hatches, with only one leg and one wing; or two neighbors divide a rooster in two; Half a Rooster finds a money purse, which is then stolen from him, and he leaves in search of the thieves. In this story, Half Chicken goes to the King to seek justice —in other words, a henhouse where she would be respected by the poultry; and in spite of the ups and downs of her stay at the King's court, she finally gains protection for herself and her friends, Shaggy Wolf, Fair River, and Burning Fire.

A German version of this tale may be found in *Folktales of Germany,* another volume in this series.

PART XI

FRANCHE-COMTÉ

·54· The Wolf and the Fox

Type 15, *The Theft of Butter (Honey) by Playing Godfather;* Type 2, *The Tail Fisher;* and Type 34, *The Wolf Dives into the Water for Reflected Cheese.*

Recorded by Jean Garneret in 1950 from Louis Mouchotte in Burgille-lès-Marnay (Doubs) in Franche-Comté.

This story is related to these three universal themes which are based on the legendary rivalry between the wolf and the fox. There are sixty versions of the first theme in French folklore, according to Delarue. In general the fox is after a pot of butter, of fat, or of honey, and while the names the fox gives his godson vary between regions, they all describe the state of the pot—in this case, Gobbled, Half, and Well-Licked.

The next trait (the wolf sent to the butcher) could be considered an alteration of the end of Type 1. The episode of the wolf fishing in a pond with a pail attached to his tail is represented by twenty-four variants in France, and was made famous by the *Roman de Renart;* in folktales it is sometimes followed by another episode in which a new tail is manufactured for the tail-less wolf (Type 40B).

The concluding episode of the wolf mistaking the moon's reflection in a well for cheese is less widespread in France (there are four versions).

Additional variants of Type 15 may be found in *Folktales of Ireland* and *Folktales of Germany,* volumes in this series.

·55· *The Wolf and the Fox in the Well*

Type 34, *The Wolf Dives into the Water for Reflected Cheese;* and Type 32, *The Wolf Descends into the Well in One Bucket and Rescues the Fox in the Other.*

Recorded by Jean Garneret in 1950 from Charles Pepin in Lantenne (Doubs) in Franche-Comté.

The second episode is represented by five versions in France, and was also made famous by the *Roman de Renart.*

·56· *The Black One, the White One, and the Plucked One*

Type 2300, *Endless Tales.*

Recorded by Jean Garneret in the winter of 1960–61 in Etrabonne (Doubs).

This little Franche-Comté story belongs to the family of those tricks used by tired storytellers when their audience urges them to tell another story. The form of these "endless tales" is also suitable to an audience of children, like the joke of the *Rouge-Cochet,* also known as the "ricochet fable," or of the *"sourneto* of the white lamb" (see my study "C'est la Fable de Ricochet," *Le Français Moderne* (Oct., 1964), 286–95). Underlying the story is the eternal theme of the wolf duped by weaker animals, in this case ewes—his natural prey—as in Type 122C, *The Sheep Persuades the Wolf to Sing* (to alert the dogs). The names of the three ewes call to mind another animal fable recorded by the same man in Franche-Comté,

La Blanche, la Noire et la "Depoilée," which belongs to Type 124. For an "endless tale" from Japan, see No. 14 in *Folktales of Japan,* in this series.

PART XII

DAUPHINE

·57· *The Girl and the Thief*

Type 956B, *The Clever Maiden Alone at Home Kills the Robbers.*

Recorded in 1954 from a farm woman, Marie Arnoux, aged sixty-one, in Abriès, in the Queyras area (Hautes-Alpes), by Charles Joisten, a young disciple of Paul Delarue who visited even the smallest villages of this department, where he gathered a collection of over five hundred folktales.

In Dauphiné this tale seems to be particularly appreciated in the Queyras and Briançonnais areas, where it is represented by five versions. Joisten writes, "The high valley of the Queyras, close to the Italian border, is one of the richest centers we have discovered in the French Alps."

Aarne-Thompson does not list any versions of Type 956B in France, though it mentions twelve Franco-American versions. However, some good variants have been recorded throughout different provinces as far apart as Lower Brittany and Corsica. The theme usually appears with more highly developed hardships than in this story. Usually there is a whole band of thieves and not just one, and the heroine's flight gives rise to a series of incidents: in Trégor, she hides in a wagon full of hay, into which the thieves stick their swords, and then she runs to a washhouse and from there goes and hires herself out to some farmers. Just as in this Dauphiné story, one of my Corsican versions also contains the motif of the mutilated hand hidden with a glove (see the commentary in my *Contes Corses,* Nos. 24 and 68, pp. 287–88).

·58· *The Devil's Boot*

Type 1130, *Counting Out Pay.*

Recorded by Charles Joisten in 1960 from a farmer, Joseph Genon-Descotes, aged fifty-five, in Miribel-les-Echelles, in the department of Isère (Dauphiné).

This theme is widespread in the Nordic areas of Europe (two

hundred variants have been listed in Finland, forty-five in Estonia) as well as in the western areas, notably in Germany (twenty-six versions) and in France (eight versions). The initial motif—a ruined young nobleman calls up the Devil, who proposes a bargain for his soul—is also found in France at the beginning of certain versions of Type 313. The appearance of the Devil with the smell of sulphur, red clothes, and horse's feet, is consistent with his traditional representation.

·59· *He Who Speaks First*

Type 1351, *The Silence Wager*.

Recorded by Charles Joisten in 1959 from an eighty-five-year-old peasant woman, Mme Octavie Jail, in Saint-Jean d'Hérans, in the Isère region.

This theme is the subject of a study by W. N. Brown, "The Silent Wager Stories: Their Origin and Their Diffusion," *American Journal of Philology,* XLIII (1922), 289–317. It fits into the cycle of domestic quarrels over some insignificant detail, such as closing the door or bringing back an object. Seven versions have been found in France, two among the Walloons, and one among the American French.

An English version of this tale may be found in *Folktales of England,* in this series.

·60· *The Fearless Shoemaker*

Recorded in Isère by Charles Joisten.

This story about a shoemaker who watches over a dead man does not fit under a type classified in Aarne-Thompson. It can be compared to an episode of Type 326, *The Youth Who Wanted to Learn What Fear Is,* in which the hero is not afraid of ghosts. In a Corsican variant of this theme (published in my *Contes Corses,* No. 48, p. 116), the hero is lured one night into a cemetery, where a sacristan hidden in a tomb speaks to him; far from being frightened, the hero instead gives him a sharp answer and throws him over the wall. This Dauphiné story, however, is about a man who pretends to be dead and who is caught in his own trap, for the hero takes him at his word and strikes him as though he were a ghost, thus making him as silent as a real corpse. This brings to mind the final episode of our Vendean version of *The Tale of Jean-le-Sot* (see No. 20 of this collection).

Charles Joisten calls to our attention two published versions of this unclassified theme: one recorded by him and published by M. L. Tenèze and Georg Hüllen in *Begegnung des Völker im Märchen* (Frankreich-Deutschland, Münster, 1961, I, 134); the other recorded and published by Yvonne Sévoz in "Contes Populaires Recueillis à Villard-Reculas, Canton de Bourg d'Oisans," *Bulletin de la Société Dauphinoise d'Ethnologie et d'Archéologie,* XX, 2–3 (April–June, 1913).

PART XIII

SAVOY

·61· *The Scalded Wolf*

Type 121, *Wolves Climb on Top of One Another to Tree* (Motif J2133.6), and Type 1875, *The Boy on the Wolf's Tail.*

Recorded by Charles Joisten in 1958 from a thirty-seven-year-old farmer, Gaston Trépier, in Aillon-le-jeune, a mountain village of the department of Savoy.

The landmarks of this village—La Fraissette, the Replat, the Col des Prés, the Croix de Fornet—provide the setting for the story, which presents Types 121 and 1875 as though they were the successive episodes of a true narrative. The episodes of Type 1875 are preceded by an anecdote about the scalded wolf which recalls the final motif of Type 123 (see Nos. 15 and 36).

Aarne-Thompson does not mention any versions of Type 121 in France. However, Delarue cites a charming variant from French Lorraine in the journal *Arts et Traditions Populaires* (1953, pp. 42–43). The story Joisten recorded in Savoy also bears witness to the fact that this theme, which is rather common in Nordic folklore and which is also known in Spain (including Catalonia) is found in southeastern France. Delarue has written several commentaries on Type 1875 (see his *Contes du Nivernais et du Morvan,* No. 21, p. 292; the *Contes de Gascogne* by Perbosc, No. 45, p. 289), for which twenty-nine versions are listed in France; and he has devoted a comprehensive study to it in the journal *Arts et Traditions Populaires* (1953, pp. 33–58), in which he remarks on how often this theme is presented as an authentic adventure, especially in literary adaptations, notably that of Mistral.

·62· *Princess Elisa*

Type 329, *Hiding from the Devil.*

Recorded by Charles Joisten in 1958 from Léonie Clerc-Pithon, aged fifty-eight, in Jarsy, in the Bauges mountain range in Savoy. The informant had learned it as a child from an old woman nicknamed La Pesoule, who died in 1918, famous for having inherited from her father the art of telling stories for an entire evening.

Until now only one version has been recorded in France, the Lower Breton version published in F. Cadic's *Contes de Basse-Bretagne* (No. 1, p. 17). It was reproduced and discussed by Delarue in his *Catalogue des Contes Français* (pp. 342–45), who reports that this theme is also found in the French West Indies (Guadaloupe) and in Canada, where until now thirteen variants have been recorded. The Savoyard version seems to fit the definition of the universal folktale type better than the Lower Breton version, but it has not preserved as well the motif of the characteristic magic gifts. The three successive heroes are helped through their test by grateful animals: the eagle, the fish, and the ant (cf. Motifs H982 and B500), like the hero of Type 302, *The Ogre's (Devil's) Heart in the Egg* (see my *Contes de l'Ouest,* No. III, p. 25).

A Chilean version of this tale may be found in *Folktales of Chile,* another volume in this series.

·63· *The Little Devil of the Forest*

Type 500, *The Name of the Helper.*

Recorded by Charles Joisten from a sixty-three-year-old farm woman, Françoise Dupérier, in Jarsy (Haute-Savoie).

This story is greatly enjoyed by storytellers and their audiences because its formulas are to be sung; thirty-nine versions of it have been recorded in France. The initial motif of the mother's deceitful boast, which is based on a play on words, is common to both Types 500 and 501.

The Devil's picturesque name, which the heroine has to guess, varies among the different regions: it is Tirlemiton-Tirlemitaine in Franche-Comté, Fanfimois or Ropiquet in Lorraine, Mirloret in Bourbonnais, Ricouquet in Guyenne, Racapé or little old man Ripopé in Poitou (cf. *Arts et Traditions Populaires,* 1960, p. 139). In a tale by Miss Lhéritier which was inspired by this theme, the Devil's name is Ricdin-Ricdon (*La Tour Ténébreuse et les Jours Lumineux,* 1705), and in a Norman folklore version it is Rindon. It is odd that in Savoy the heroine's diabolical helper has the feminine name of Mimi Pinson, which suggests the famous song by Alfred de Musset, "Mimi Pinson is a Blonde." Cosquin (*Contes Populaires de Lorraine,* No. 27, I, 268–272) has discussed several French versions of this theme in relation to one recorded in Montiers-sur-Saulx.

An English version of this tale may be found in *Folktales of England,* in this series.

PART XIV

PYRENEES

·64· *The Charcoal Burner*

Type 159A, *Animals Warm Selves at Charcoal Burner's Fire.*

Recorded in 1953 by Charles Joisten from a seventy-one-year-old farm woman, Veuve Marie Rouzaud, in Montgailhard, Vaut par Nalzen, in the district of Lavelanet (Ariège).

This is a very rare theme which has been found only in southwestern France and in Catalonia. It is a kind of antithesis to Type 130, *The Animals in Night Quarters.* In this case, it is the cold which drove the bear, the wolf, the fox and the hare to the charcoal burner's hut in the mountains. In opposition to Type 130, at first they are well received and are able to warm up at their leisure. But the food they bring their host by way of acknowledgment arouses his greed, and they are the ones who are attacked in contrast to the four associates of Type 130, who throw the owners out of the house and take it over. This theme can also be compared to Motif W154.8, *Grateful Animals; Ungrateful Man.* Delarue has made a record of the French versions of this tale (see his commentary on Perbosc's *Contes de Gascogne,* p. 273) and has proposed the number 162 for this theme, which is also found in Joan Amades' *Folklore de Catalunya* (Barcelona: Rondallistica, 1950, No. 278, I, 586).

·65· *The Three Deserters*

Type 566, *The Three Magic Objects and the Wonderful Fruits* (*Fortunatus*).

Recorded by Charles Joisten in 1953 from a farmer, E. Bonnet, aged sixty-three, in Luzenac, in the district of Cabannes (Ariège).

Twenty-seven versions of this theme have been recorded in France, thirteen among the American French, and five in the French West

Indies. The great folklorist Cosquin discussed this theme at great length in relation to a variant recorded in Montiers-sur-Saulx, *La Bourse, le Sifflet et le Chapeau* (cf. his *Contes Populaires de Lorraine*, No. 11, I, pp. 121–132). In his commentary on a Nivernais version (cf. his *Contes du Nivernais et du Morvan*, pp. 281–285), Delarue states that "in France, the recipients of the gifts are usually three soldiers, sometimes brothers, either discharged or deserters, sometimes three brothers to whom their father leaves the magic objects; or finally, a young girl imprisoned in a castle gives these objects to the soldier who releases her after three nights of trials." Interestingly enough, in our Pyrenees version the three magic objects —the purse which is always full, the napkin which lays the table, the coat which carries you wherever you want to go—are furnished by the Devil when the three soldiers keeping watch in the haunted castle allow him to come in to look after a treasure. The motif of the nose which grows longer or shorter does not appear as often in folktales as does the motif of horns sprouting on the dishonest Princess' head.

·66· *The Laurel Flower*

Type 780, *The Singing Bone*.

Recorded by Charles Joisten in 1953 from the same informant as No. 64.

The little verses in rhyme or assonance—sometimes sung—which link the different episodes of this theme give it a certain charm, while they also help to fix the story in the listeners' minds. It is therefore one of the themes that are told to children in spite of its cruelty. Thirty-six versions of it have been counted in France. There are three brothers in our Pyrenees version, the youngest of whom is polite and kind, and therefore succeeds where his older brothers failed. This motif, which is widespread in French folklore (Luzel has grouped a whole series of his *Contes de Basse Bretagne*, II, cycle VII, 123–250, under the "cycle of the three brothers"), serves as a beginning for variants of rather different folktale types (cf. *Motif-Index*, Q2, "Kind and unkind"). The desired wonderful object, in this case the laurel flower, is almost everywhere a rare plant: the *Rose de Pimprenelle* (see my *Contes de l'Ouest*, p. 157, No. 16), the *Rose de Montperlé* (Maugard, *Contes des Pyrénées*, No. 4, p. 25; he also cites the *Rose de Pimperlé* or the *Herbe de la Salogne*).

PART XV

CORSICA

·67· *The Legend of the Oxen's Pass*

Recorded from Jeanne Alfonsi, from Albertacce, in Corsica.

Corsica is not lacking in mountain legends, for it is a mountainous island where the shapes of peaks and rocks and the lake beds give rise to popular explanations. The most famous is undoubtedly the legend of Spusata, in the Sartene region, which explains how a young hard-hearted wife was turned to stone, for she took everything away from her poor mother, even down to the little scraper from the family kneading trough. An old storyteller from Niolo, who came from the same village as the informant, told me a much more complicated story on the same subject of the pass, in which Saint Martin's presence is placed in opposition to the Devil's senseless anger (see my *Contes Corses*, No. 53, p. 129; commentary, p. 307). The legendary explanation for the hole through the *Capu Tafonatu*, and for the rocks in the shape of petrified oxen, already appeared in Saint-Germain's *Itinéraire de la Corse* (1868) and in Mortillet's *Rapport sur les Monuments Mégalithiques en Corse* (1893), and in the works of still other more recent authors.

·68· *The Fox and the Blackbird*

Type 56B, *The Fox Persuades the Magpies into Bringing Their Young into His House.*

Recorded from a shepherd, Henri Rossi, from Albertacce (Niolo), in Corsica.

I have already published a Corsican variant of this type, *Le Chien Cippone,* from Castagniccia (cf. my *Contes Corses*, No. 6, p. 12; commentary, p. 271). The emphasis on the blackbird's revenge, which is legitimate since the fox cruelly deprived her of her offspring, is in keeping with the Corsican mentality. The universal theme can be compared to a little scene from the *Roman de Renart* in which the sparrow Droïn, tricked by the fox, who offered to guard her young, asks the dog Morhout to help her gain revenge. In the Corsican story, the blackbird pretends to limp to attract the shepherd's attention; in the *Roman de Renart,* the sparrow flutters about in front of a peasant's cart, and their trick has the same result. The dog takes advantage of the man's diverted attention to steal his food; his strength thus increased, the dog grabs the fox by the throat and avenges the wronged bird.

·69· The Shepherd and the Snake

Type 670, *The Animal Languages.*

Recorded in 1955 from a ninety-year-old shepherd, François Castellani, originally from Rutali (Nebbio) in Corsica.

Aarne-Thompson lists only two variants of this theme in France; however, I have already recorded two versions, one of which has been published in my *Contes Corses* (No. 2, commentary pp. 268–69).

In these Corsican stories, the episode of the hero learning about the existence of hidden treasure from the crow is perhaps borrowed from Type 673, *The White Serpent's Flesh,* in which the rooster's example incites the man to punish his wife for her curiosity about his secret. However, the motif exists independently of this theme: Straparola (*Facétieuses Nuits,* VII, Fable 5) tells the story of "three poor brothers, the youngest of whom learned the birds' language, and thus found out the existence of a hidden treasure"; and before him, Morlini (*Novella* 80) tells the same story.

The basic content of the theme of Type 670 already appears in the Middle Ages in the *Gesta Romanorum* and the *Roman des Sept Sages,* and among the Italian storytellers of the Renaissance, Morlini (*Novella* 71: *Du Pouzzolan' Qui Entendait le Langage des Bêtes*) and Straparola (XIIth Night, Fable 3: *Histoire de Frédéric du Petit Puys*), who attribute similar adventures to imaginary heroes.

Other versions of this tale may be found in *Folktales of Germany* and *Folktales of Ireland,* companion volumes in this series.

·70· The Child Promised to the Devil

Type 811A, *The Boy Promised (or Destined) to Go to the Devil Saves Himself by His Good Conduct.*

Recorded in 1955 from a housewife in the suburbs of Bastia.

In my comments on another Corsican tale recorded in Castagniccia, *Ambrunu* (cf. my *Contes Corses,* No. 21, p. 47; commentary, p. 283), in which the theme of *The Boy Promised to Go to the Devil* precedes Type 400, I have already mentioned a third variant, *L'Enfant et les Croix d' Asphodèles,* recorded by Charles Giovoni in the Taravo valley. Whether the story is about a fisherman in despair because he cannot catch any fish, or a compulsive card player, or a wife distressed over her sterility, the child, promised to the Devil either before or after his birth, makes up for his parents' rashness or sin by his valorous conduct. In this story, the young man gets rid of the Devil through a real duel with swords.

Bibliography

AARNE, ANTTI, and STITH THOMPSON. *The Types of the Folktale.* (Folklore Fellows Communications, No. 184.) Helsinki, 1961.

ARONCO, GIANFRANCO, D'. *Le Fiabe di Magia in Italia.* Udine, 1957.

Arts et Traditions Populaires. Paris, since 1953. (A continuation of *Mois d'Ethnographie Francaise.*)

BASILE, GIAN ALESIO ABBATUTIS. *Lo Cunto de li Cunte, overo lo Trattenemiento de' Peccerille.* Naples, 1637. (Known as the *Pentamerone* since the edition of 1674.)

CADIC, FRANÇOIS. *Contes de Basse-Bretagne.* Paris, 1955.

Collection de Contes et Chansons Populaires. 44 vols., Paris, Leroux, 1881–1930.

COSQUIN, EMMANUEL. *Contes Populaires de Lorraine.* 2 vols., Paris, 1886.

DELARUE, PAUL. *Catalogue des Contes Français.* Vol. I, Paris, 1957. Vol. II was prepared by his associate, Marie-Louise Tenèze. Paris, 1964.

———. *Contes Merveilleux des Provinces de France.* 7 vols., Paris, 1953–56. Published under the general editorship of Paul Delarue, as follows: Nivernais-Morvan (A. Millien-P. Delarue); Ouest (G. Massignon); Gascogne (A. Perbosc-S. Cezerac); Pyrénées (G. Maugard); Auvergne (M. A. Meraville); Basse-Bretagne (F. Cadic); Haute-Bretagne (A. de Félice). (Issued in two editions, with and without notes.)

FÉLICE, ARIANE DE. *Contes de Haute-Bretagne.* Paris, 1954.

HOEPFFNER, ERNEST. *Les Lais de Marie de France.* Strasbourg, 1920.

HUET, GEDEON. *Les Contes Populaires.* Paris, 1923.

Les Littératures Populaires de Toutes les Nations. 47 vols., Paris, 1883–1903.

MASSIGNON, GENEVIÈVE. *Contes Corses.* Aix-en-Provence, 1963.

———. *Contes de l'Ouest.* Paris, 1953.

———. *Contes des Teilleurs de Lin du Trégor.* Paris, 1965.

MAUGARD, GASTON. *Contes des Pyrénées.* Paris, 1955.

Mélusine, 11 vols., Paris, 1877–1901.

Mémoires de IVe Congrès des Investigateurs de Contes Populaires, Kiel & Kopenhagen, 1959. Berlin, 1961.

MERAVILLE, M. A. *Contes d'Auvergne.* Paris, 1956.

Les Mille et Une Nuits. trans. Galland. 12 vols., Paris, 1704–17.

MILLIEN, A., and PAUL DELARUE. *Contes du Nivernais et du Morvan.* Paris, 1953.

MORLINI, GIROLAMO. *Novelle.* Naples, 1520 and 1524.

OESTERLEY, HERMANN (ed.). *Gesta Romanorum.* 2 vols., Berlin, 1872.

PERBOSC, ANTONIN, and SUZANNE CEZERAC. *Contes de Gascogne.* Paris, 1954.

RANKE, KURT. *Die zwei Brüder.* (Folklore Fellows Communications, No. 114.) Helsinki, 1934.

Revue des Traditions Populaires, succeeded by *Revue d'Ethnographie et des Traditions Populaires.* Paris, 1886–1919; 1920–29.

Le Roman de Renart. Edited by Mario Roques. Paris, 1948.

ROOTH, ANNA BIRGITTA. *The Cinderella Cycle.* Lund, 1951.

STRAPAROLA, GIOVANNI FRANCESCO. *Le Piacevole Notte.* Venice, 1552–53. In French, *Les Facétieuses Nuits.*

THOMPSON, STITH. *The Folktale.* New York, 1946.

———. *Motif-Index of Folk Literature.* 6 vols. Rev. ed. Bloomington, Ind., and Copenhagen, 1955–58.

VAN GENNEP, ARNOLD. *Manuel de Folklore Français Contemporain.* Vol. IV, Paris, 1938. (Bibliography, pp. 654–715, nos. 3720 to 4279.)

NOTE: See "Foreword" for additional titles on French folklore.

Index of Motifs

(Motif numbers are from Stith Thompson, *Motif-Index of Folk Literature*
[6 vols; Copenhagen and Bloomington, Ind., 1955–58].)

Motif No.	B. ANIMALS	Tale No.
B11.2.3.1	Seven-headed dragon	8
B11.10	Sacrifice of human being to dragon	8
B11.11.1	Fight with dragon	8
B103.1.1	Gold-producing ass. Droppings of gold	51
B165.1	Animal languages learned from serpent	69
B165.2	Animals languages learned from frog	18
B171	Demi-coq	53
B177.1	Magic toad	18
B211.1.8	Speaking cat	25
B211.3.4	Speaking parrot	29
B216	Knowledge of animal discovers treasure	69
B253	Secrets discussed in animal meeting	45
B261	War of birds and quadrupeds	49
B291.1.6	Parrot as messenger	29
B296	Animals go a-journeying	52
B313	Helpful animal an enchanted person	23
B322.1	Hero feeds own flesh to helpful animal	46
B325.1	Animal bribed with food	11
B350–399	Grateful animals	6
B375.1	Fish returned to water: grateful	62
B375.3.1	Released: grateful	62
B411	Helpful cow	43
B422	Helpful cat	23, 25
B435.1	Helpful fox	53
B451	Helpful eagle	46
B469.5	Helpful cock	69
B482.2	Helpful dungbeetle	14
B491.1	Helpful serpent	69
B493.1	Helpful frog	29
B541	Animal rescues man from sea	17
B542.1.1	Eagle carries men to safety	17, 46
B548.2.2	Fish recovers [key] from sea	11
B551.1	Fish carries man across water	62
B562.1	Helpful animal discovers treasure	69

C. TABU

D. MAGIC

E. THE DEAD

J. THE WISE AND THE FOOLISH

T. SEX

V. RELIGION

W. TRAITS OF CHARACTER

X. HUMOR

Z. CUMULATIVE TALES

Index of Tale Types

(Type numbers are from Antti Aarne and Stith Thompson, *The Types of the Folktale* [Helsinki, 1961].)

General Index

Aarne, Antti (Finnish folklorist), xxx

Agreement: between fox and wolf, 192

Amades, Joan (Spanish folklorist), 286

Anger: first to show it is punished, 61

Animals: help old woman, 68, 180–81

Ant: helps to hide man, 208; transformed into boy, 95

Aronco, Gianfranco d' (Italian folklorist), 256

Arrogance: cause of poverty, 101

Aulnoy, Madame d', vi, 262

Baby: born in well, 143

Ball: leads girl to brothers, 146

Balys, Jonas (Lithuanian folklorist), 249

Banishment: of daughter by father, 16

Bark of oak: used to restore eyesight, 154

Basile, Gian Alesio Abbatutis (Neapolitan tale collector), 248, 266, 267

Bear: mistreats beetle, 173

Beast: speaks to girl, 40

Bed: happens to be in well, 143

Bédier, Joseph, x

Beetle: declares war on bear, 169

Beggar: frightened by hen, 105

Bench: leaps, 123; speaks, 123

Benfey, Theodor, viii, xi

Bet: between bird and boy, 54–55; between master and tenant farmer, 161

Bird: bets with boy, 54–55; turns into human, 54

Blackbird: killed by dog, 238; speaks, 347

Blémont, Emile (French folklorist), xii, xix

Blind boy: abandoned, 49; giant makes wishes for him, 49; overhears animals' conversation, 153; regains sight, 50, 154

Blood: brings marble statue to life, 14

Boasting: causes wolf to be hurt, 87; of daughter by mother, 210

Body: parts fall from chimney, 4–5; assembled parts become Devil, 5

Bones: used to make ladder, 25

Box: contains endless cloth, 90

Boy: asks fairy for help, 30; becomes bishop, 79; cures girl, 78, 154; defeats Devil, 243; deserted by friends, 160; disguised as priest, 82–84; eaten by beasts, 155; forces Devil to sign pact, 5, 7; given choice of King's daughters, 97; given impossible task, 24, 50, 56, 57, 58; hears voice of the dead, 4–5; helped by cat, 96–97; helped by crow, 58; helped by God, 155; helped by supernatural mule, 50; helps town to get water, 154; hides in cabbage, 80;